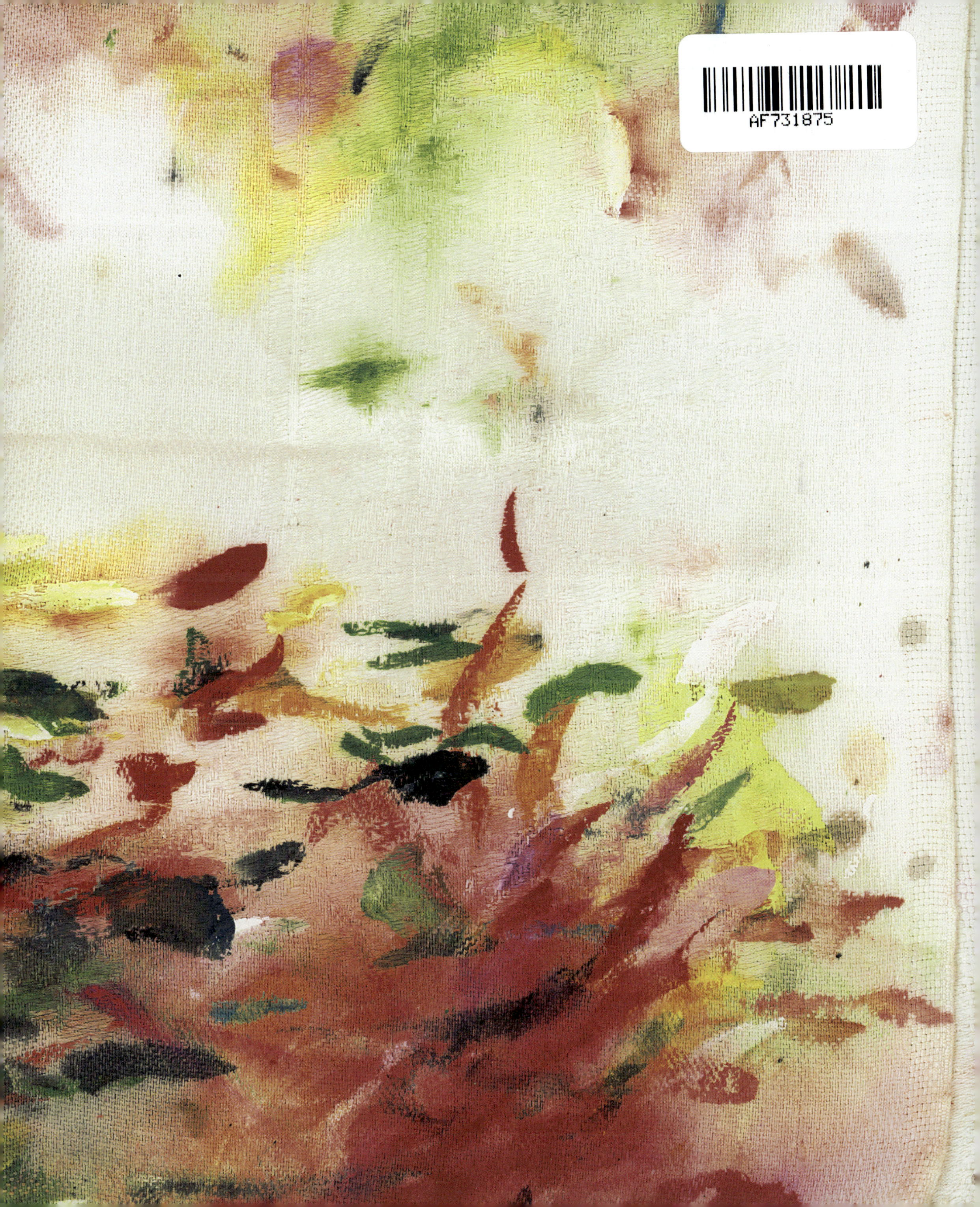

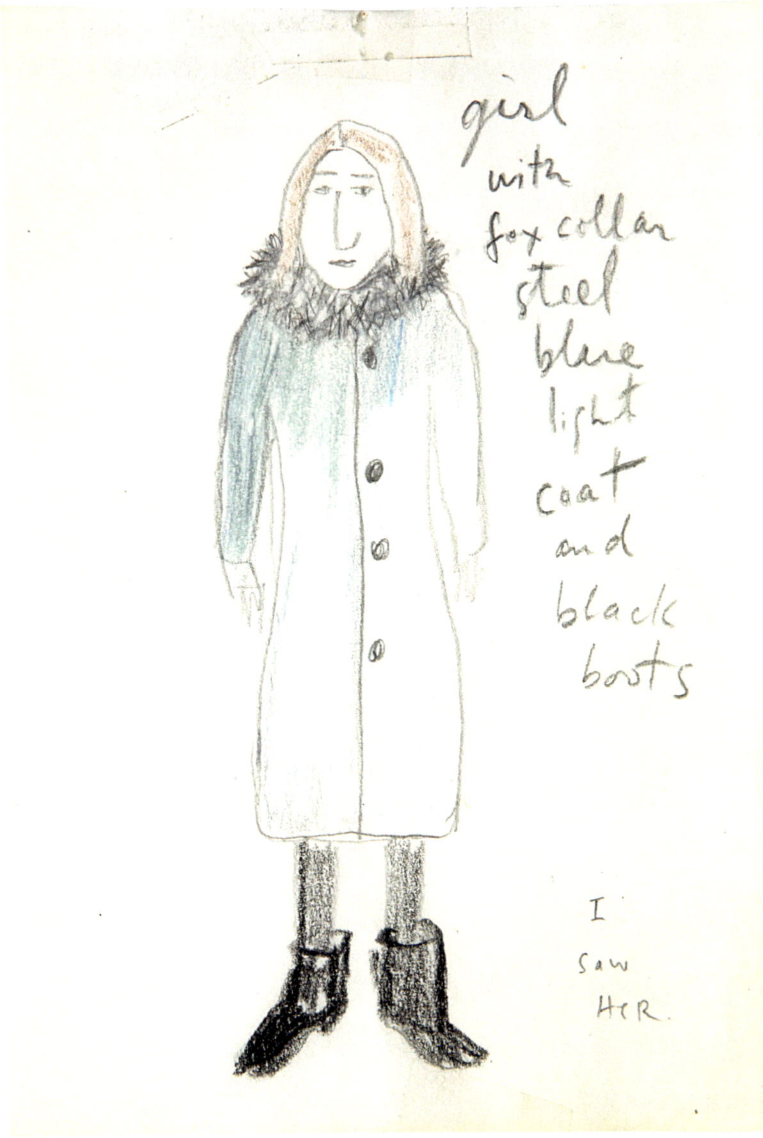

I Saw Her, 1996

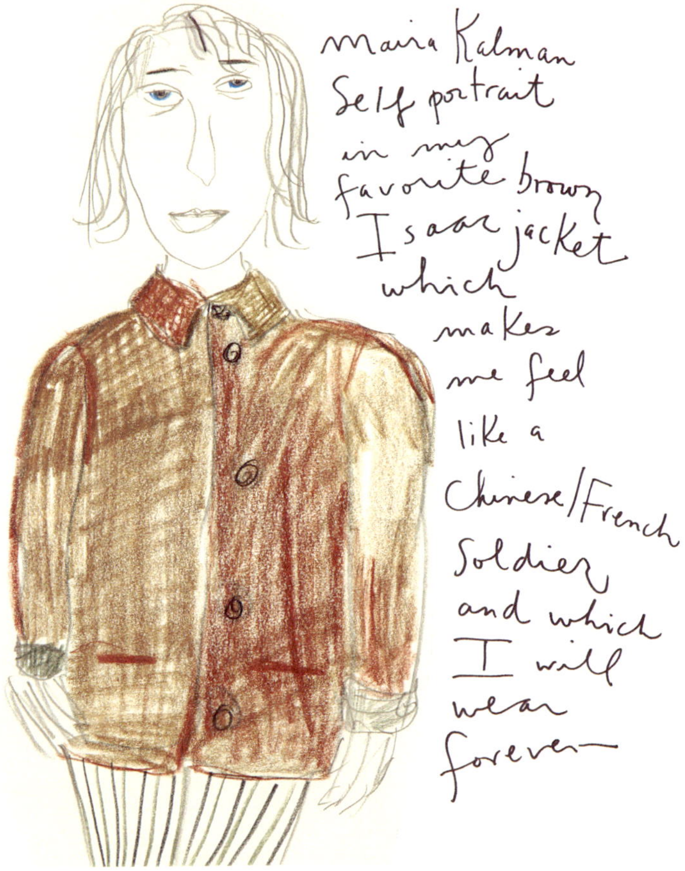

Self-Portrait (Favorite Jacket), 1991

Maira Kalman
Various Illuminations

(of a Crazy World)

Ingrid Schaffner

With contributions by
Donna Ghelerter, Stamatina Gregory,
and Kenneth E. Silver

Institute of Contemporary Art, University of Pennsylvania

DelMonico Books • Prestel
Munich Berlin London New York

Published on the occasion
of the exhibition
**Maira Kalman:
Various Illuminations
(of a Crazy World)**

Organized by Ingrid Schaffner,
Senior Curator, Institute of
Contemporary Art
University of Pennsylvania,
Philadelphia

EXHIBITION ITINERARY
Institute of Contemporary Art
University of Pennsylvania,
Philadelphia
January 14–June 6, 2010

Contemporary Jewish Museum,
San Francisco
July 1–October 26, 2010

Skirball Cultural Center,
Los Angeles
November 16, 2010–
February 13, 2011

The Jewish Museum,
New York
March 13–July 31, 2011

Published by Institute of
Contemporary Art and
DelMonico Books, an imprint of
Prestel Publishing

Institute of Contemporary Art
University of Pennsylvania
118 South 36th Street
Philadelphia, PA 19104
www.icaphila.org

Prestel, a member of Verlags-
gruppe Random House GmbH

Prestel Verlag
Königinstrasse 9
80539 Munich
Germany
Tel: 49 89 242908 300
Fax: 49 89 242908 335
www.prestel.de

Prestel Publishing Ltd.
4 Bloomsbury Place
London WC1A 2QA
United Kingdom
Tel: 44 20 7323 5004
Fax: 44 20 7636 8004

Prestel Publishing
900 Broadway, Suite 603
New York, NY 10003
Tel: 212 995 2720
Fax: 212 995 2733
E-mail: sales@prestel-usa.com
www.prestel.com

The paper in this book meets
the guidelines for permanence
and durability of the Committee
on Production Guidelines for
Book Longevity of the Council of
Library Services.

Second printing 2010

Printed and bound in Singapore

ICA gratefully acknowledges
Leonard and Louise Riggio and
The Andy Warhol Foundation for
the Visual Arts, Inc., for generous
support of this exhibition. ICA
acknowledges Barbara B. &
Theodore R. Aronson for their
sponsorship of the exhibition
catalogue. We are also grateful
for the support of Mari & Peter
Shaw, Carol T. & John G.
Finley, BZ & Michael Schwartz,
Erica & Eric Schwartz, and
Anthropologie, Inc.

ANTHROPOLOGIE

Additional support has been
provided by the Barbara &
Richard S. Lane Fund; Howard
A. Silverstein & Patricia B.
Silverstein Exhibition Endowment
Fund; Joan & Hyman Sall; The
Horace W. Goldsmith Foundation;
the Commonwealth of
Pennsylvania Council on the
Arts; The Dietrich Foundation,
Inc.; the Overseers Board for
the Institute of Contemporary
Art; friends and members of
ICA; and the University of
Pennsylvania. ICA is also grateful
to The Chodorow Exhibition
Initiative Fund for support of
this exhibition’s tour. ICA also
thanks the Julie Saul Gallery for
in-kind support. (As of 1-8-10)

ISBN: 978-3-7913-5035-6

British Library of Cataloguing-
in-Publication Data: a catalogue
record for thisbook is available
from the British Library;
Deutsche Nationalbibliothek
holdsa record of this
publication in the Deutsche
Nationalbibliografie; detailed
bibliographical data can be
found under: http://dnb.ddb.de.

Curator: Ingrid Schaffner
Designer: Beverly Joel, pulp, ink.
Editor: Elisa Urbanelli
Printer: CS Graphics
Paper: GardaPat 13 Kiara
Type: Mr. Eaves Modern and
Wessex

Front cover: *Woman with Face
Net*, 2000

Endpapers: paint rags from the
artist’s studio, gouache on linen

Facing page: *Self-Portrait (with
Pete)*, 2004–5

PHOTOGRAPH AND
REPRODUCTION CREDITS
All works by Maira Kalman are
© 2010 Maira Kalman

Pages 116, 117: Images
courtesy of The Robin Hood
Foundation. Photographs
© Peter Mauss/Esto

Pages 126–34: Installation
photography by Greenhouse
Media

Library of Congress Cataloging-in-Publication Data

Schaffner, Ingrid.
Maira Kalman : various illuminations (of a crazy world) / Ingrid Schaffner ;
with contributions by Donna Ghelerter, Stamatina Gregory, and Kenneth E. Silver.
p. cm.
Issued in connection with an exhibition held Jan. 14–June 6, 2010,
Institute of Contemporary Art, University of Pennsylvania, Philadelphia,
and at three other institutions at later dates.
Includes bibliographical references.
ISBN 978-3-7913-5035-6 1. Kalman, Maira—Exhibitions. I. Ghelerter, Donna.
II. Gregory, Stamatina. III. Silver, Kenneth E. IV. Kalman, Maira.
V. University of Pennsylvania. Institute of Contemporary Art. VI. Title.
N6537.K236A4 2010
709.2—dc22

2009053004

FSC www.fsc.org
MIX
Paper from
responsible sources
FSC™ C007776

Contents

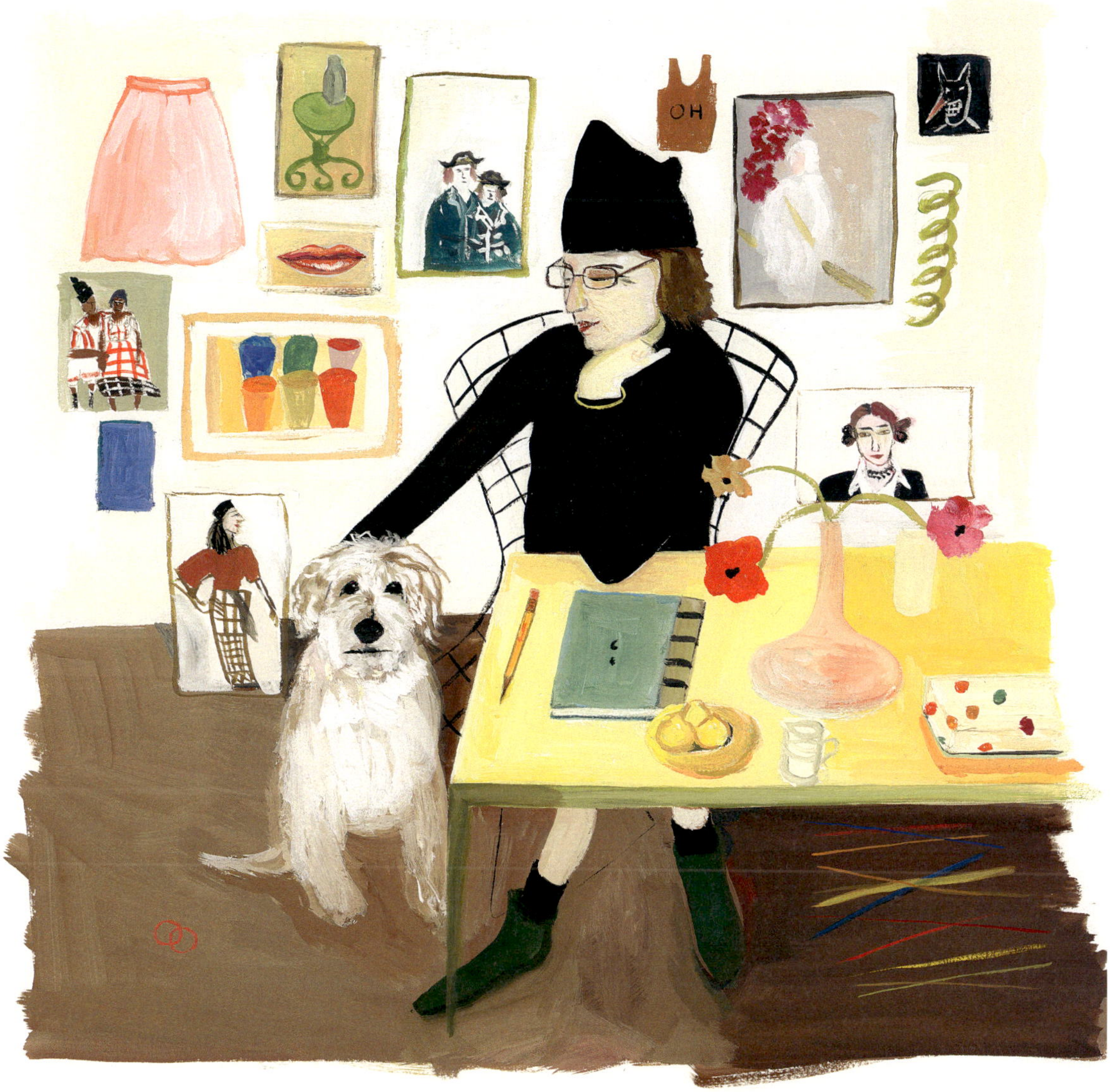

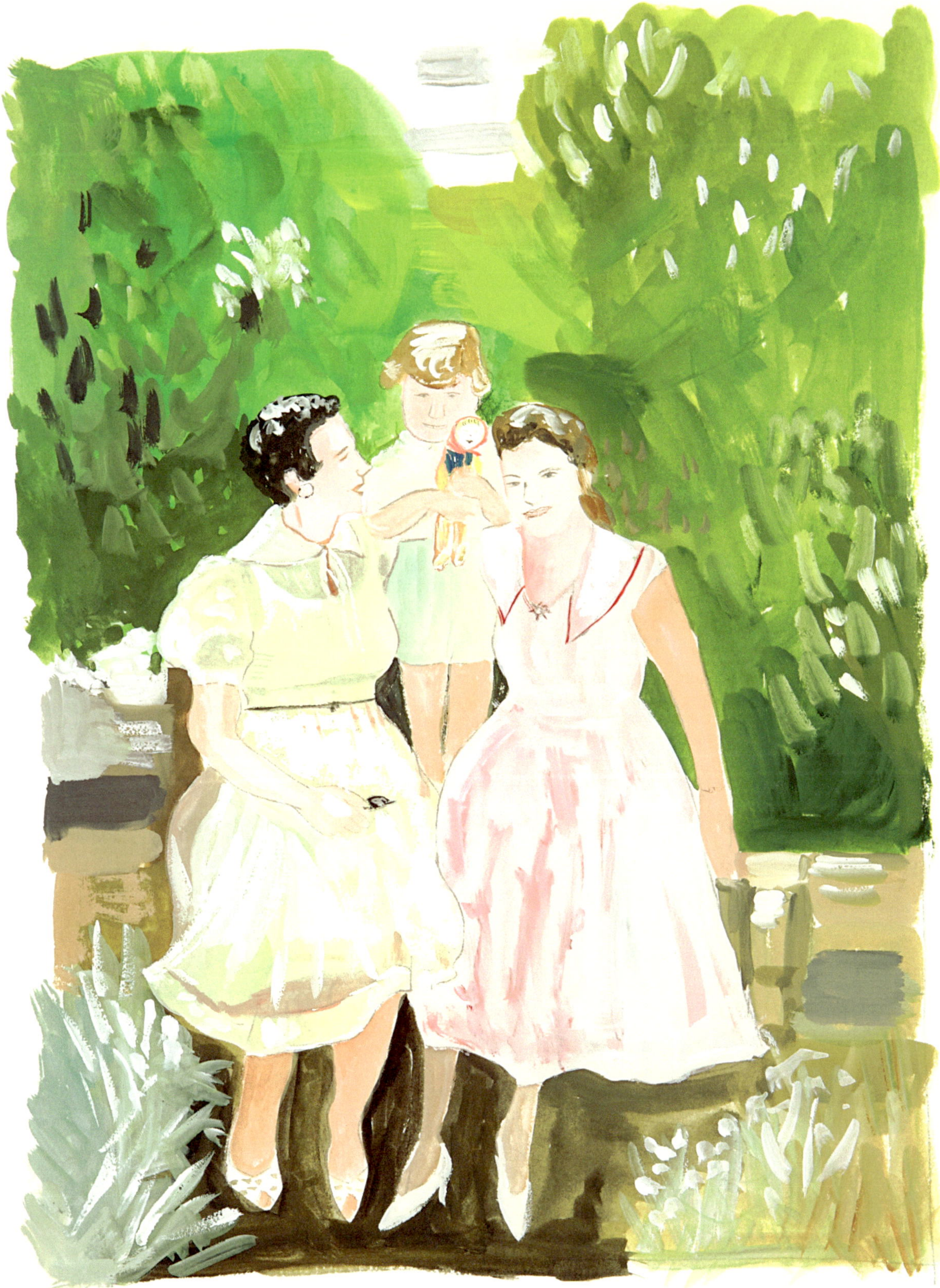

My Mother in Organza, 2003

Ooh-la-la Acknowledgments

NOT SO LONG AGO—WELL, MAYBE SEVENTEEN YEARS ago—the "R." family, as I will call them, had a son named Max. This first and only son of a liberal Jewish New York family had, as you might imagine, many expectations laid out for him. Having known the boy's mother since I was eight, and hoping to ease the educational burden that would soon fall upon his parents' shoulders, I went to the store looking for some books. I was delighted to find several very witty illustrated children's books (designed to appeal to adults, too) about another Max, Max Stravinksy the Poet Dog, by the writer and illustrator Maira Kalman. I bought them all, hoping they might have a positive and liberating influence on Max R.'s life. And they did. Lines from **Ooh-la-la (Max in Love)** (1994) became R. family mantras: "Your Hotty Spotty Body Makes Me Tingle with Joy!" Now seventeen, Max still uses the mantras—even more fun once you can whisper the words to your teenage girlfriend.

Max in Hollywood, Baby (1992) also had its effect. The R. family had a house on the ocean, and imagine the parents' surprise when their little boy, decked out in bright green sunglasses, dragged a canvas deck chair very much like Max Stravinksy's down to the beach and began calling everybody "Baby," as he continues to do even today—even when it's not appropriate—but who cares, he mumbles, now that he is seventeen.

It's **Max Makes a Million** (1990), however, that may end up having the most lasting effect on Max R. "I'm going to make a million with flair and panache," he declares. He knows a million in 1990 dollars is not the same as a million today, but he likes the sound of the words as they roll off his tongue just as much as he did when he was three. Max R. has applied for early decision to study business at the Wharton School at the University of Pennsylvania, and his family and I credit Maira Kalman for his taking the leap. This is the way an artist can get inside a life and transform it. Ooh-la-la!

Ingrid Schaffner, curator of this Maira Kalman survey, gave me Kalman's **Principles of Uncertainty** (2007) for my birthday one year. Timing is everything and Ingrid has perfect timing. I opened the book and we exclaimed in unison that she should do an exhibition with Maira Kalman, and *voilà*! Another example of how Maira has influenced all of us; this time, however, we may be influencing her, too. I would like to thank Ingrid for bringing this amazing exhibition to the ICA,

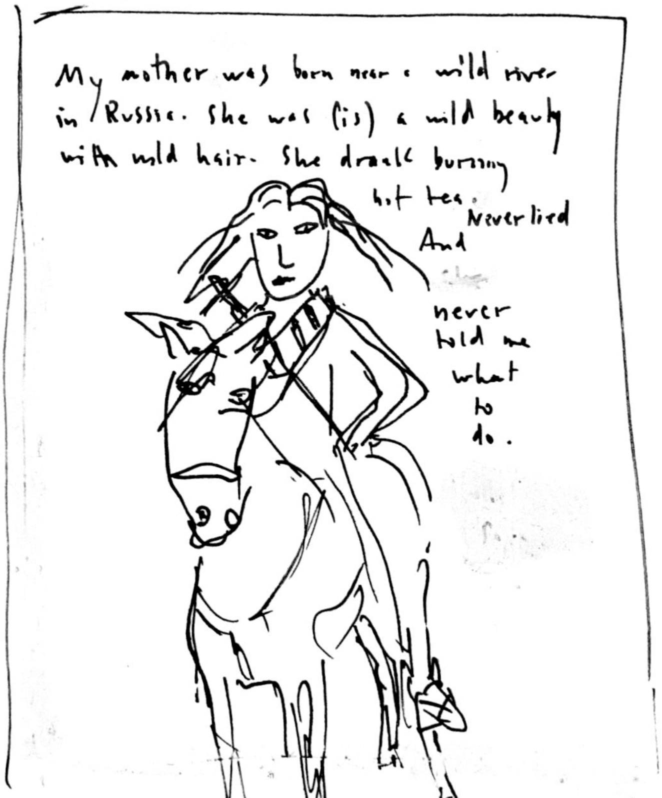

My Mother in Palestine, 1998

and Maira for allowing others to interpret her musings. Of course, Ingrid has a particular flair and panache as a curator for artists like Maira: in other exhibitions at the ICA, she has helped visitors see the work of Karen Kilimnik and Sarah McEneaney – artists with affinities to Kalman – through her eyes.

Our exhibitions would be impossible without the cooperation and team spirit of the whole ICA staff. Robert Chaney, Director of Curatorial Affairs, always manages to make us feel things are easy even when we know they are not; I personally appreciate this gift, as well as his work organizing the incredible tour of *Maira Kalman: Various Illuminations (of a Crazy World)*, which is traveling to the Contemporary Jewish Museum, San Francisco (Connie Wolf, Director and CEO); the Skirball Cultural Center, Los Angeles (Uri D. Herscher, Founding President and CEO; and Grace Cohen Grossman, Senior Curator); and The Jewish Museum, New York City (Joan Rosenbaum, Helen Goldsmith Menschel Director; and Ruth Beesch, Deputy Director for Programs). Thanks to all those who have been involved in arranging for Maira and her gifts to grace these major American cities – we feel very fortunate.

At ICA, Head Preparator Shannon Bowser and her installation crew have worked so long and well together that they are part of the lifeblood of the organization. Assistant Curator Kate Kraczon provided invaluable support for the show and an excellent chronology for the catalogue. Lucy Gallun, Whitney Lauder Curatorial Fellow, and Lizzie Frasco, ICA's Spiegel Fellow, have carried out a series of public programs related to this exhibition that is quite fantastic – a lineup including a marathon reading of Maira's children's books; an evening with artist Sarah McEneaney; a conversation about Maira and M&Co with experts Michael Bierut and Chee Pearlman; and a series of events in the spirit of "Milton" (a conceptual project of Maira's) curated by students in Kenny Goldsmith's Penn undergraduate class, "Writing through Culture and Art." Already on campus there is a lot of excitement about Maira's presence here at ICA, and we are grateful to her for taking time to meet with students in the Fine Arts and English departments and at Kelly Writer's House. It is also wonderful to have this opportunity to engage with our colleagues Derrick Dreher, Director of the Rosenbach Museum and Library, and Bill Adair, formerly of the Rosenbach and now at The Pew Center for Arts & Heritage, through Maira's **Finding Lincoln** contribution to the Rosenbach's "21st-Century Abe" program. ICA's Maira Kalman exhibition is also part of the citywide exposition *Philagrafika* that explores print in its many forms. We are pleased to be part of this citywide festival and to be sharing Maira's work.

Jill Katz, ICA Director of Marketing and Communications, continues to cultivate press for our exhibitions and public programs and is an invaluable resource on community relations. All of the curators at ICA help each other when they are organizing exhibitions, and with this in mind I would like to thank Jenelle Porter for providing support and for guiding the publication of this catalogue. The catalogue itself has been creatively conceived and designed by Beverly Joel of pulp, ink. Donna Ghelerter, Stamatina Gregory, and Kenneth E. Silver contributed wonderful essays. Elisa Urbanelli's deft editorial hand is an invisible presence throughout. We are delighted to be copublishing the catalogue with Mary DelMonico of DelMonico Books • Prestel.

William Hidalgo, ICA Visitor Services and Education Assistant, is a more than welcoming personality at our front door. Our team of interns provides staff with invaluable support at every stage of exhibition planning and execution. Thank you to Grace Ambrose and Rachel W. Higgins, who have worked hard on the catalogue and checklist, and to Dong Chen, Patricia Cuevas-Gomez, Hannah Gilbert, Kristen Kinstrey, Claudia Lauture, Evan Litvin, Ben Loughin, Sarah Margolis-Pineo, Linnea Rading, Rokssana Sukkur, Desiree Thompson, Angela Washko, and Francesca Zanghi for their help.

I am grateful to Marilyn Pollick, Director of Development and Alumni Relations, Development Associate Jamie Gorman, Staff Writer Rachel Pastan, and Major Gifts Officer Christianna Miller who have helped us identify sources of funding for this project. On the administrative side, my assistant Eliza Coviello is invaluable to me. I would also like to acknowledge our newest staff member, Business and Building Administrator Nikyia Rogers.

The Guzelofkowitzes Visit Daughter Veronica Guzé (Know Your Roots), 1978

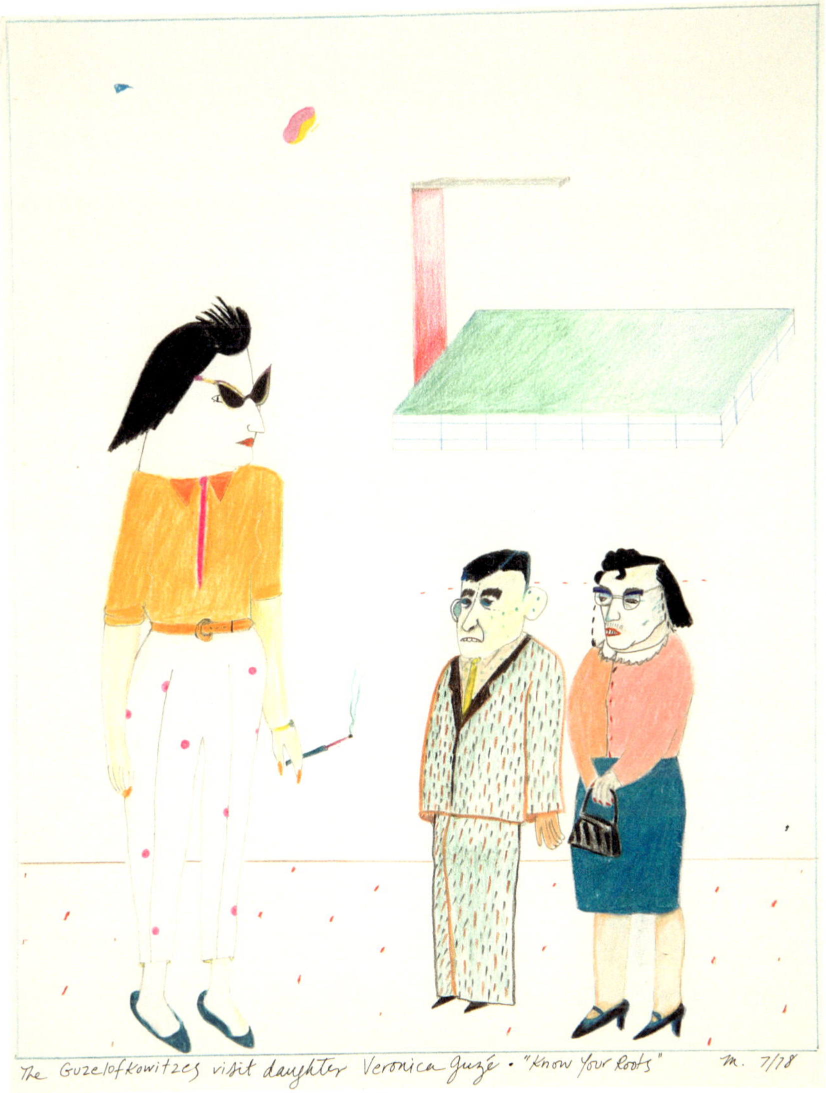

ICA is very thankful for funding for this exhibition from Leonard and Louise Riggio and the Andy Warhol Foundation for the Visual Arts, Inc. ICA acknowledges Barbara B. and Theodore R. Aronson for their sponsorship of the exhibition catalogue. We are also grateful for gifts from Mari and Peter Shaw, Carol T. and John G. Finley, BZ and Michael Schwartz, Erica and Eric Schwartz, and Anthropologie, Inc. Additional contributions have been provided by the Barbara and Richard S. Lane Fund; the Howard A. Silverstein and Patricia B. Silverstein Exhibition Endowment Fund; Joan and Hyman Sall; the Horace W. Goldsmith Foundation; the Commonwealth of Pennsylvania Council on the Arts; the Dietrich Foundation, Inc.; the Overseers Board for the Institute of Contemporary Art; friends and members of ICA; and the University of Pennsylvania. ICA is grateful to the Chodorow Exhibition Initiative Fund for support of this exhibition's tour. ICA also thanks the Julie Saul Gallery for in-kind support. Thanks as well to all the lenders to this exhibition; as a noncollecting institution we rely on you, and we appreciate your permitting your artworks to travel to ICA and the other museums hosting this show.

Julie Saul, Maira's art dealer in New York, has been enormously helpful in identifying possible sources of funding for this show, and her passion and dedication for Maira's work are immeasurable. I want to personally thank her for the time she has given this project, along with her staff, Edna Cardinale and Phil Whitman. Rick Meyerowitz, Maira's collaborator on the now famous **New Yorkistan** cover, has also played a vital behind-the-scenes role in this show, and I would like to thank him for his contributions. We are most grateful to United Pickle for all of the wonderful labels; thank you, Steven Leibowitz! And of course, I want to thank Max R. for being the inspiration for my introduction to Maira Kalman.

Patricia B. Silverstein heads our board, and I would like to thank her and all of our board members, as well as Amy Gutmann, President of the University of Pennsylvania, and Vince Price, Provost, for giving us the freedom to develop our ideas on paper and in the gallery. Finally, to Maira Kalman for her unabashed wit, flair, and YES, grand panache and enthusiastic ooh-la-la's: for sharing your work with us and the rest of the world, thank you.

Claudia Gould
THE DANIEL W. DIETRICH, II DIRECTOR

Little Baby Goes Wooo/All Night Long, 1985

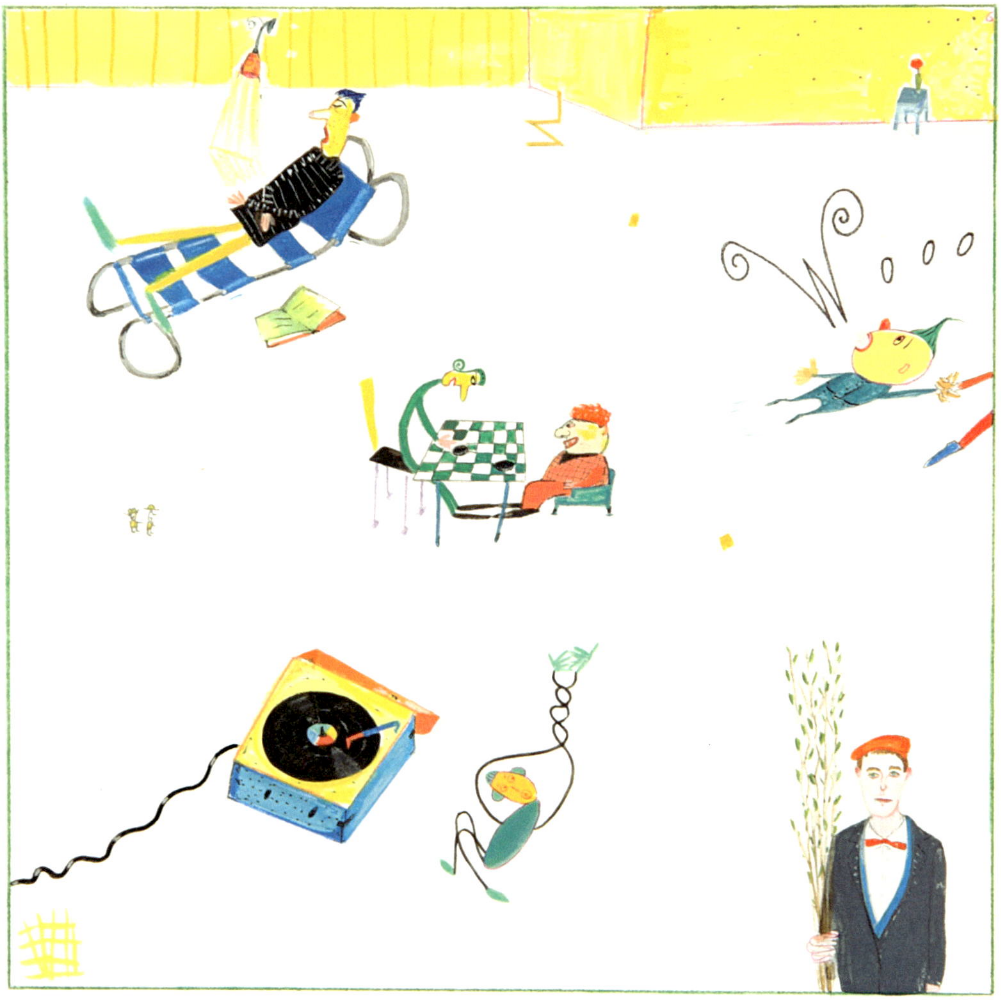

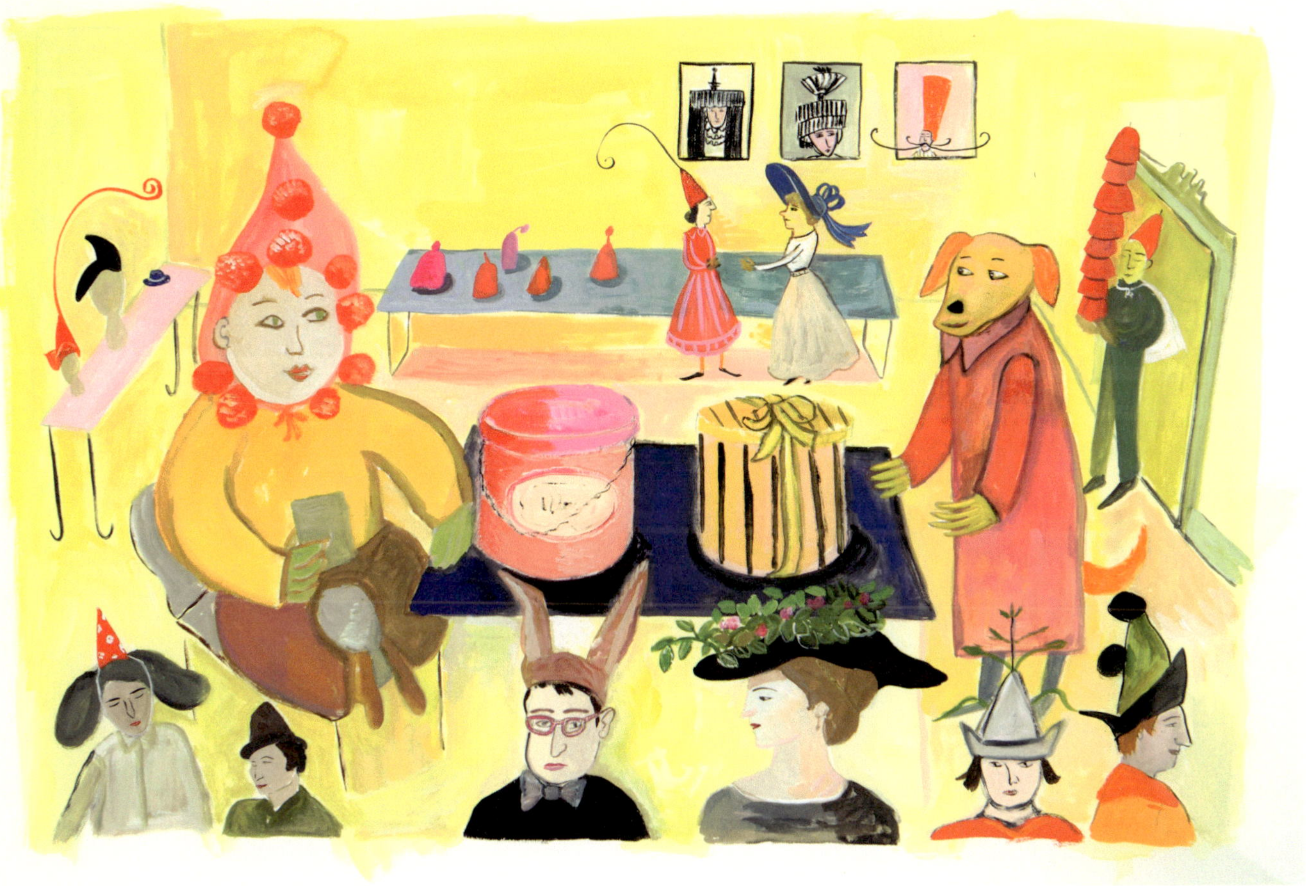

Panache, 2009

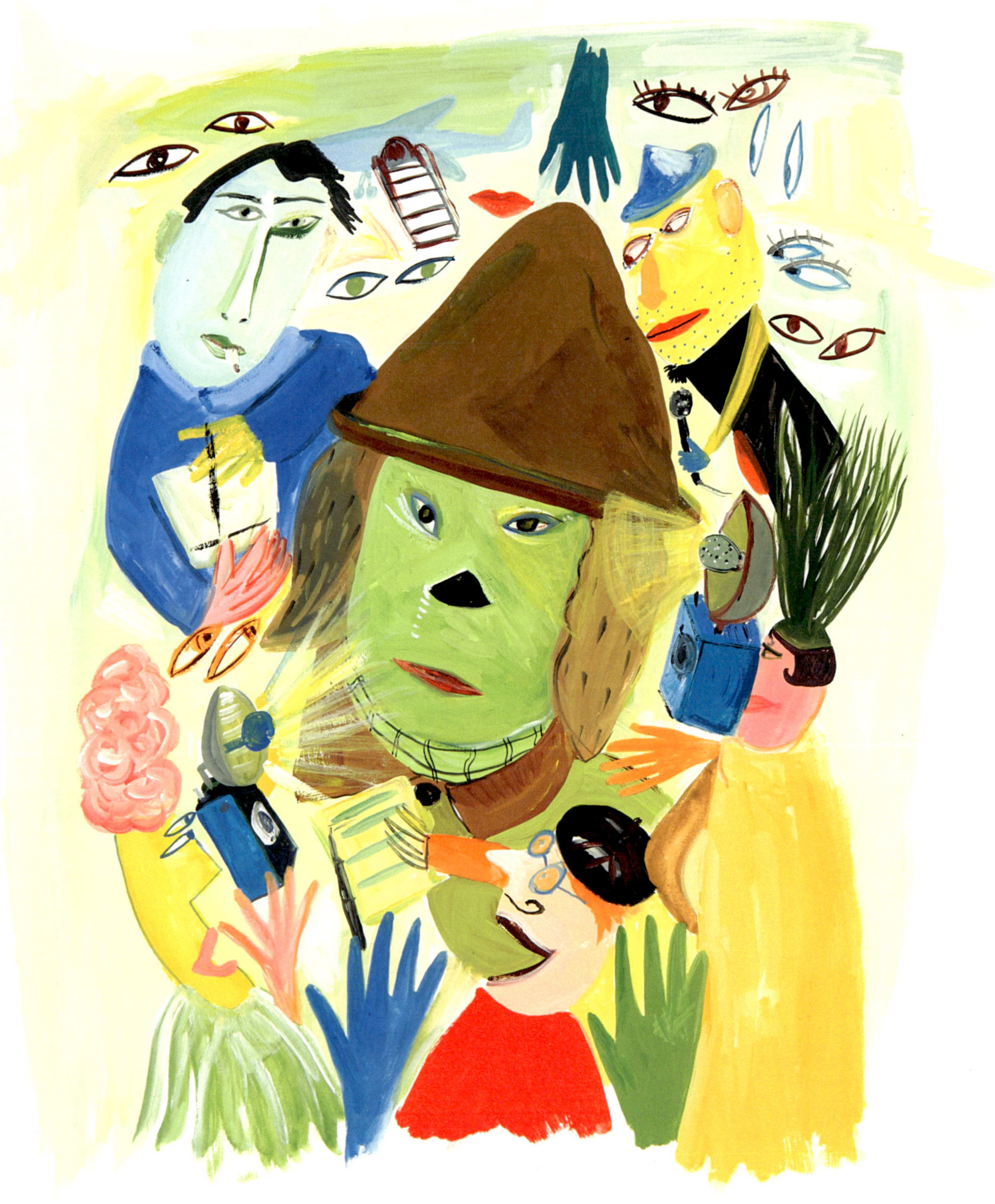

Max, 1991

Exaltations/Observations

Ingrid Schaffner

HERE'S A ROUTINE THAT'S BEEN IN REHEARSAL IN the wings of the museum for nearly two years now. It begins with you asking me what I've been working on. I say, "A Maira Kalman show." You say, "Who's Maira Kalman?" I say, "You know Maira Kalman, *the illustrator*." Occasionally, the routine ends here, wreathed in smiles, while you say: "Oh! Maira Kalman, I love her work." More typically, it continues with my answering your inquiring look. Maira Kalman is the author of twelve children's books and creator of Max Stravinsky, the dog poet of **Ooh-la-la (Max in Love)**. Among her adult classics is an illustrated edition of William Strunk Jr. and E. B. White's timeless grammar **The Elements of Style**. Her book **The Principles of Uncertainty** is a series of picture essays, a memoir of thoughts and reflections à la Montaigne, but illustrated. (Incidentally, Montaigne was also sure that nothing in life is certain.) Kalman's book is based on a yearlong column she created for *The New York Times* online.[1] In December 2009, she completed a second column called "And the Pursuit of Happiness" about democracy and history in America. The series opens with her coverage of President Obama's inauguration ceremony in Washington, D.C., and the handwritten word "Hallelujah!"

As an illustrator and writer, Kalman has done a lot of editorial work for the *Times* over the years, as well as for *The New Yorker*. Born in Israel in 1949, she has lived in New York since the age of four. Her most famous work is a cartoon map of **New Yorkistan** [page 26] that shows the boroughs divided into tribes, like Pashmina on the Upper East Side, Taxistan in the Bronx, Irate and Irant in Brooklyn. It ran on the cover of *The New Yorker* in December 2001; in the midst of the aftermath of 9/11, it was many people's first burst of laughter. It was pored over, quoted, analyzed, translated. (Did you know that *Fashtoonks* is Yiddish for stink?) In short, the map became a public distraction. As one commentator said of the panacea effect of New York's Afghanization: "If the world gives you Kandahar and Chechnya, send them back Khandibar and Kvetchnya."[2]

The **New Yorkistan** map is actually a collaborative work by Kalman with Rick Meyerowitz. A writer and illustrator who has contributed prolifically to *National Lampoon* since its inception, Meyerowitz is also a children's book author. Since they met in 2000, the couple has created a number of illustrated editorials, my favorite being "Things to Do on Valentine's Day," which ran in the *Los Angeles Times*[3]; suggestions include "make up new nicknames"—Sprinkles and Caligula, for instance. Sweet. *The New Yorker* cover started as car-ride banter as they drove out of the city; Kalman called out "Bronxistan" and Meyerowitz responded, "Yes, but a small section of Bronxistan [is] called Ferreristan" after borough president Freddy Ferrer.[4] (This tribe ultimately never made it onto the map.) To lay the terrain on paper, she did the pen and he the brush of the watercolor

Susan, 2004–5

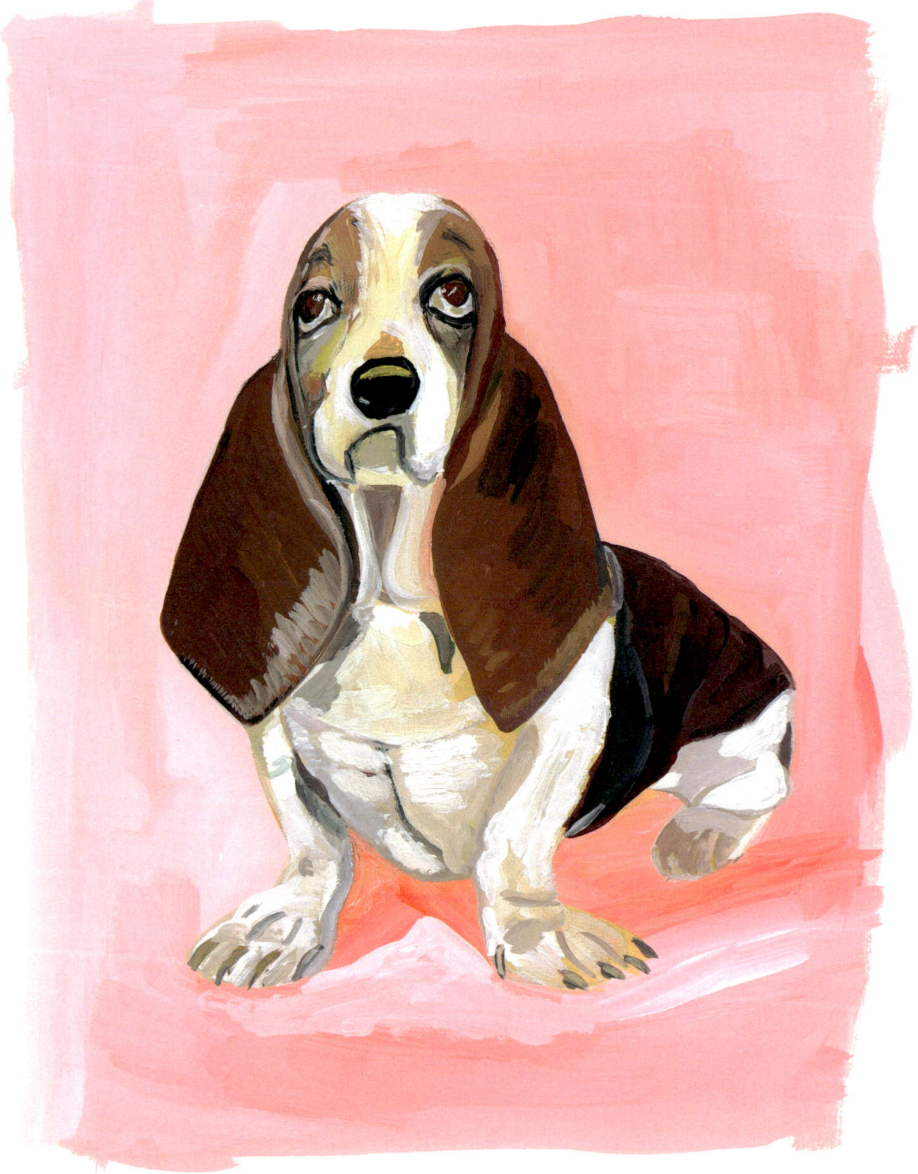

drawing. Universally known, the **New Yorkistan** map doesn't register much name recognition; also obscure is the original context, since the map has since been widely disseminated as everything from a puzzle to a shower curtain. The general lack of correspondence between the illustrator's reputation and her work only makes this exhibition project more gratifying. Because now it's my opportunity to introduce you to one of today's most idiosyncratic and revered creative artists.

Maira Kalman: Various Illuminations (of a Crazy World) is the first major museum survey of the work of Maira Kalman, whose narrative art illuminates so many aspects of contemporary life. Since the 1990s, her children's books have been acclaimed for their syncopated nuttiness and sophistication. A dog named Max arrives in Paris and checks into the *Bleu* suite at the aromatic Miss Camembert's hotel. The room is flatly drawn and dreamily composed, with objects floating across the picture plane and everything painted in an expressive palette of blues. Will children get the blue-period Picasso joke? Probably no more than they are likely to eat Camembert cheese. Indeed, so might parents be hard pressed to keep up with the verbal and visual fusillade of references to art, literature, music, movies, dance, architecture, design, and fashion that catapult Kalman's books right off any shelf built to hold conventional genre. Although she emerged as a children's author, Kalman's audience today is largely adult. And though her style has become less cartoony and more painterly over time, her work's appeal remains spontaneous. Apparently, exploding the modernist canon proves fun for all ages.

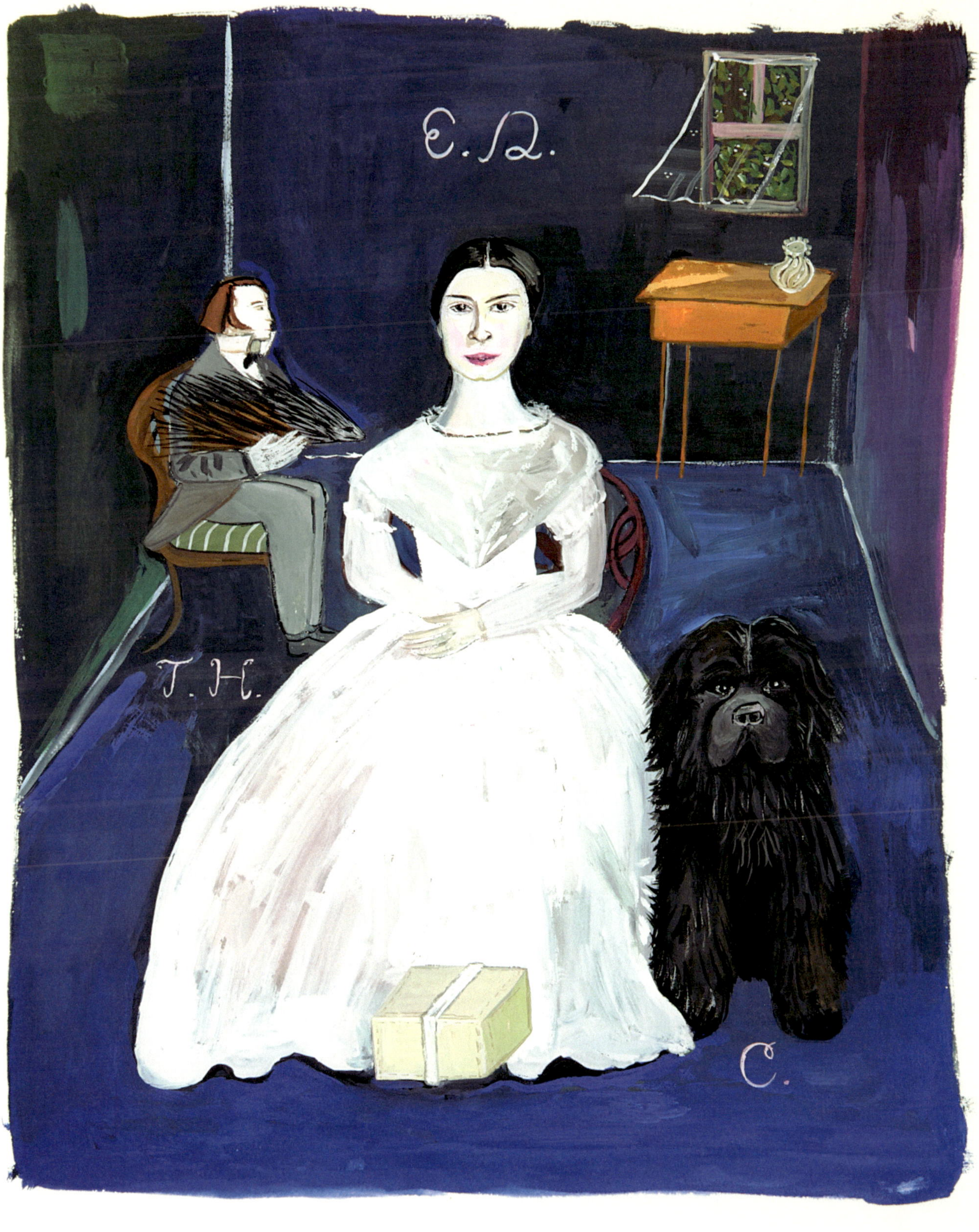

Emily Dickinson, 2008

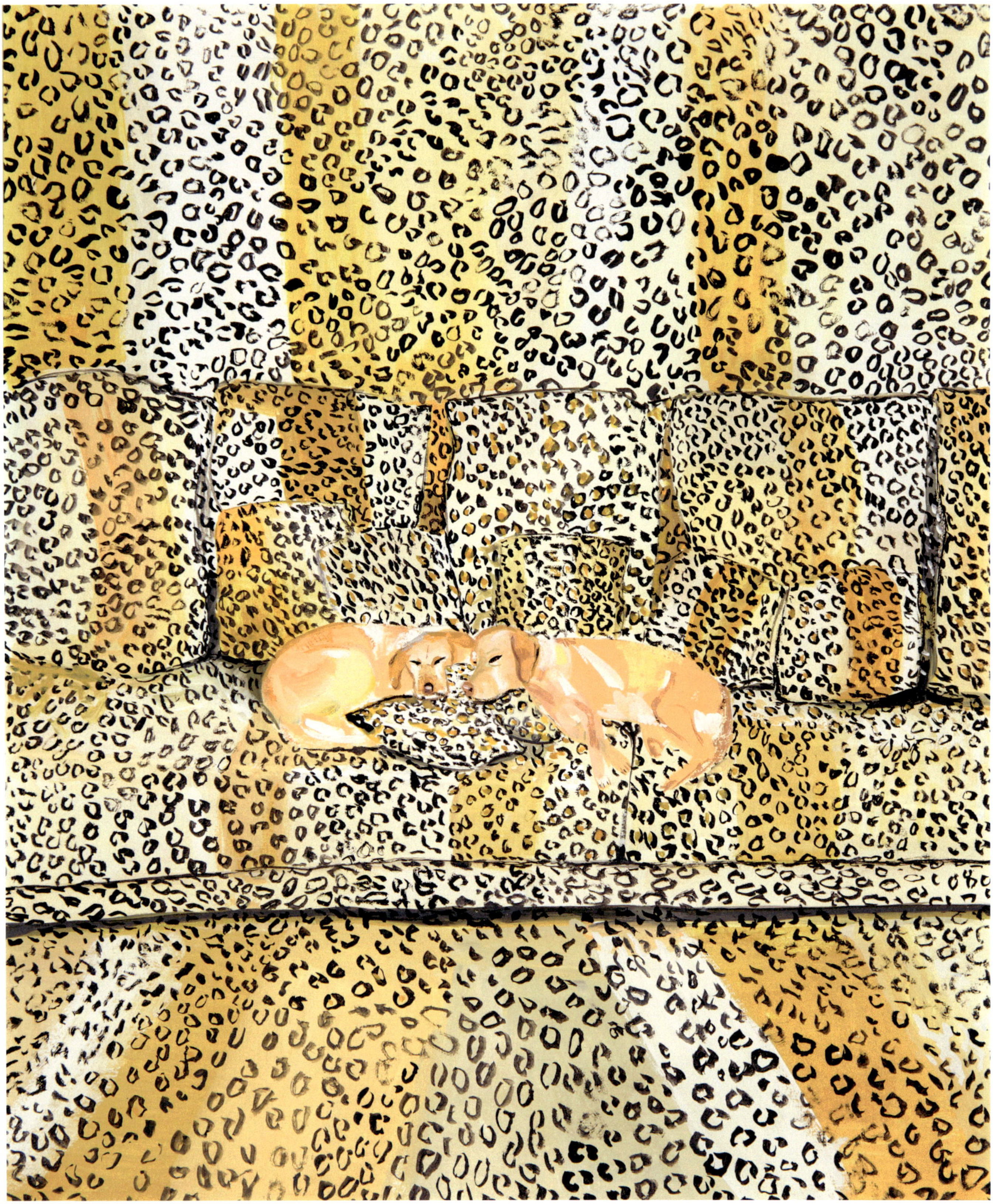

Labs on Cheetah Print (Dolce and Gabbana's Yellow Labradors, Lola and Dalí), 2000

Packed with diverse cultural references, digressions, curlicues, and question marks, Kalman's work seems quintessentially postmodern. And yet, there is nothing arch or ironic in, say, her portrait of Le Corbusier's kitchen sink [page 56], which first appeared in her online column in November 2006. She later described seeing the sink as a "heart-stopping" moment, a moment she hoped to transmit to her reader through her work's depiction as "an earnest and loving presentation to you of this thing that I fell in love with."[5] Kalman's work is always colored by strong emotions, like love and loss – how empty stands Corbu's sink – even while valorizing the most ordinary objects and moments of everyday life. We don't see the studio in which one of modern architecture's great purists worked, but rather the porcelain fixture in which he washed his hands. Talk about truth to material. This light touch is typical of the humor that gives Kalman's work its vitality and charm. Paradoxically, its lightness is also what gives her work the capacity to be so profoundly moving. As in medieval times, when gold was used to bring light to the pages of illuminated manuscripts, so today Kalman's vaguely absurd illuminations bring daily exaltations to light.

Funny that a sink, or a hat, or a box can be so transcendent an image, but that's an achievement of Kalman's work: to surprise expectation. Consider her métier. Because it presumably bends to popular tastes and is crafted in response to a dominant text, illustration is traditionally regarded as a decorative form of picture making. (Never mind if the illustrator is also the author, especially if the readers are children; then we are talking seriously *minor* arts.) Well, so be it. By identifying herself as an illustrator, Kalman may eschew high art's claims of cultural seriousness and name recognition, but the work is no less ambitious or authoritative, just truer to its own aspirations of creative freedom. As viewers, suffice to say, joy is where you find it – usually on the shelf right next to sadness.

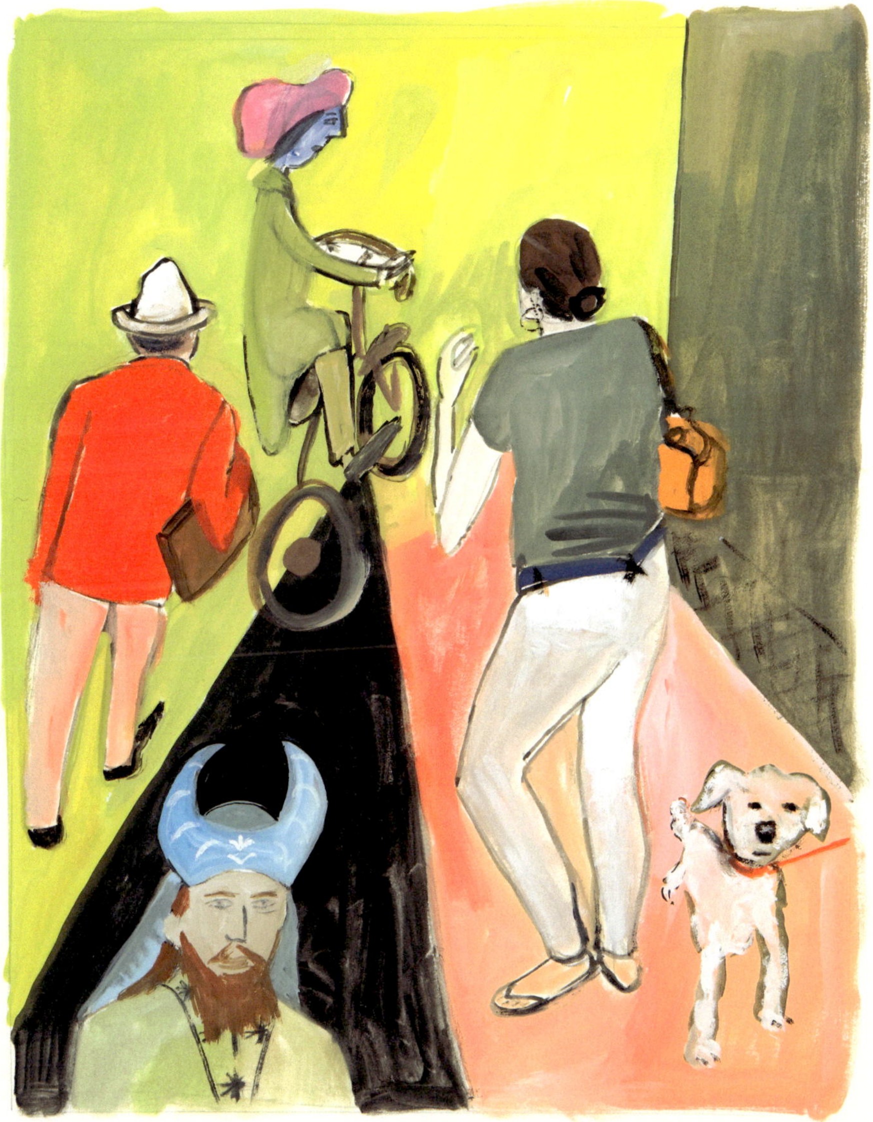

Red Jacket, 2009

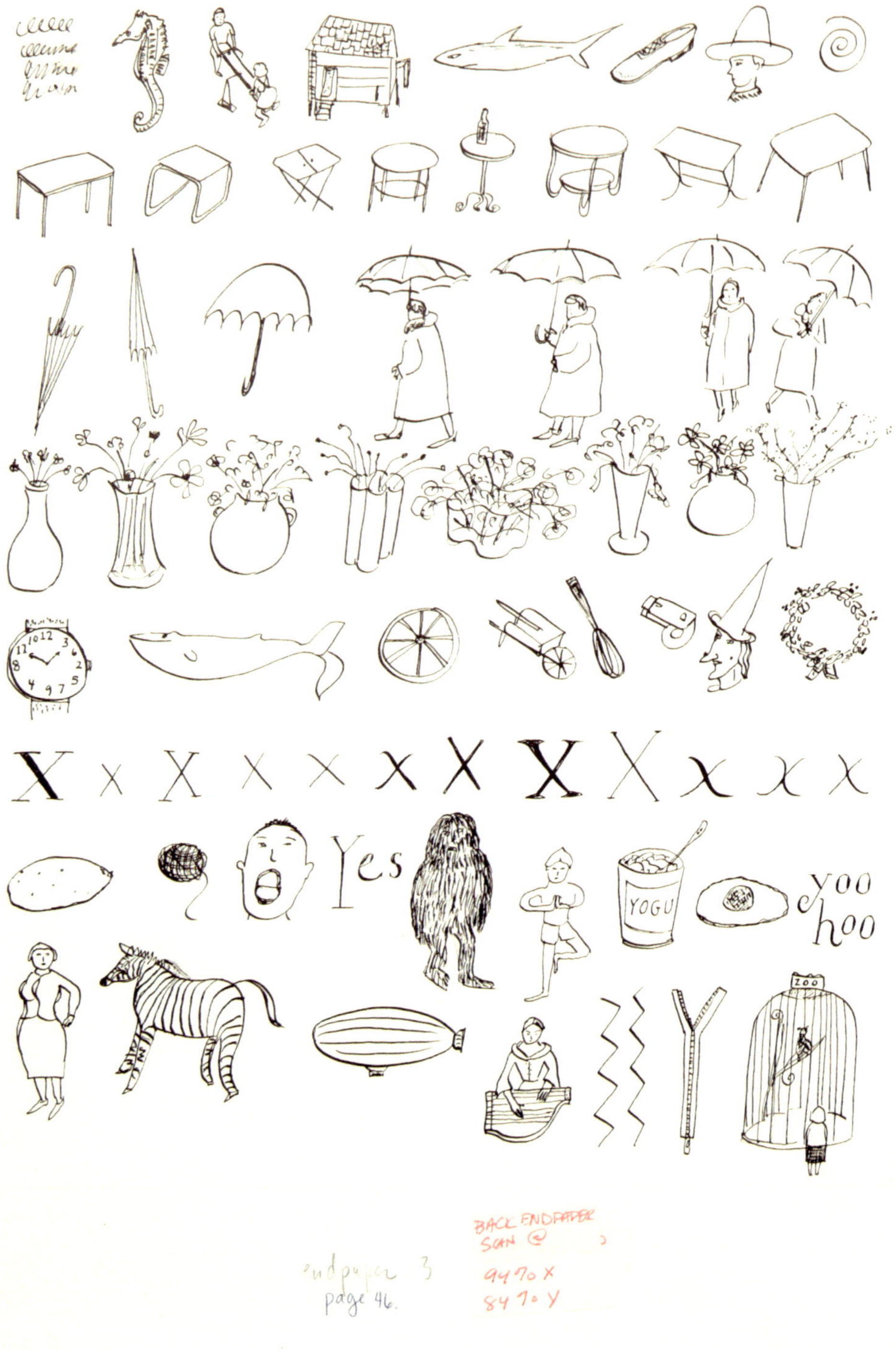

Endpaper (What Pete Ate), 2001

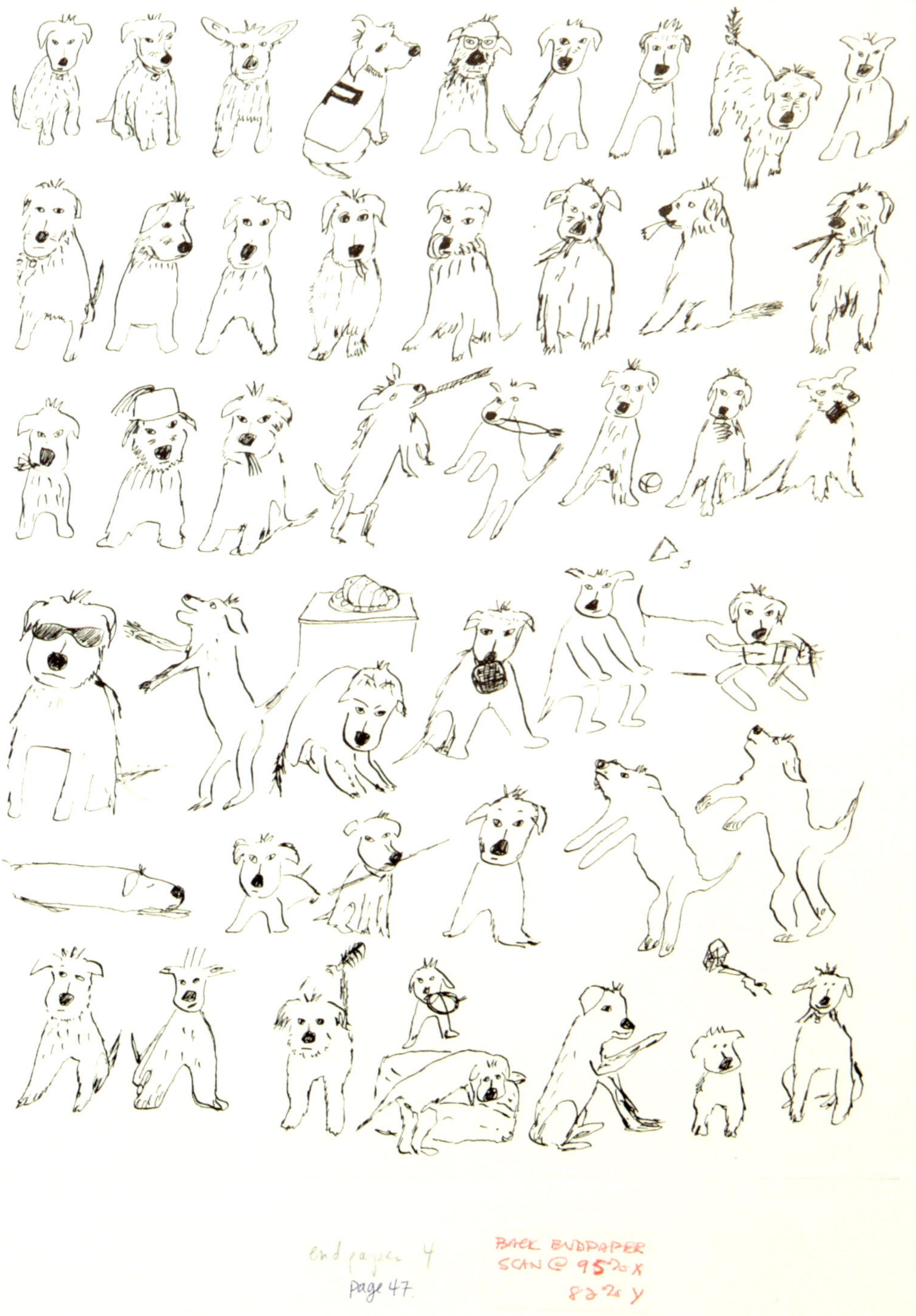
end paper 4
page 47
BACK ENDPAPER
SCAN @ 95% X
82% Y

I Saw Her

THE CURRENT EXHIBITION FEATURES ONE HUNDRED original drawings and paintings that span thirty years of illustration for publication. Drawn largely from the artist's studio and including a generous number of loans from private collections, the selection is composed thematically – as opposed to chronologically, stylistically, or by publication project. It begins and ends approximately with self-portraiture. The first picture is a pencil sketch of a girl wearing galoshes and a blue coat with a fur collar; she is faintly drawn on a pocket-size sketchbook page, inscribed with the words: "I saw her." This modest work (with its whiff of menace) signals so much to follow, from Kalman's journalistic approach to the act of voyeurism it sanctions. "There is a strong personal narrative aspect to what I do. What happens in my life is interpreted in my work. There is very little separation. My work is my journal of my life."[6] By the time we reach the last picture in the exhibition, we know that dog reading a book at the table, paw resting next to a strong cup of coffee, is also a self-portrait of Maira Kalman. We see her.

As beginning and end points, the two pictures – one a sketch the other a painting, both from the 1990s – bracket a selection that moves into the present, while showing a full spectrum of process in between. Preparatory drawings hang next to finished paintings on paper. There are traces of mechanical reproduction, such as Wite-Out erasures and scotch-taped additions, as well as marginal notes to printers and editors. Likewise, stylistic changes that occurred over decades jostle randomly from picture to picture. This corresponds with Kalman's own tendency to work in a number of different styles and media at any given moment within a curatorial narrative that unfolds, quickly and quixotically, along these

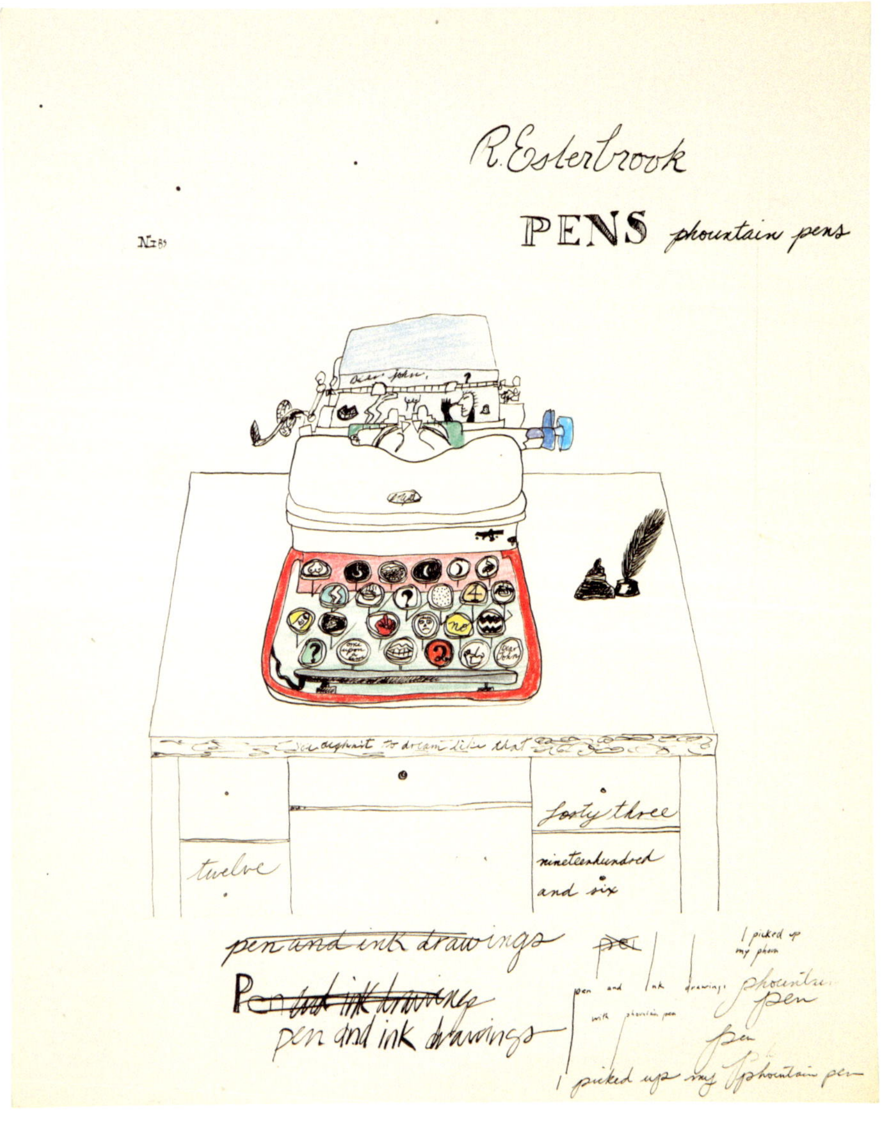

R. Esterbrook Pens, 1977

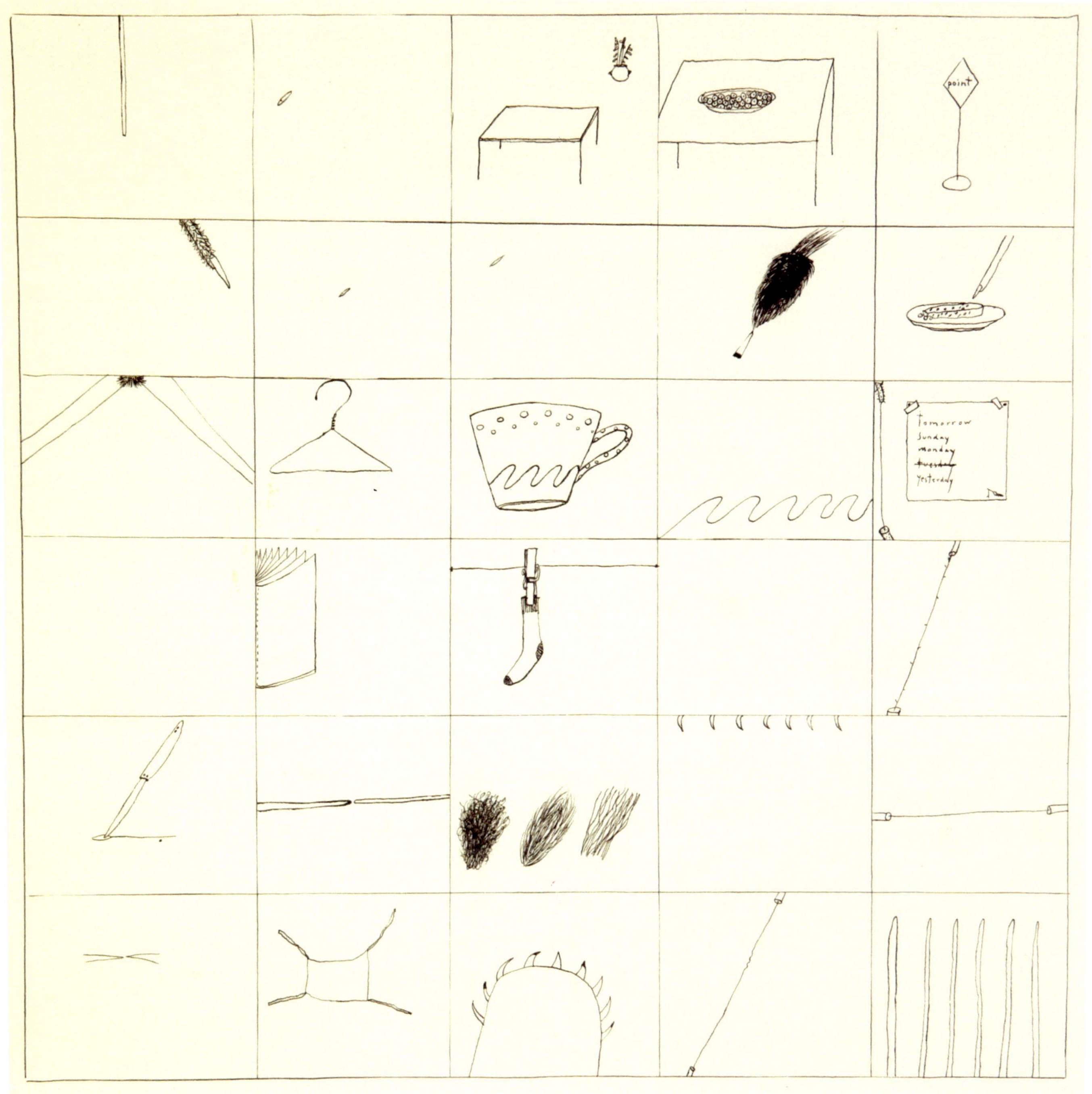

In the Apartment, 1972

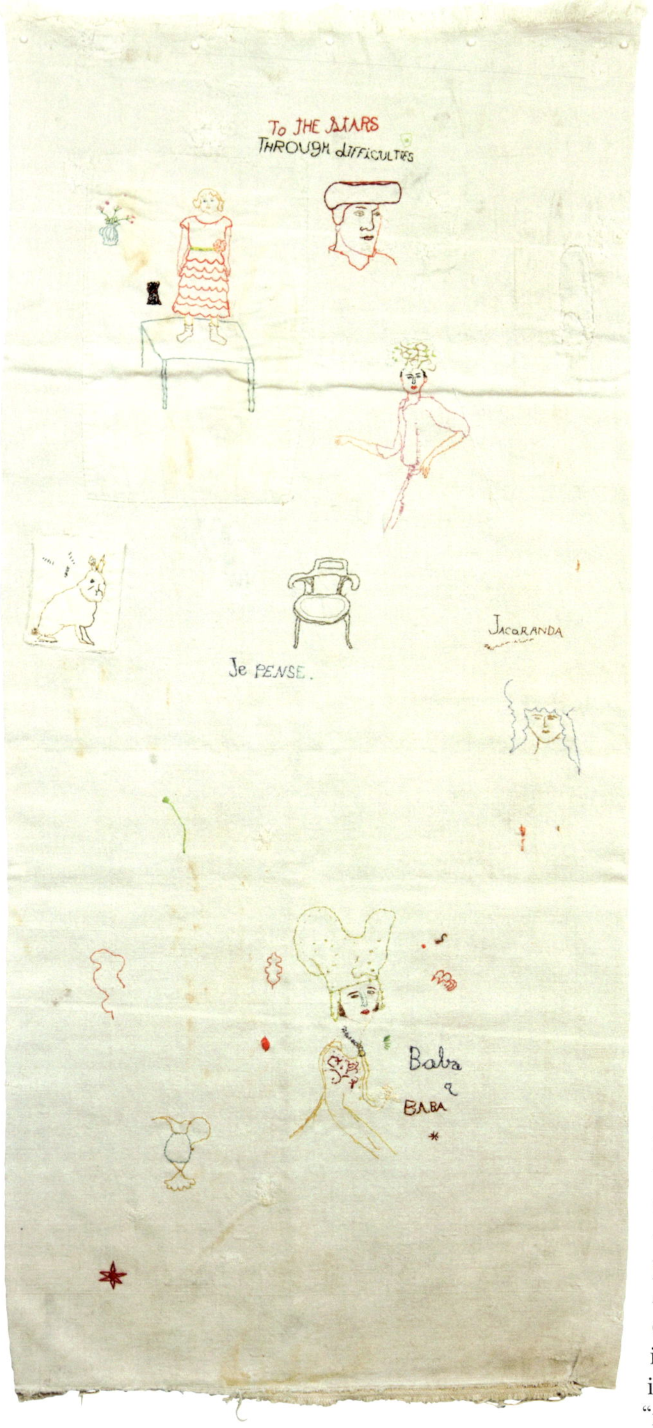

To the Stars, 2005

pictorial lines: self-portraiture; family; dogs; writing, drawing, and mapping; cities. Pause for a glass of water. Resume: portraits of objects; landscapes; dreams; flowers; still life and food; interiors. Attention, when you get to the Rajastani room, keep your eye on the miniature portrait and jump-cut to Abraham Lincoln; faces, fashions, and uniforms; performance; art; books. What emerges is a sense of how consistently Kalman has worked a full range of themes, while concentrating on certain images, to realize her idiosyncratic point of view. Another constant is chaos. Be it crazy and madcap, or simply devastating, chaos erupts from within and pressures against the exterior framework of Kalman's world. Even as her work appears to hold it at bay, chaos ebbs without ever fully waning.

But this is just the beginning of what's on view. Beyond the illustration for which she is best known, Kalman's work in other media – photography, embroidery, textiles, and performance – is represented. So are books and other publications, as well as design objects. As a context for this sweeping total production, Kalman has created a special installation [pages 126–35]. The space is furnished with chairs, ladders, and "many tables of many things," to quote Kalman, who has judiciously ransacked her own studio, household, basement, and storage to arrange it. Among the many things are fezzes, bobby pins, balls of string, lists, things that have fallen out of books, rubber bands. (Kalman is a cofounder with the artist Alex Melamid of the Rubber Band Society, which disbanded when the group became too popular.[7]) There are bits of moss tucked into envelopes that are neatly labeled in Kalman's hand with the names of places such as Matisse's grave, Marfa, Falling Water, Jerusalem, and Sissinghurst. Kalman's collection is based on someone else's she had found at an antique store. Hanging on a nearby wall is Kalman's painting [page 47] of the shoebox containing **Mosses of Long Island**. Why is this so tender an image? Perhaps it is its evocation of the word "amateur"–from the Latin "to love"–that ennobles every hobbyist pursuit to connect with the world in some small way. Some of the many things Kalman has collected are encased in two vitrines that were made years ago by her son, when he was thirteen. Painted blue, one of these vitrines holds a wooden box, painted black, made by her daughter when she was eight. All of it appears expressive of Kalman's habits as a collector, traveler, reader, and avid walker. To wander amidst this theatrical tableau is to catch a glimpse of the world as Kalman sees it, both inside and outside the studio.

M&Co

ANOTHER STUDIO LOOMS LARGE IN THE FOREGROUND, the revolutionary design firm of M&Co. Founded in 1979 by Maira Kalman's late husband Tibor Kalman, M&Co's challenging principles of un-design, blunt vernaculars, and socialist agenda are widely credited for having changed the look and profession of contemporary graphic art. For instance, Benetton's *Colors* magazine, the firm's most infamous work, emblazoned itself in mass cultural memory with in-your-face portraits

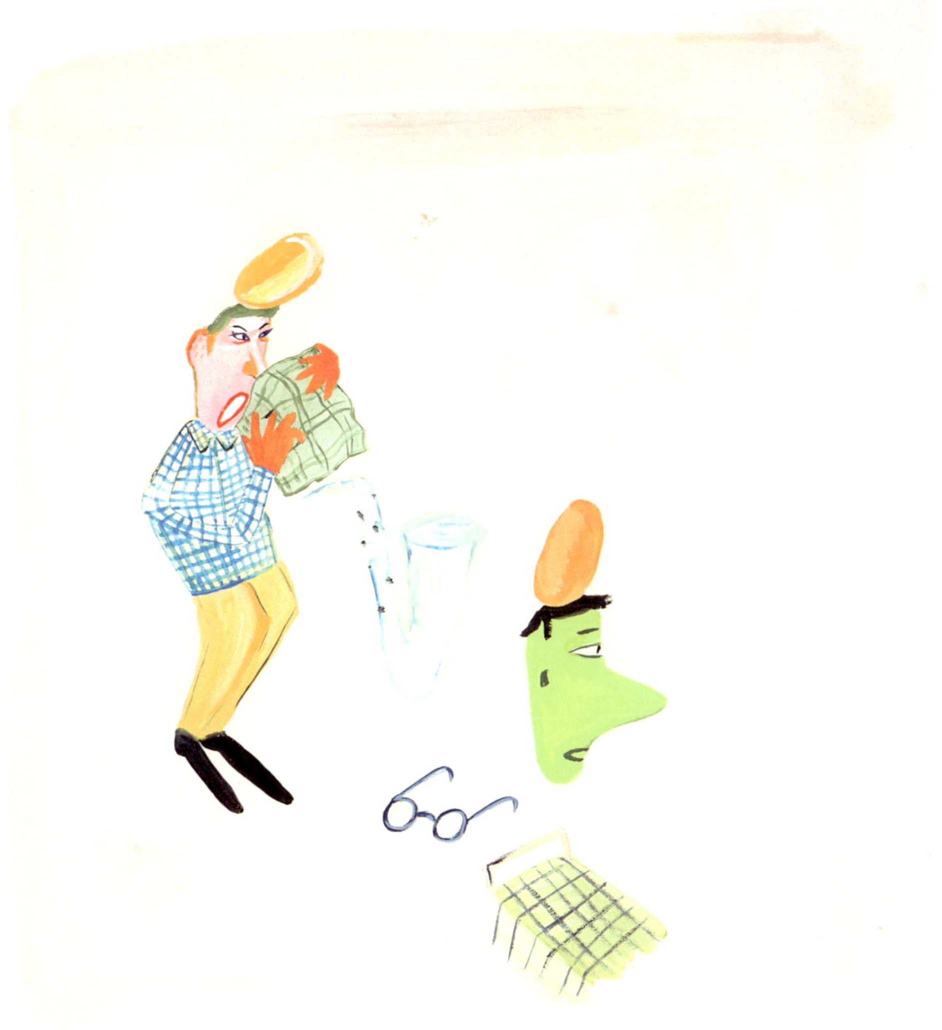

Blow the Saxophone, 1988

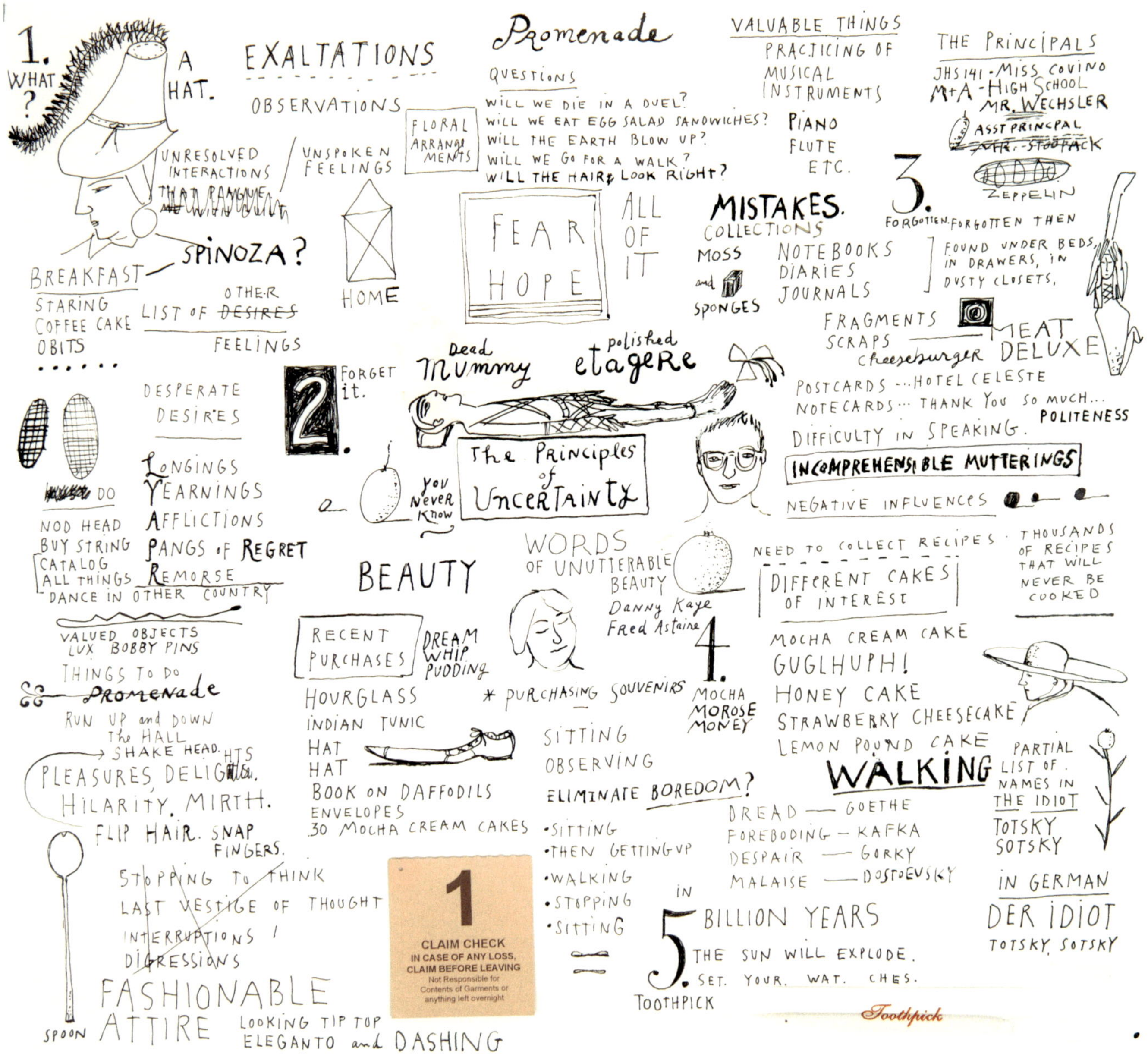

Exaltations/Observations, 2006

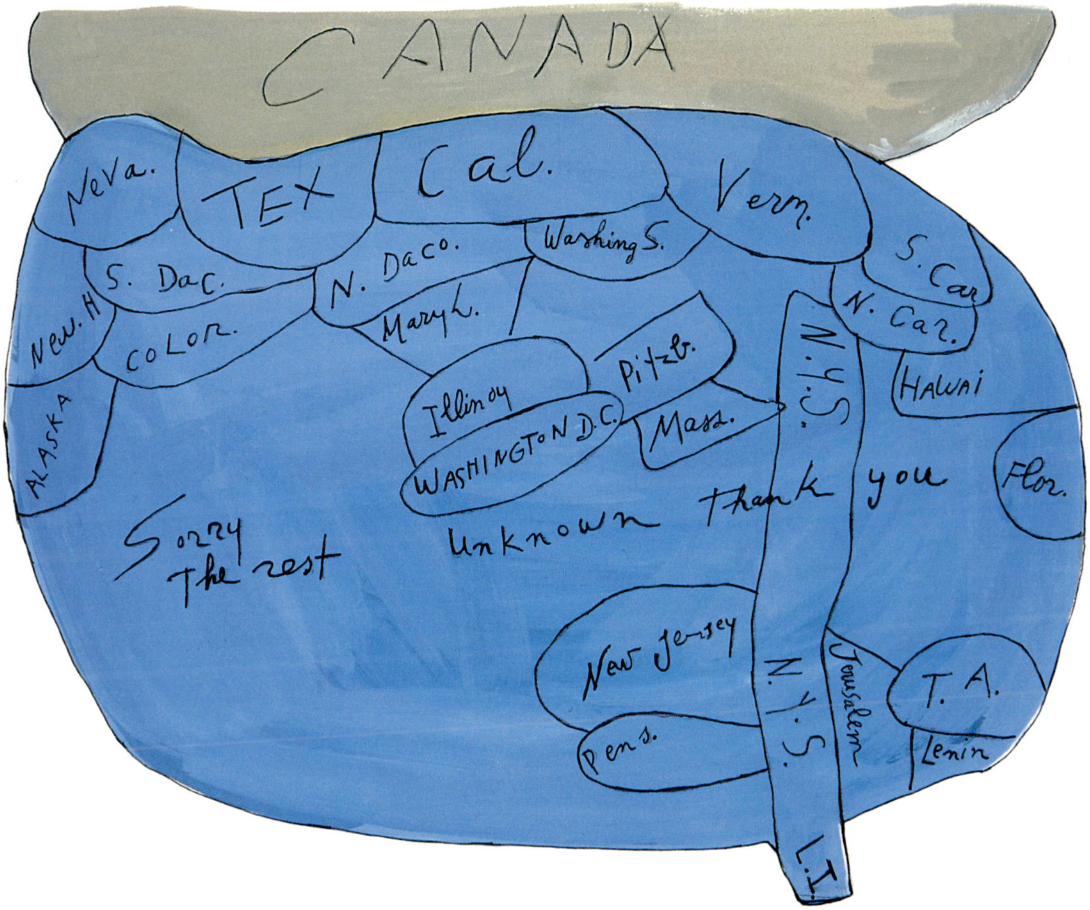

My Beautiful Mother's Map, 2006

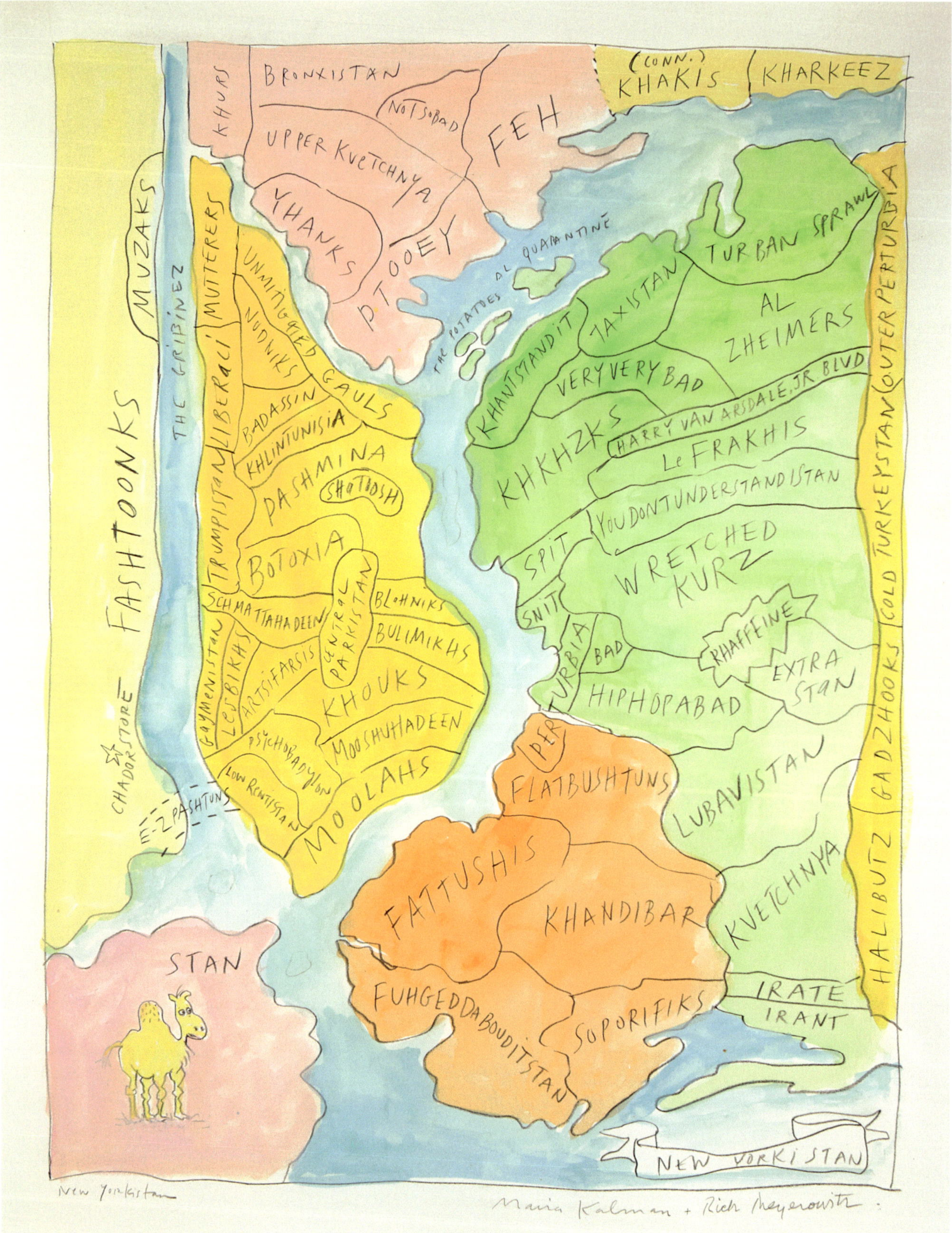

New Yorkistan, 2001

of Queen Elizabeth as a black woman and President Reagan scourged with the AIDS virus. Hip, humorous, radical, and angry, *Colors* delivered one-two graphic and political punch. Created to sell Italian sportswear, it was also rife with the contradictions of pairing a "bad boy" designer with a corporate sponsor. That said, *Colors* was a first big gulp of multiculturalism and issues of globalism within the popular media. No wonder Maira called Tibor a "perverse optimist." He called her "M" and named his company after her.

Tibor Kalman and Maira Berman met in 1968 when both were eighteen-year-old students on the verge of flunking out of New York University. Both were children of families who immigrated to the United States in the 1950s, which may explain a mutual love of things American—coffee shops in particular. In the background of Maira's 1998 portrait of Tibor hangs a small, greasy trophy—Tibor collected onion rings—from the just recently closed Joe Junior, their favorite New York City neighborhood coffee shop. Another painting, a portrait of a Snickers bar [page 70], pays homage to Maira's love of American snack foods. Growing up as outsiders, however, also means otherwise ordinary things and daily language may seem curious, alien, or just plain funny. This is how things often look as seen through the Kalmans' respective bodies of work, as if you are seeing something for the first time. (Look, a glass of water [page 41].) Jokes are also big.

As students, neither Maira nor Tibor trained in art or design, a lack that turned out to seem purposeful, given Tibor's reputation for fearlessness and Maira's hallmark naïveté. Not knowing the rules of how something should be done or should look leaves one free to make

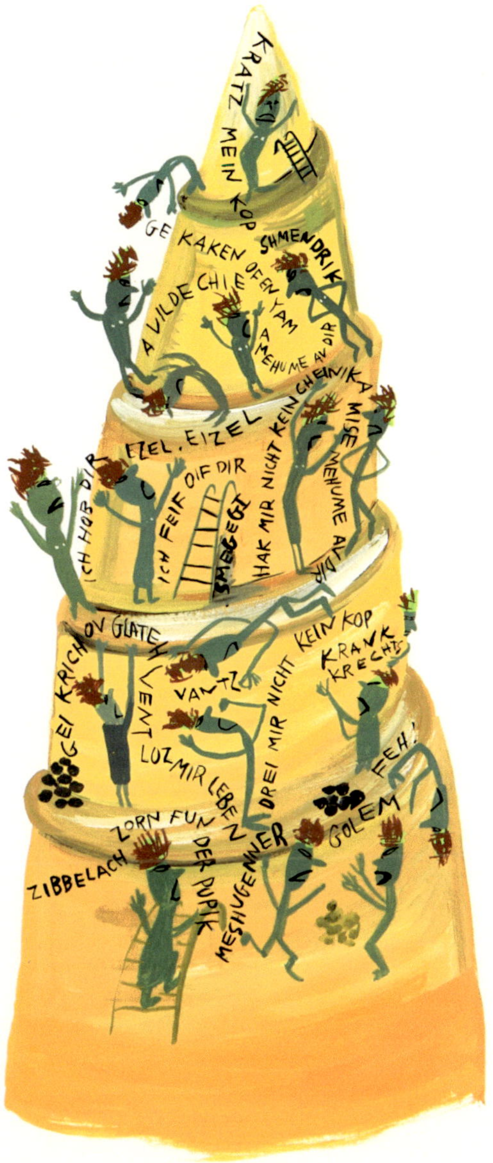

Tower of Babel, 1989

The Planes Attacked, 2002

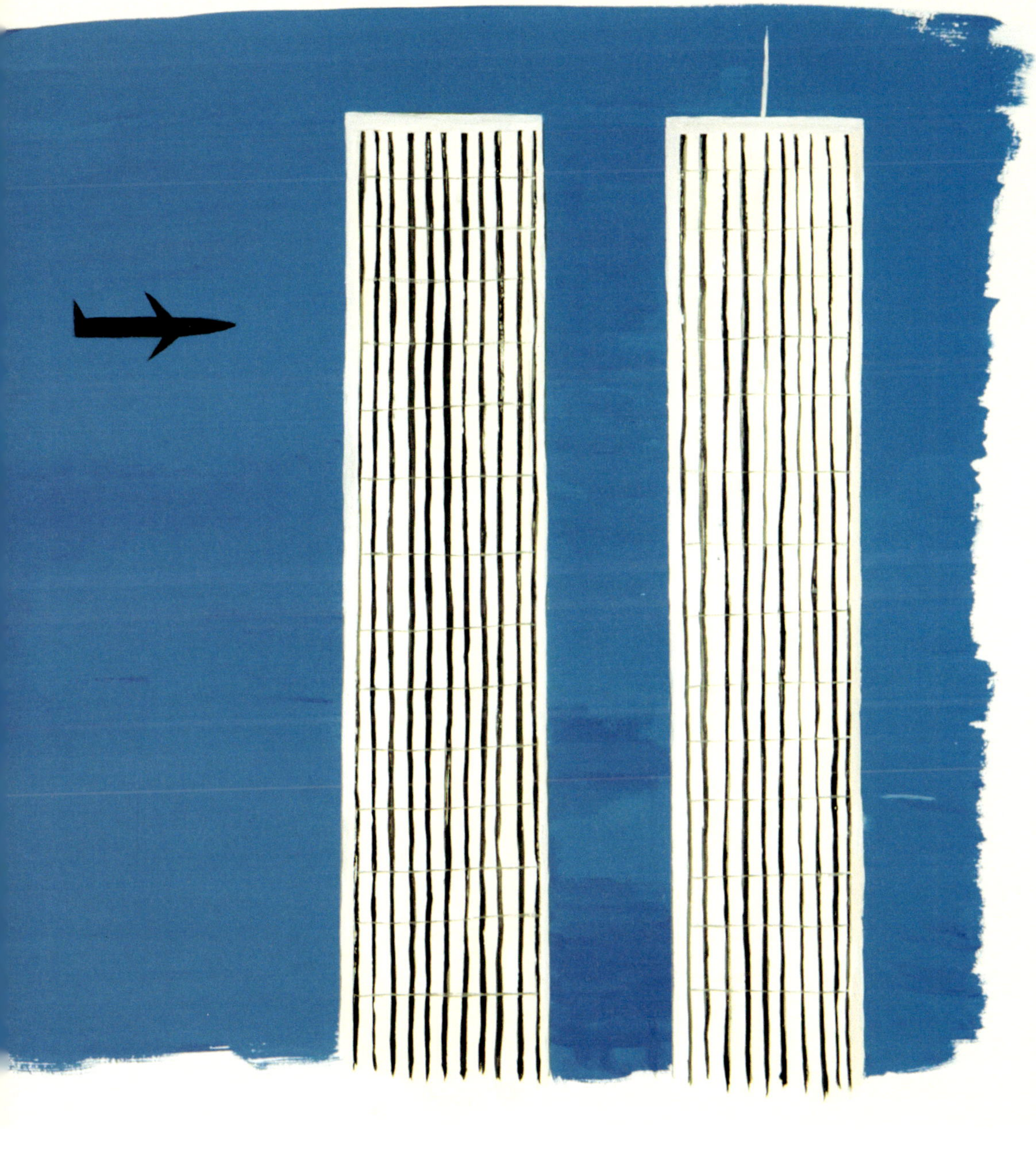

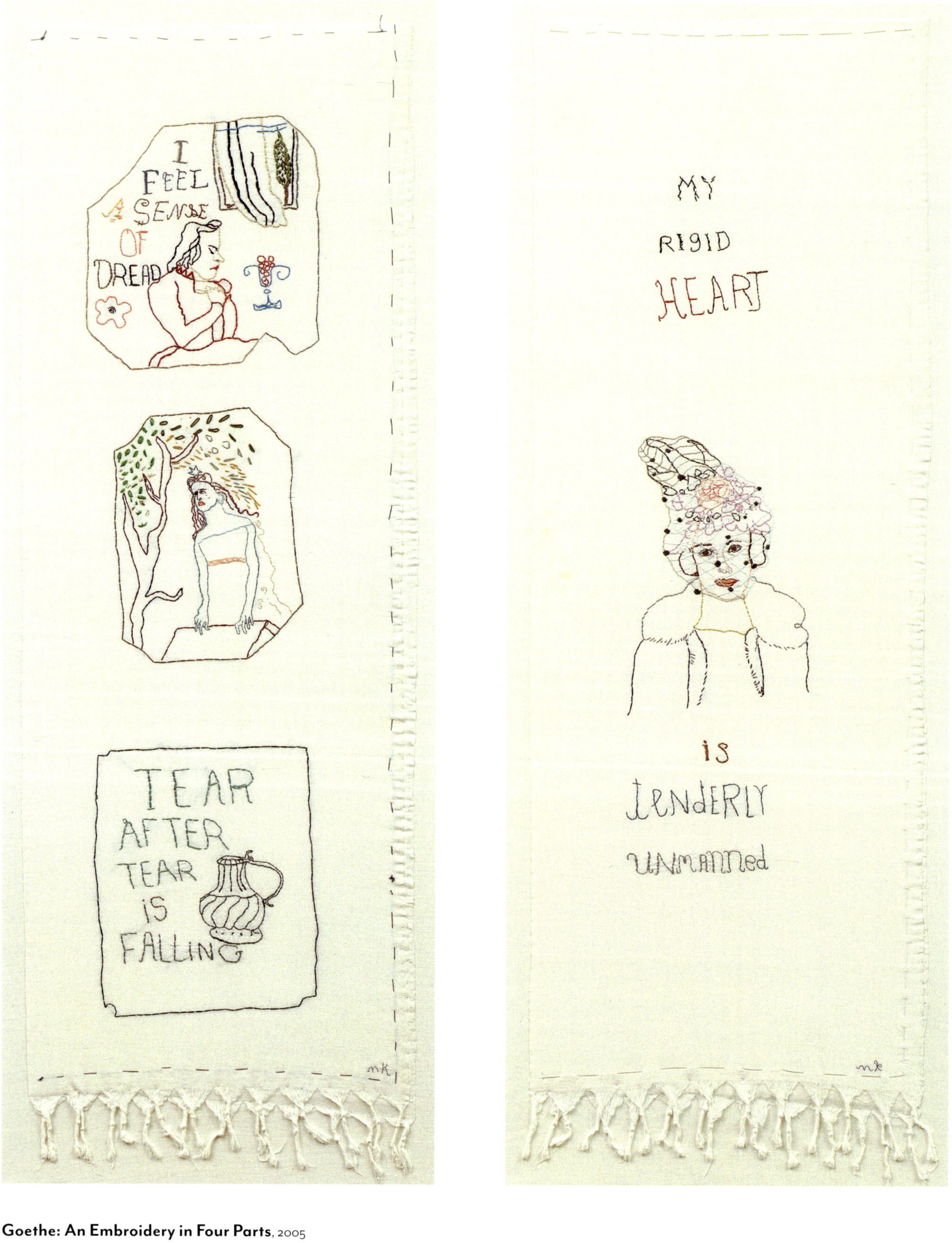

Goethe: An Embroidery in Four Parts, 2005

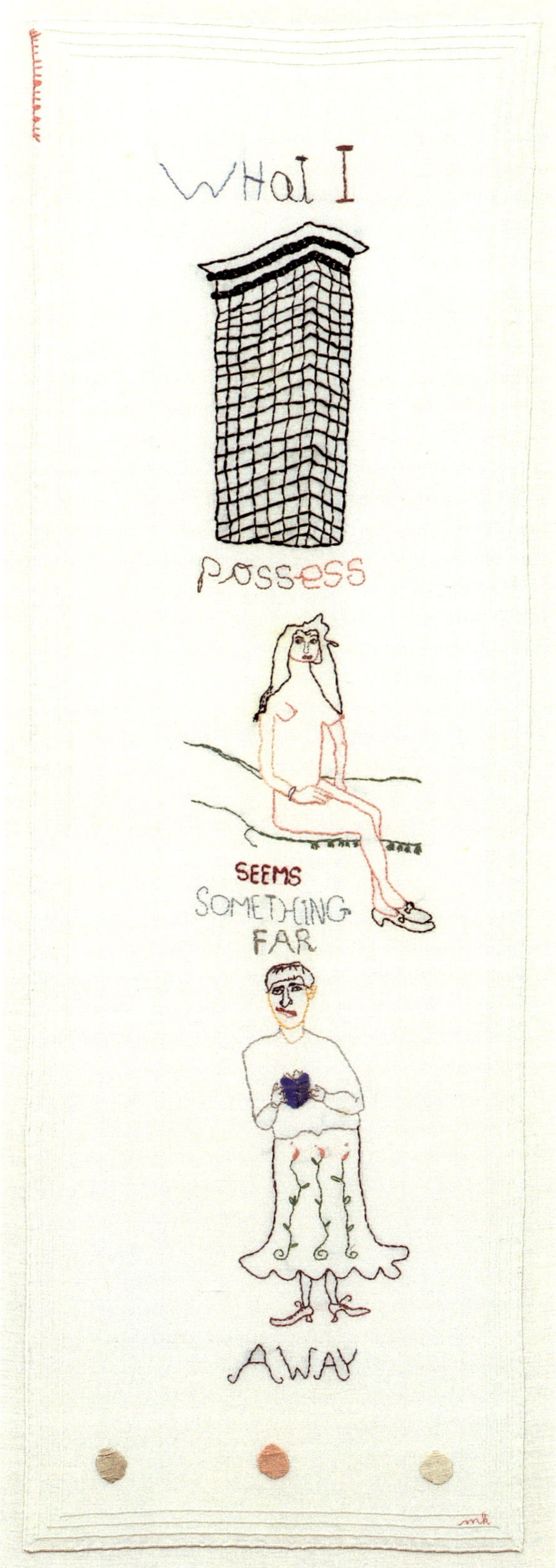
WHAT I
possess
SEEMS
SOMETHING
FAR
AWAY
mk

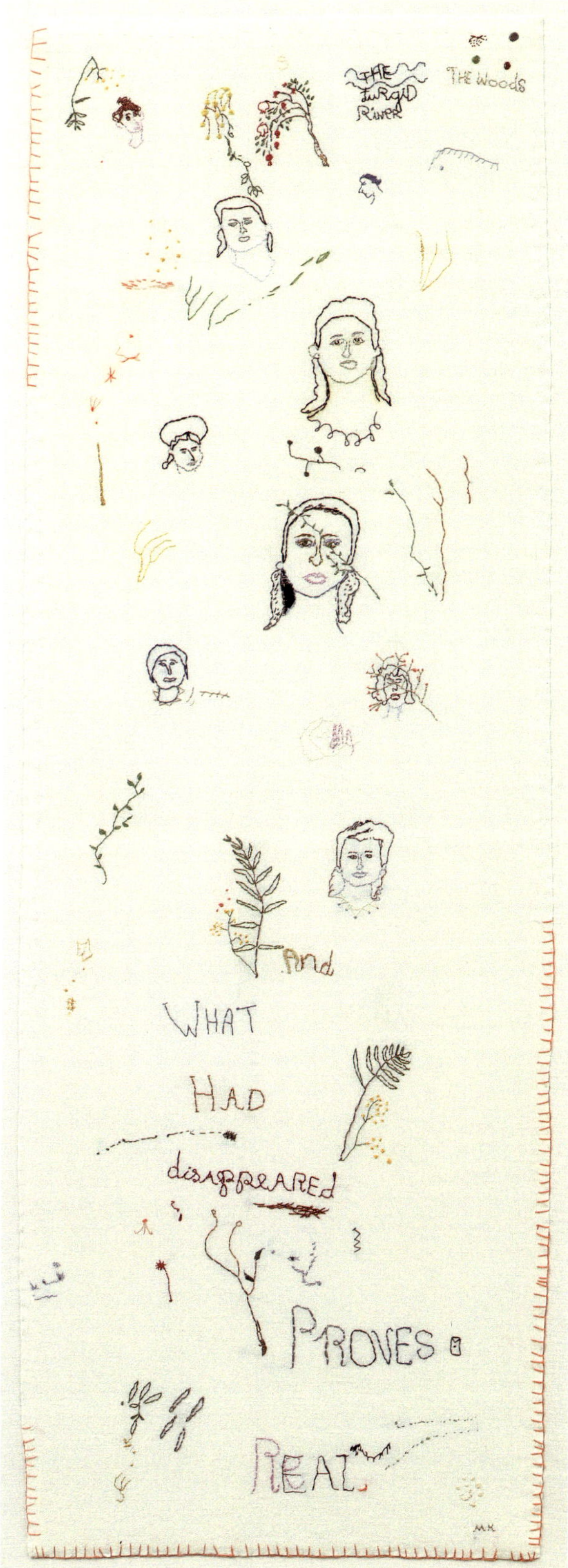
THE turgid River
THE Woods
And
WHAT
HAD
disappeared
PROVES
REAL
M.K.

2 Million People, 2009

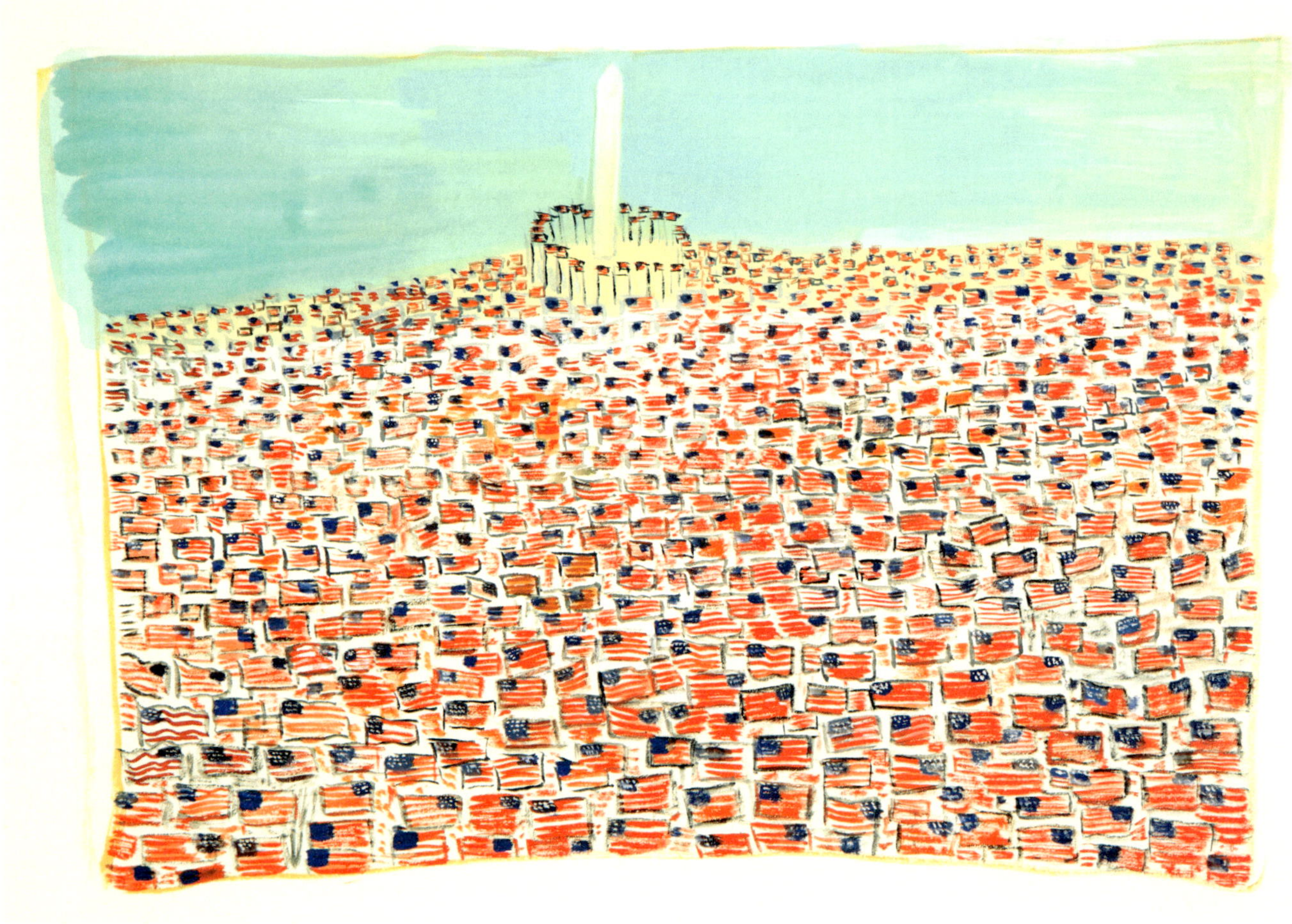

things up for one's self. By encouraging each other to have the confidence to follow intuition, the Kalmans evolved creatively in a dialectical bond, as if by design. While Tibor as a young man was busy getting radicalized (he joined Students for a Democratic Society and cut sugar cane in Cuba), Maira says she was home "knitting sweaters for him. (Feminists hated us.)."[8] However, what seemed like a conventional relationship from the outside was anything but, when one considers the work this partnership engendered.

Maira was never officially a part of M&Co, but at the same time she was intrinsic to it. No profile of the studio is complete without acknowledging her role. As design historian Steven Heller summed up: "Maira Kalman—as muse, sounding board, wacky-idea generator—has been instrumental in most of M&Co's major projects."[9] Among the most beloved is a series of design objects that M&Co produced, including watches, clocks, paperweights. And among the most popular of these is the 10-One-4 watch. Now in the collection of the Museum of Modern Art, it is based on a sketch Tibor spotted in one of Maira's journals of a clock with a few random numbers sprinkled on the face.[10]

Even before Tibor started the studio, Maira was a contributor. For a guide to New York he designed in 1973, she wrote the text. Her vision rings clear in the introduction, which reads like a voice-over for her myriad illustrations of the city to come: "There's nothing special about New York. Sure it's the banking, finance, art, entertainment, media, trade capital of the world. So what? It's just a façade. New York is really just a fascinating fabric of small towns. What's nine million people but lots of humanity living together."[11] From **New Yorkistan** to Grand Central Station to **Annual Misery Day Parade**, it's all in the script [pages 26, 36–37, 39].

Among M&Co's early clients was the musician David Byrne. For the cover of his 1981 solo record

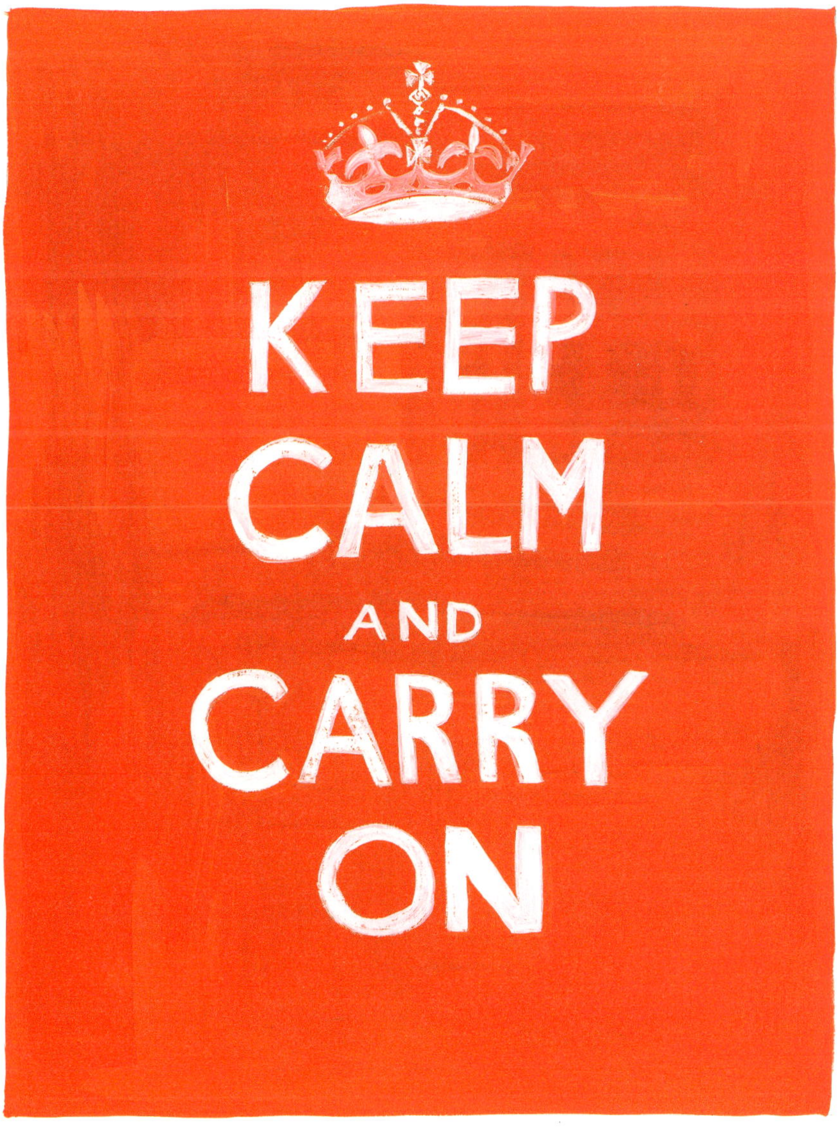

Keep Calm, 2007

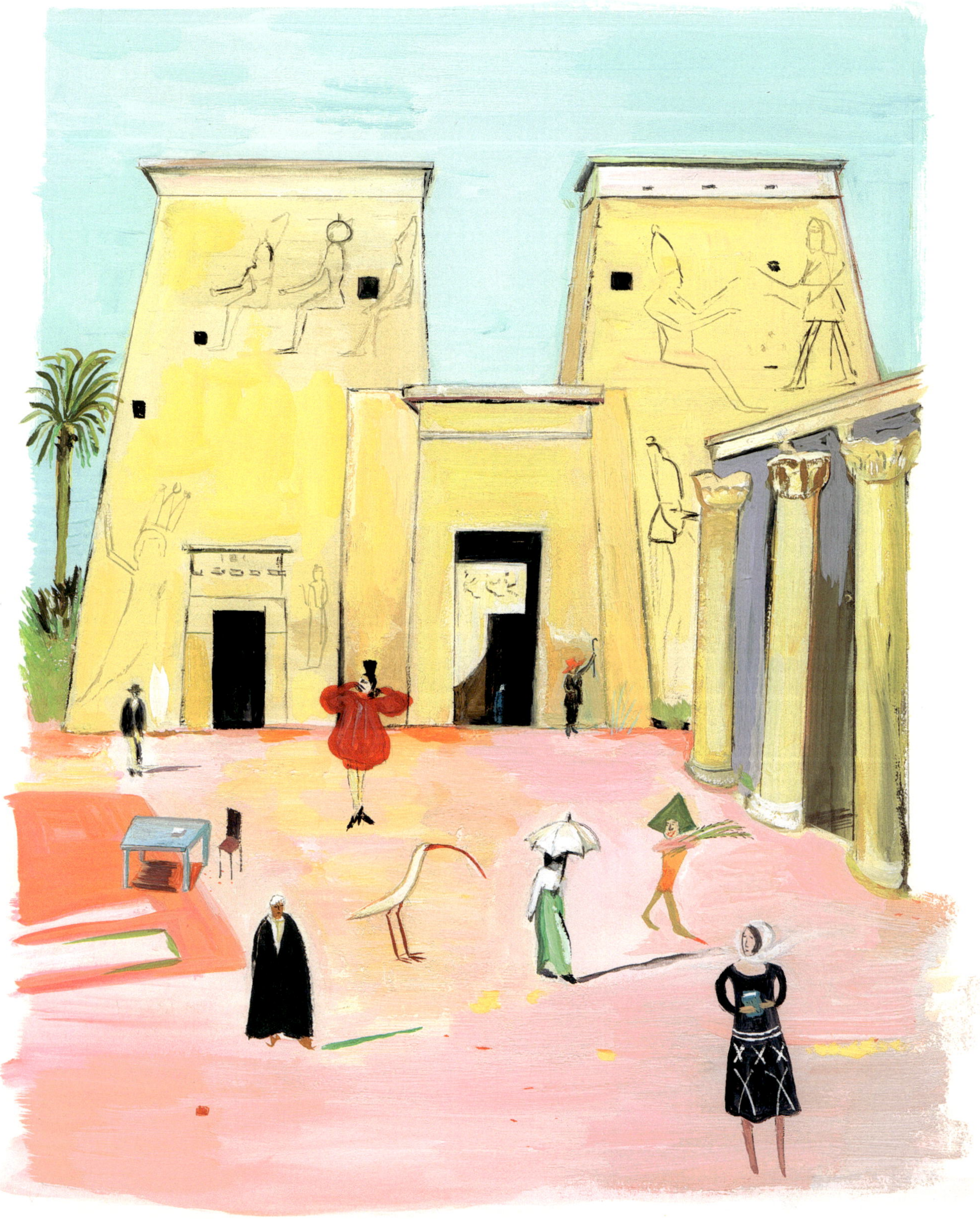

The Temple of Isis, 2004–5

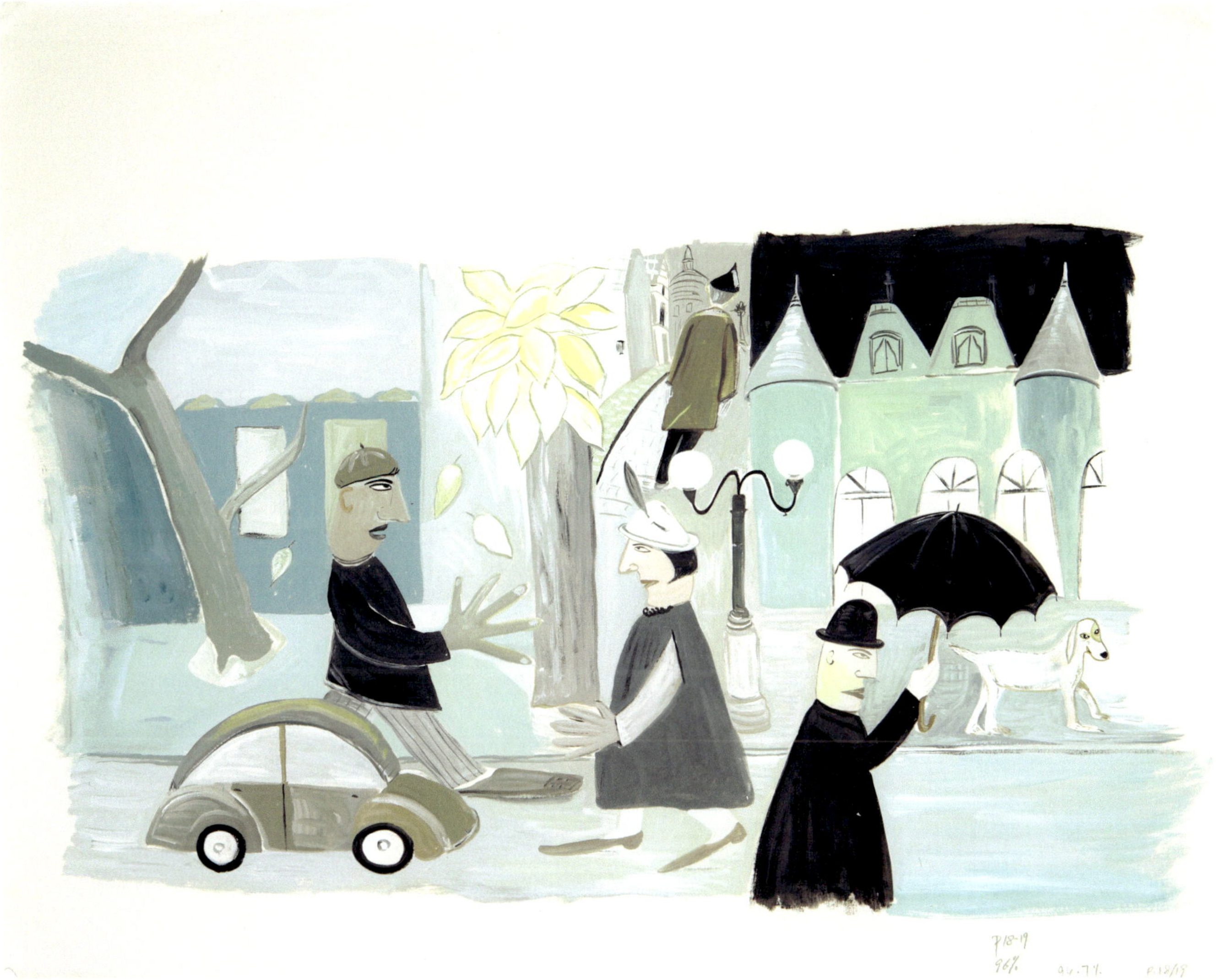

The Poet Wrote on the Sidewalk, 1991

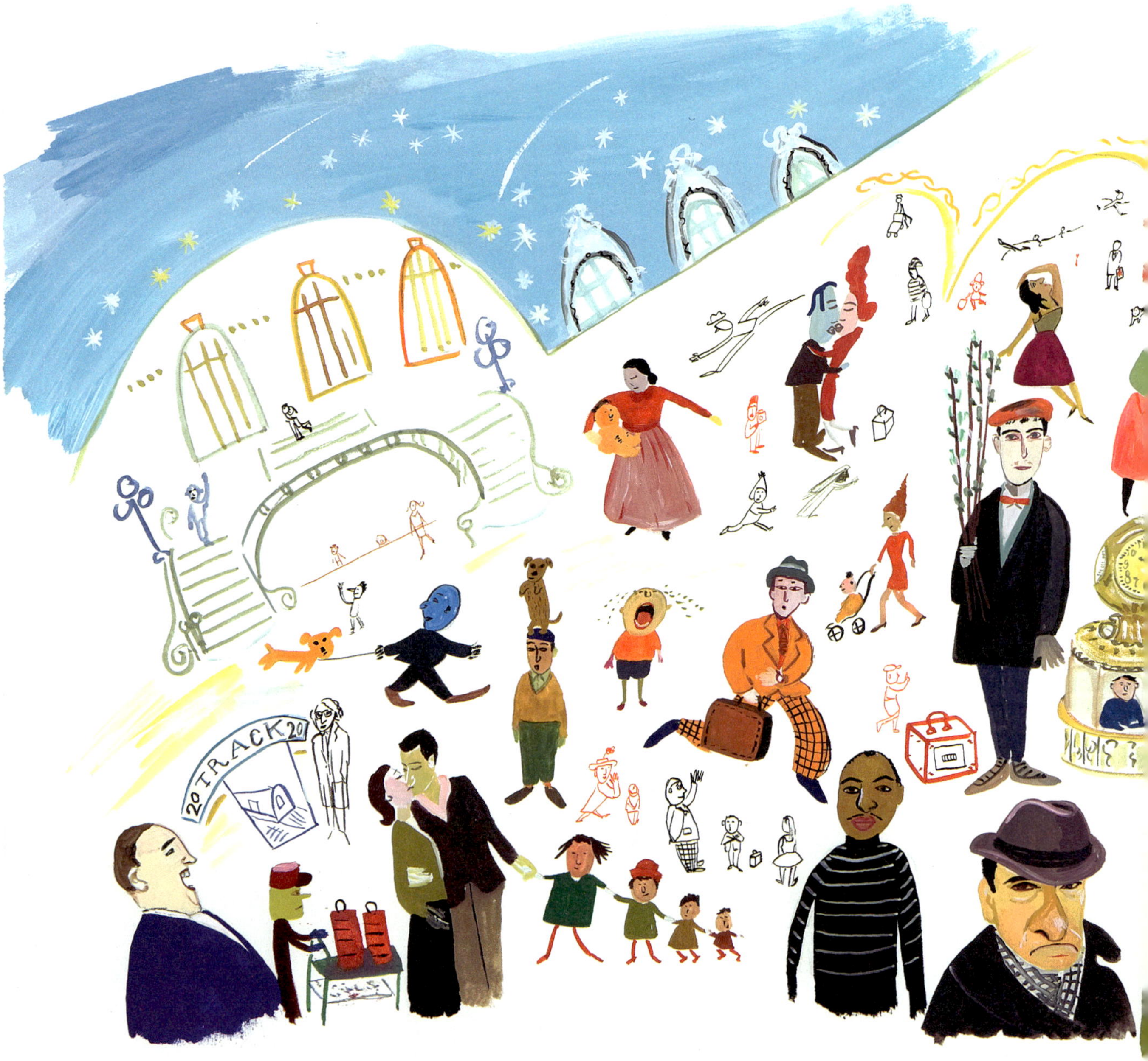

New York, Grand Central Station, 1999

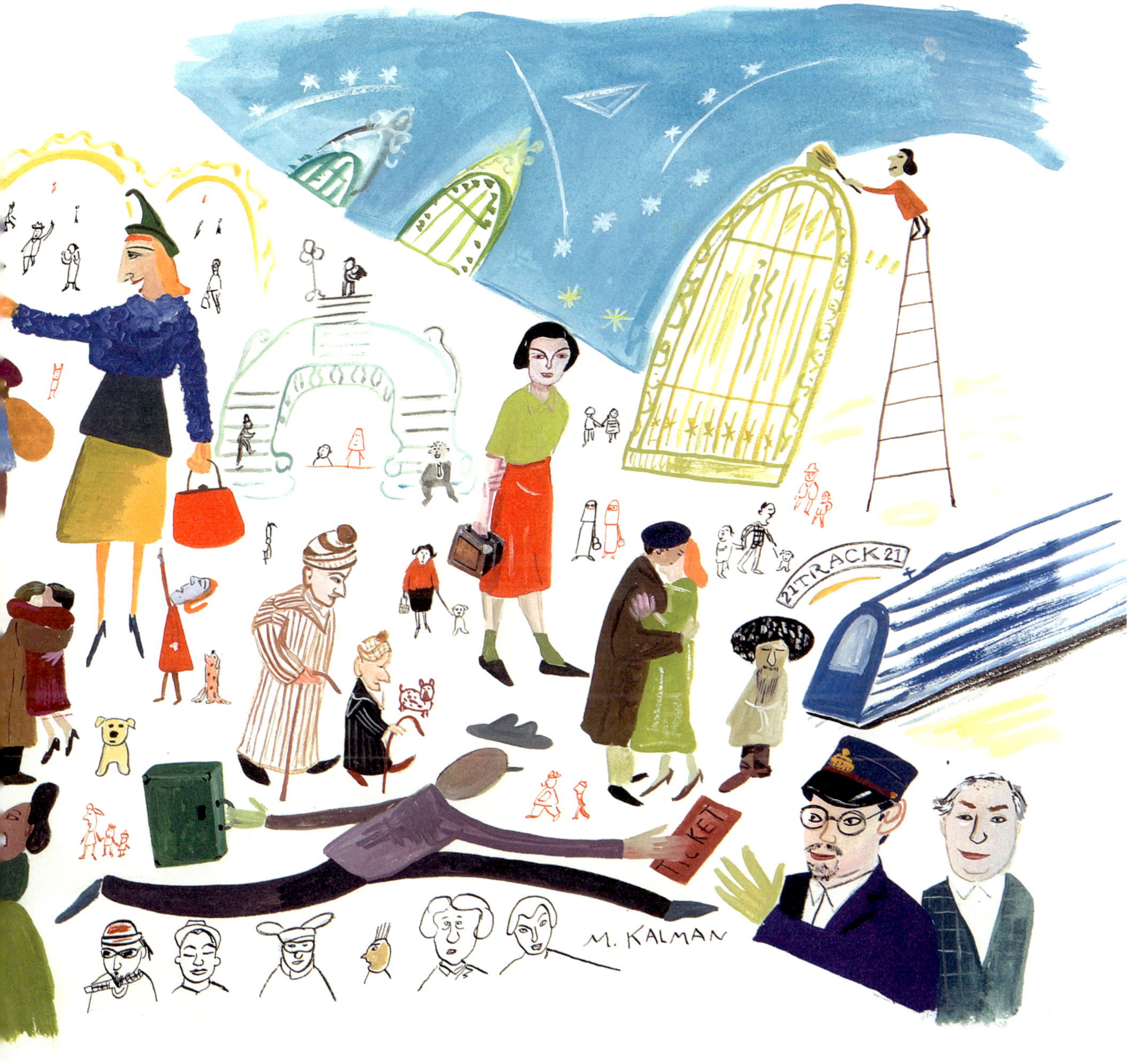
21 TRACK 21
TICKET
M. KALMAN

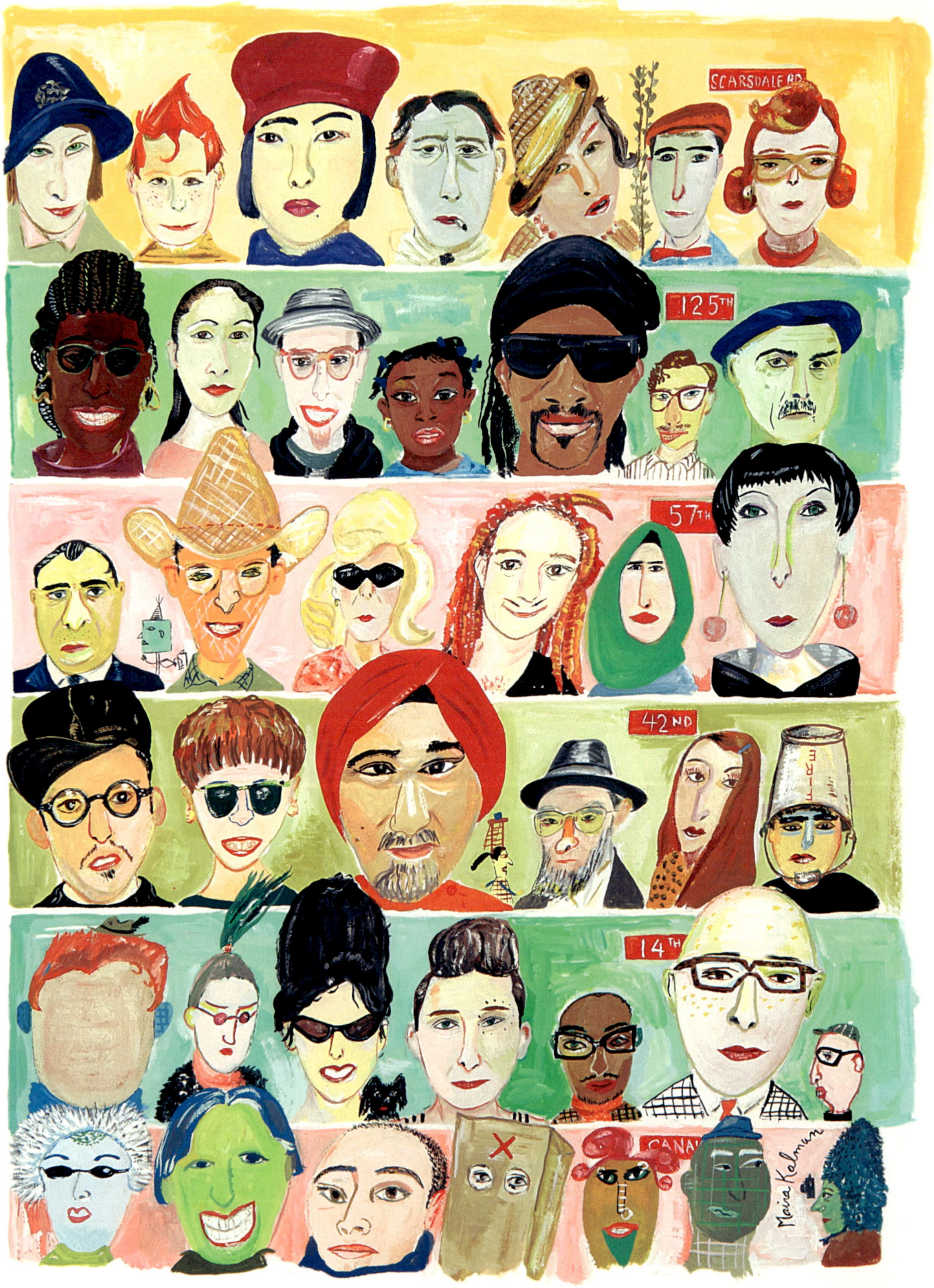

Crosstown Boogie Woogie, 1995

Three Big Songs, Tibor chose four doodlelike drawings by Maira. It was also Tibor who brokered Maira's first children's book into being. ("Schmuck, it's time for you to do a book," she says were Tibor's exact words.[12]) Published in 1987 with text by David Byrne and pictures by Maira Kalman, **Stay Up Late** is a New Wave children's book—and not just because the words are the lyrics for the anthem song by New Wave's signature group Talking Heads, but because of the illustrations' electrified compositions, synthetic colors, and big-shouldered, skinny-legged characters, waving noodlelike arms, mouths agape in jubilant ululations, while the whole family dances around a living room amidst bobbing bits of furniture, a tiny TV, and a pet robot. Even baby is geek chic with its itty-bitty green hair. Sound like the neighbors of one's East Village heyday?

Maira Berman

FOR ADULTS, MAIRA'S EARLY ILLUSTRATION STYLE WAS more on the punk side. Weasel Wendy, Imogen Placenta, Letitia Air, and Maria Crass are among an irony-clad cast of characters that turn up in an undated illustration for *National Lampoon*.[13] Kalman worked for the magazine as a pasteup artist from 1979 to 1981, while establishing herself as a freelance graphic artist. Her work of this period is signed with her maiden name, Berman. Another early colored-pencil drawing [page 74] features a blood-oozing suitcase in the center of a room full of dolled-up men. Well serving the David Lynch-like drama, the floor pitches forward. More generally,

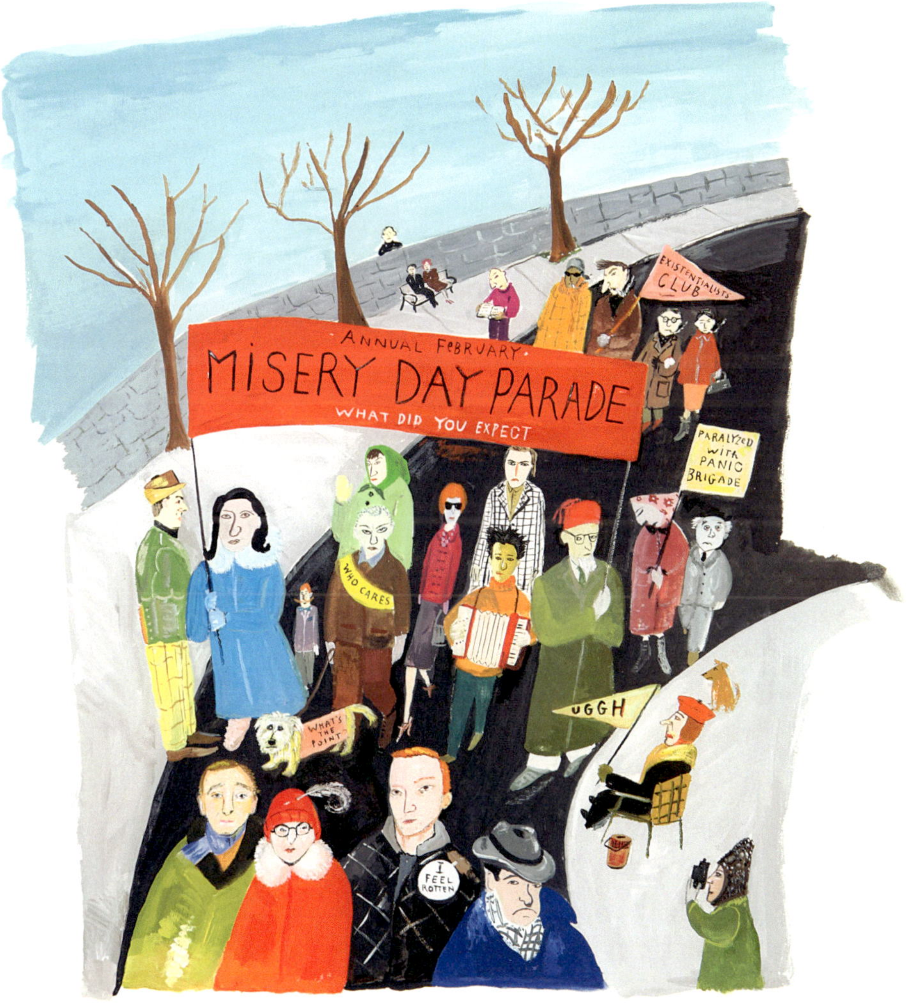

Annual Misery Day Parade, 2001

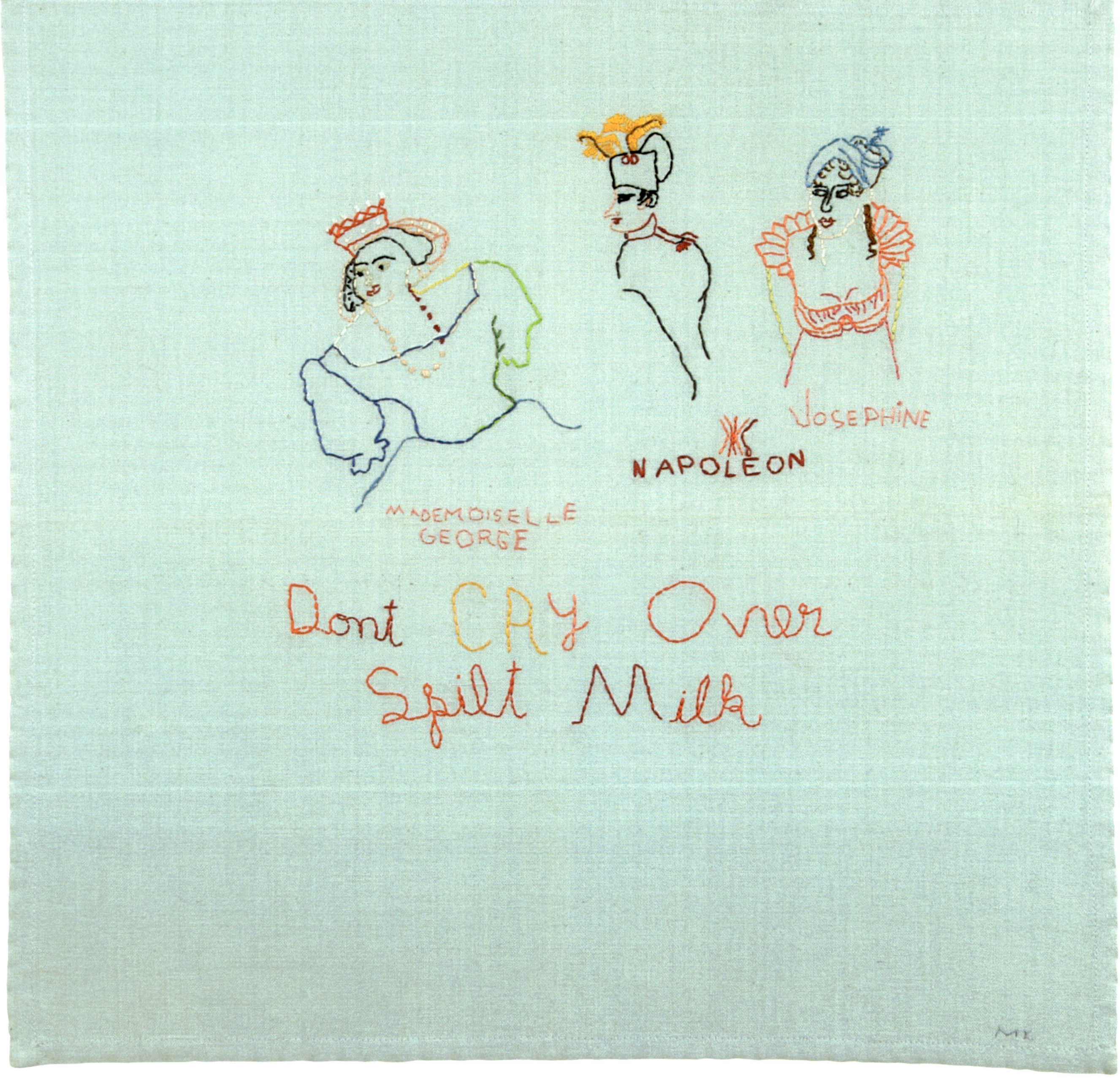

Don't Cry Over Spilt Milk, 2005

Glass, 1996

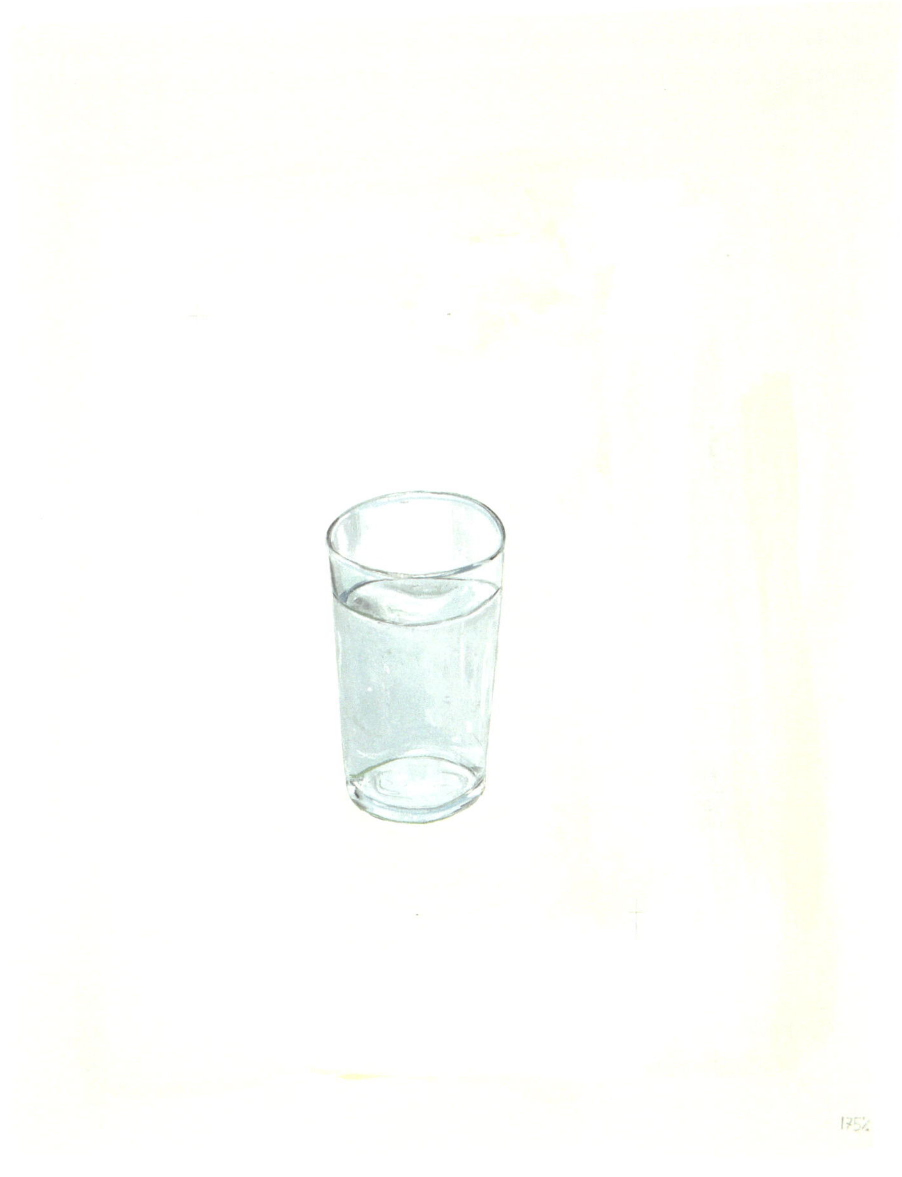

however, this tipped-up perspective shows the world come unglued and things gone topsy-turvy. "I can see a crazy world.... It is a violent, comical and funny feeling," she said in a 1983 interview.[14] It's also patently surreal.

Kalman's pictorial space is dream space, wherein visual non sequiturs and stream-of-consciousnes narratives are the disorderly order of the day – and, according to her, the everyday reality of life with children, which, by the time **Stay Up Late** was published, the Kalmans had two of: Lulu Bodoni (after a favorite typeface) and Alex Onomatopoeia (one of several middle names). "If you live with children, the kinds of conversation you have during the day range from the surreal to the mundane to the insane to the pedantic."[15] Following the successful collaboration with Byrne, Kalman went solo. Her next two books are discombobulating tales of adventure as told by a girl named Lulu to help her brother, Alex, fall asleep (or stay up late). The fictional children have a pet dog, Max, whereas their namesakes did not. (The Kalmans eventually did get a dog, whose appetites are the subject of another children's book, **What Pete Ate**.) Real Kalman family travels are woven throughout these books. **Sayonara, Mrs. Kackleman** was published in 1989, the same year as Maira's solo exhibition at the Ginza Art Space in Toyko. Writing for the brochure, curator Hiroko Tanaka gently stirs, "You might feel a little awed or even frightened when an adult draws like a kid, since there is so little pretention." She continues, "Her work is so unrestrained that you might even feel jealous." And concedes, "Maira Kalman, your pictures are so crazy that everyone wants to hug them."[16]

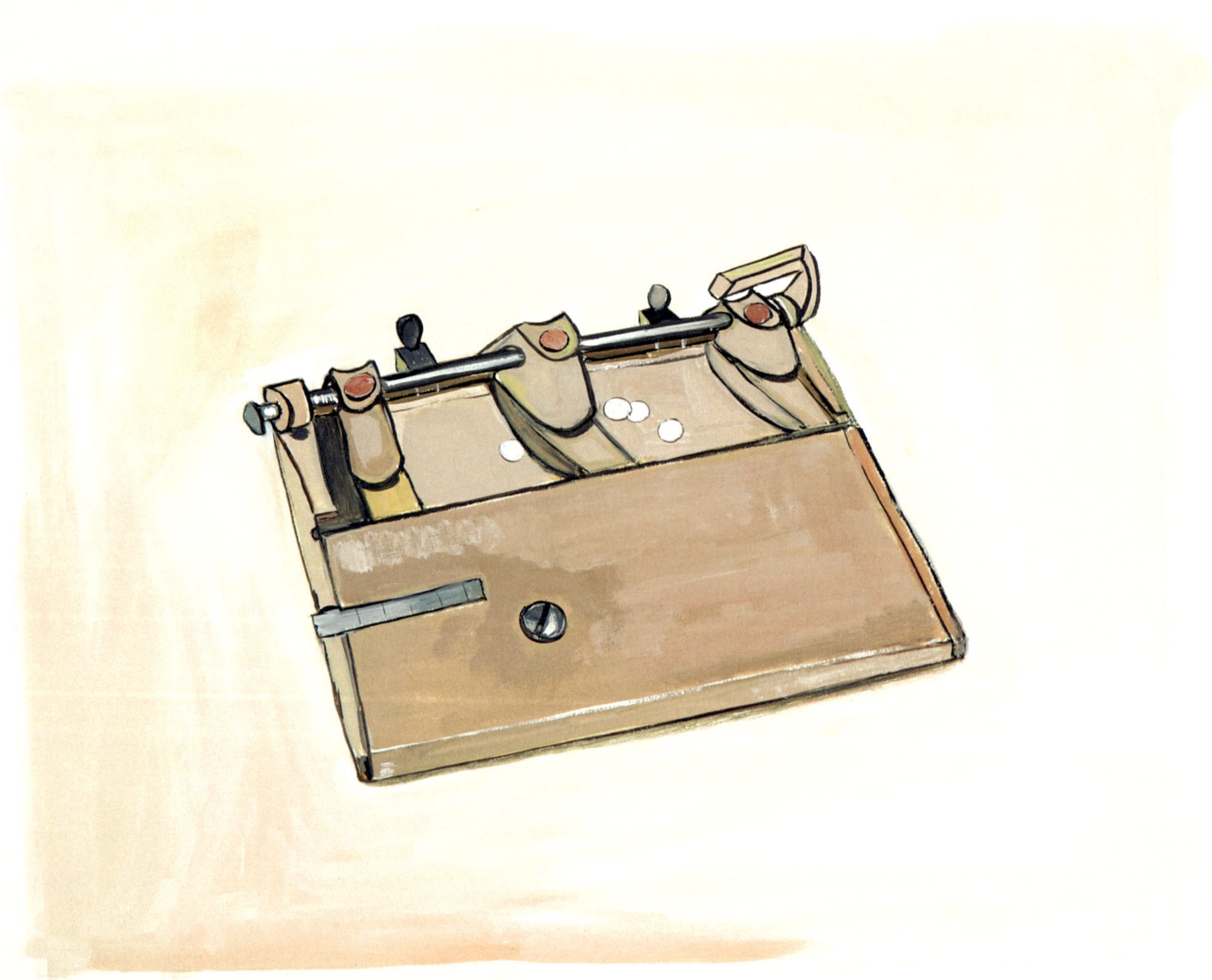

Hole Punch, 2009

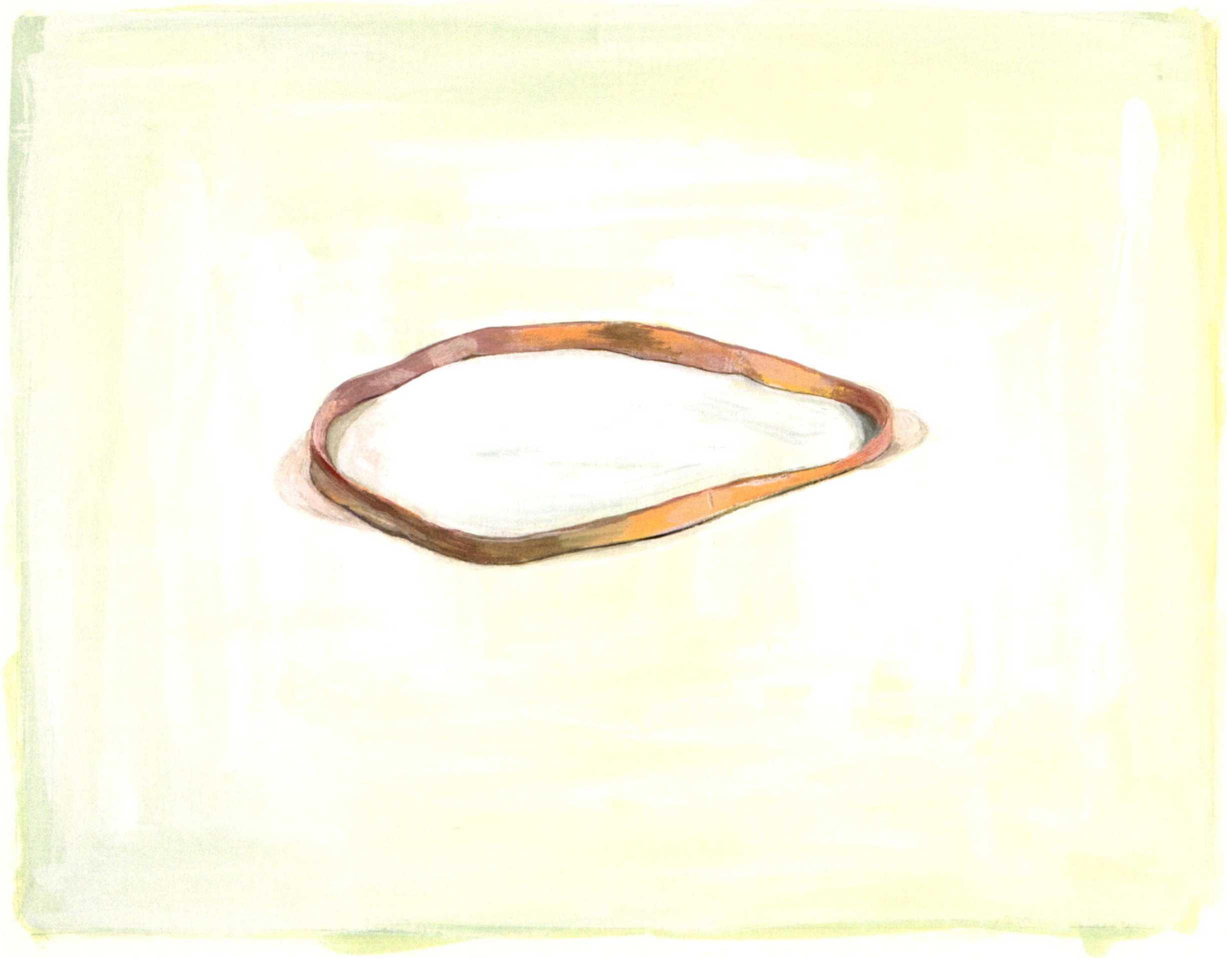

Rubber Band, 2009

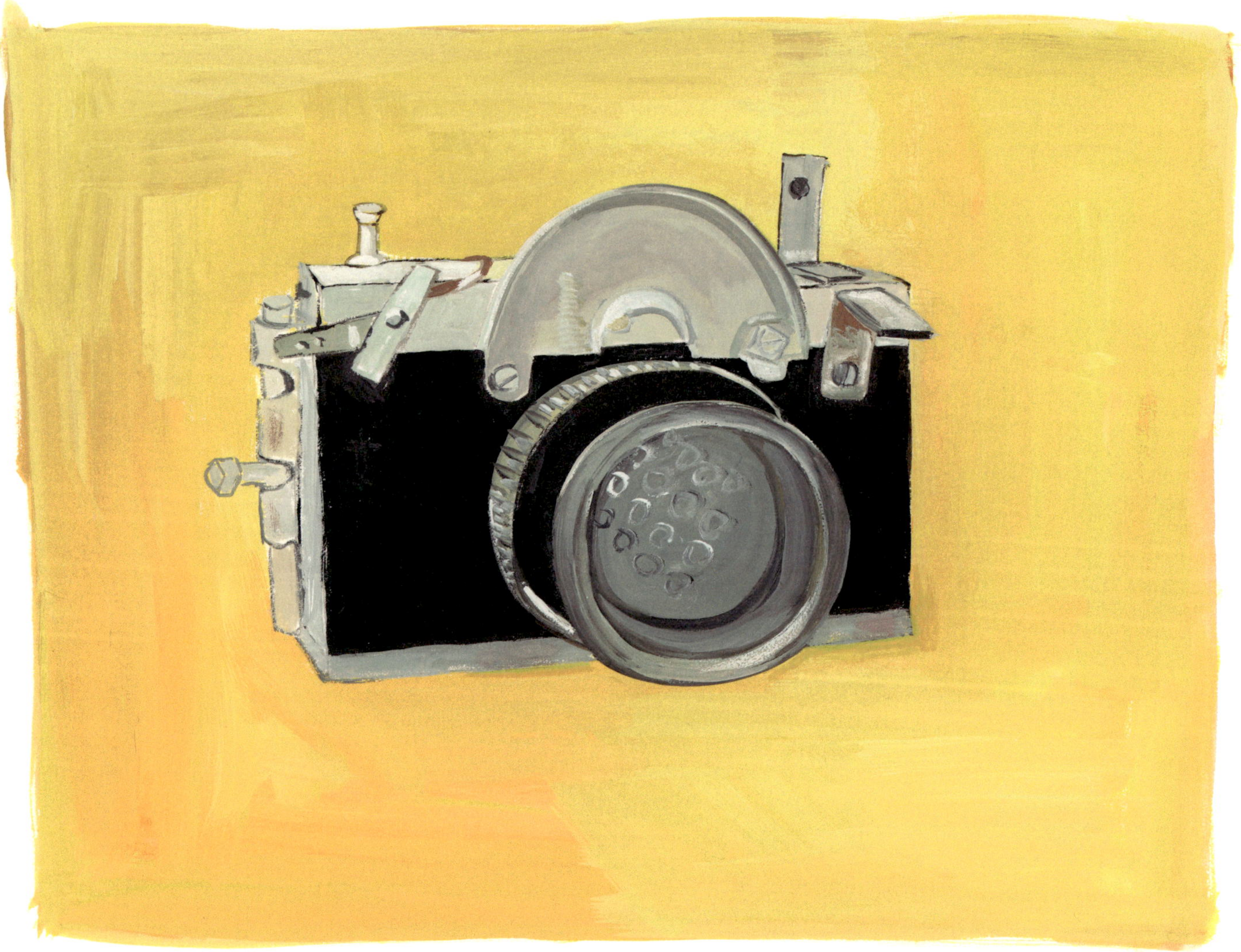

Steinberg Camera, 2007

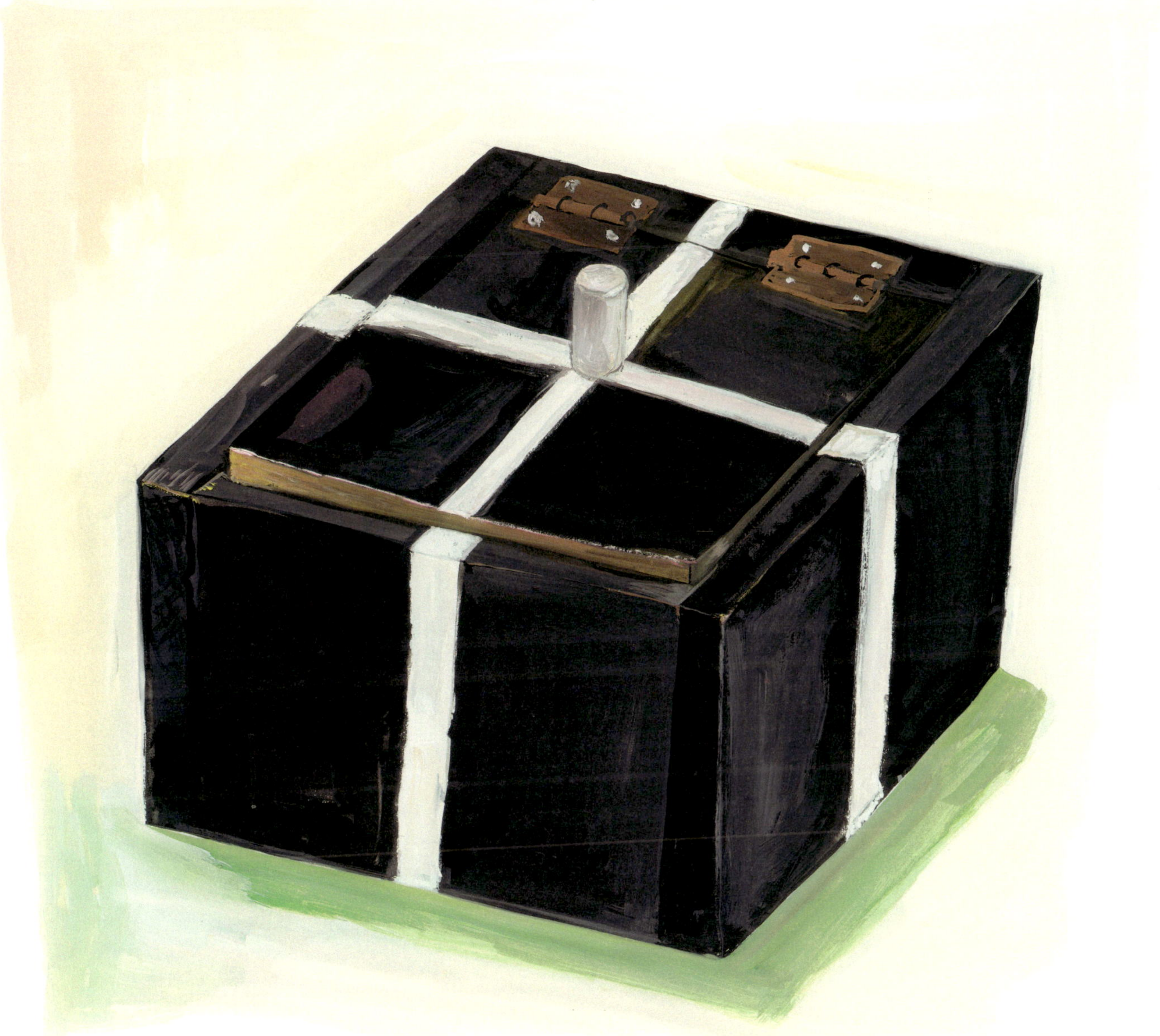

Wooden Box, 2006

Max

Max is me . . .
[but] People see a lot of themselves in Max.
Wry and sophisticated. Insecure and courageous.
Humanist and irreverent.[17]

SWAMI ON RYE FINDS THE DOG POET IN INDIA ON a spiritual quest for the meaning of life—puppies, or, in other words, family. It is the penultimate of Maira's books designed by Tibor with M&Co. The process was as intense as a tango, as he describes, "She would write the text and start to sketch, and I would sketch type over her pencil drawings . . . and she'd have to cut copy or I'd say, this type could go here and it'd be nicer if this character could raise their arms so we could tuck the type in their armpit. It was a completely integrated process, and there was lots of trust."[18]

Cardboard Box, 2004–5

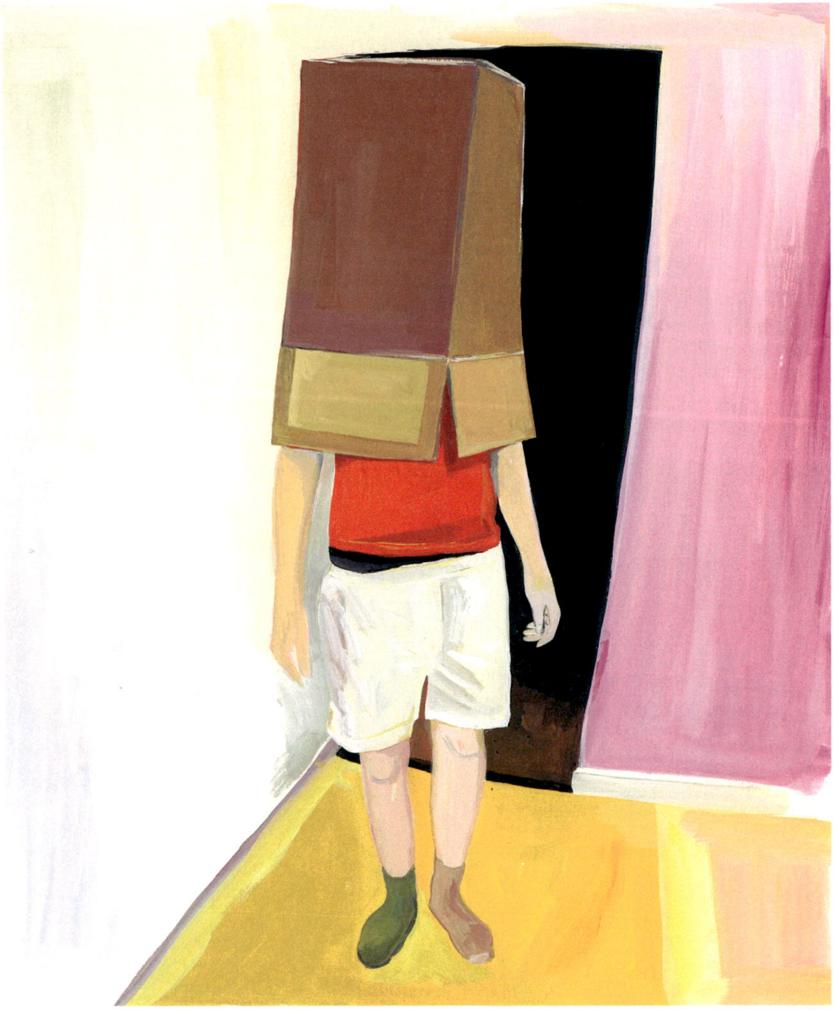

And lots of play with type, too. The couple drew, Maira says, from a "big library full of our favorite work of Dadaists and Futurists and lots of other 'ists.' And we both like the surprise of vernacular design and hand-lettered typography. . . . The text was a piece of the art."[19] Nowhere is this more apparent than in **Roarr: Calder's Circus**, in which both the sense and the structure of the words on the page shimmy with movement and shimmer with sound, sounds like "Zing" that ping with echoes of some Futurist manifesto past.[20]

A planned-for children's book that never came to be is "Max in Rome."[21] In 1993, Tibor sold M&Co to run *Colors* from Italy. For Maira, the deeply cultured city was Manhattan dolce—with the human kerfuffle of coffee shops only amplified by the marble interior of the espresso bar. For Tibor, the civilized pace was too close to a standstill. After two years, suddenly it was imperative to return to America. Following a four-year battle with cancer, Tibor Kalman died on May 2, 1999. It had always

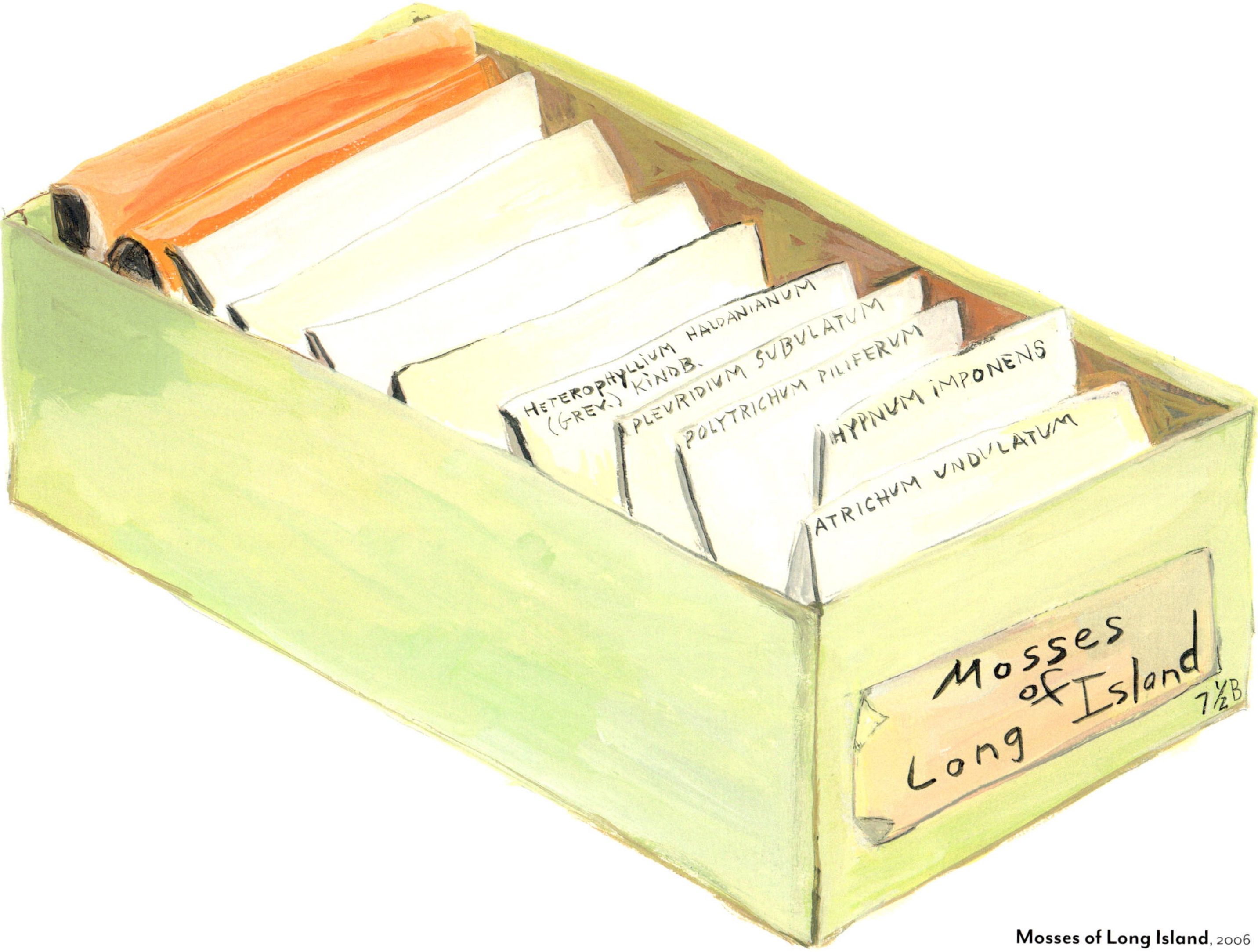

Mosses of Long Island, 2006

been his wife's habit to start the day reading the obituaries: "Well life is short and . . . being reminded of that every morning grounds me. Or gives me something kind of larger than life beginning–with my cup of coffee. And then you find out all kinds of fantastic tidbits about crazy things that people did. It's a very emotional way to begin the day."[22] That Maira began the following year in a very emotional way is still an understatement, considering the obituary she wrote and illustrated for *The New York Times Magazine*'s January 2000 tribute to the notables who died in the previous year.

The piece appears as the magazine's endpaper; small paintings illuminate the page. One shows Tibor floating in the Caribbean, where the family traveled to spend his last days together. Another shows Maira's grandparents "floating in heaven watching." She writes, "Tibor died in a whisper. The children and I went down to the ocean. . . . Swimming in a sea of tears, not comprehending how this extraordinary man, this life force, could die, I saw a fish. . . . Happily swimming alone. Fearless. 'It's Tibor,' I shouted to the children. 'Tibor is still here.' You bet he is."[23]

As personally devastating as it gets, the page is a prayer, a public offering of the solace to be found in life's distractions. Which is not the same as distraction from life, but exactly the opposite. "How to live and how to die," that's what Kalman says occupies her thoughts all the time and every day, "and have some snacks and yell at my children."[24] Keeping things light, in light of the crushing void–and the chaos, depression, anxiety, nightmare, and worse that fill that void–is the meaning of finding distraction. And in Kalman's work both the difficulty and imperative of doing so is right there on the page, along with the cakes, the kids, the family, the fish.

In the story of Maira Kalman's life, Tibor is epic. And vice versa. Together for thirty-two

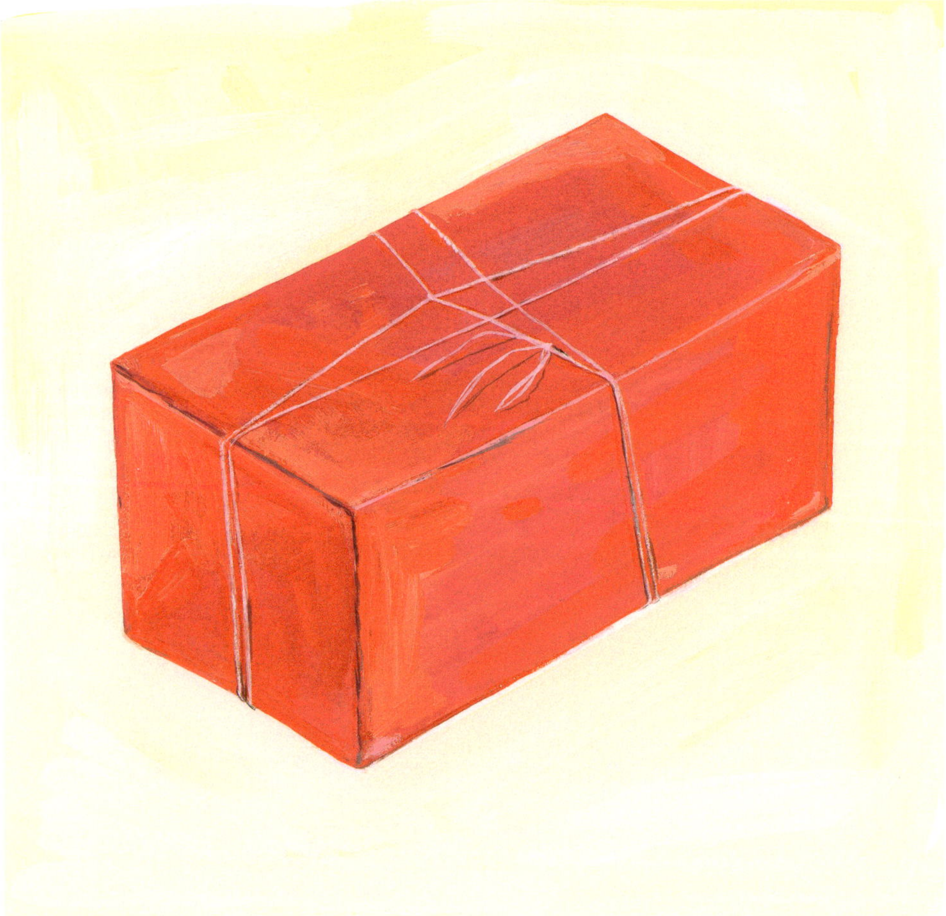

Pink Package, 2004–5

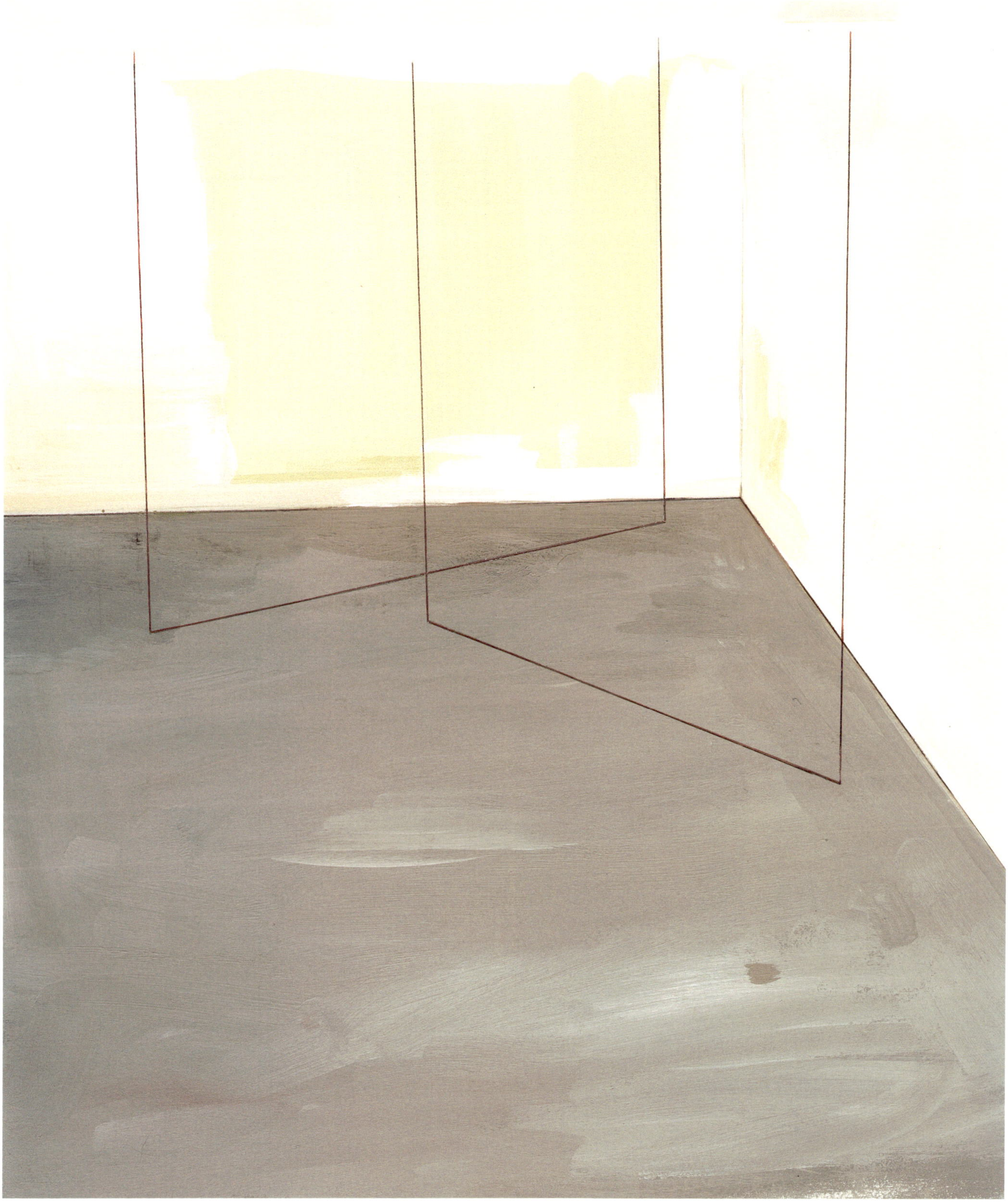

Fred, 2003

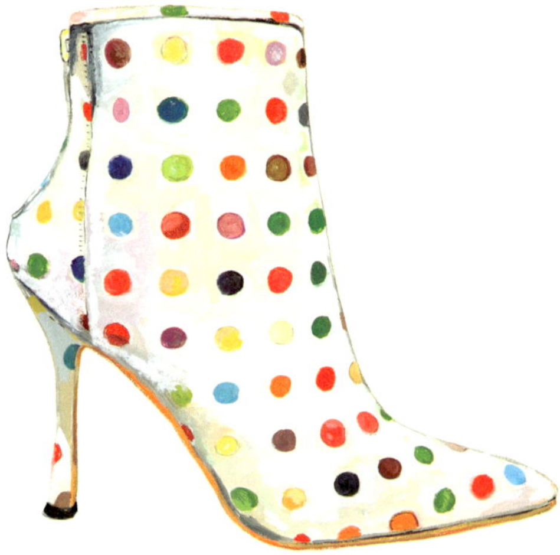

years, each was integral to informing the other's life, work, and identity. To Tibor's politics with a capital *P*, Maira may have professed passionate indifference – "I approach everything from the personal point of view, and I reject everything that doesn't interest me, politics being top of the list."[25] And yet, over the past decade, Kalman's work has made her an increasingly public citizen, and through it, she has created a form of compassionate engagement through media culture that is the very core of Tibor Kalman's activism by design.

Dreams

Dreaming has always been a highly productive mode for Maira Kalman. Dreams provide her work with its surreal imagery and structure. And dreams literally provide passage into it: so many of her stories open with a dream sequence that segues seamlessly into Kalman's skew on reality. Take her picture essay "Mad about the Met," which begins with Kalman sleepwalking the halls of the Metropolitan Museum of Art: "Something is wrong. I am distraught. Unable to open my eyes. Blinded by the beauty. It is a tragedy."[26] The spell is broken by the splash of ice blue that is Ingres' portrait of Princesse Albert de Broglie [page 90], allowing for Kalman's highly subjective tour to begin. Among the highlights: run, don't walk, to see the Manolo Blahnik boot with Damien Hirst dots [left] in the Met's Costume Institute, where Kalman confesses she can barely restrain herself from snatching the Schiaparelli *Shoe Hat* and making a break for it.

Other times, dreams are just there, like rooms we enter – sometimes unwittingly. Of a not particularly strange painting of a man and woman in a pink hotel room [page 76], she informs, "I had this dream [in Venice] I was wearing this fantastic green dress and looking out the window."[27] Capping off this (Maidenform) fantasy, she adds the bald man's hair was also part of the dream. Dreams are signaled metaphorically by streams

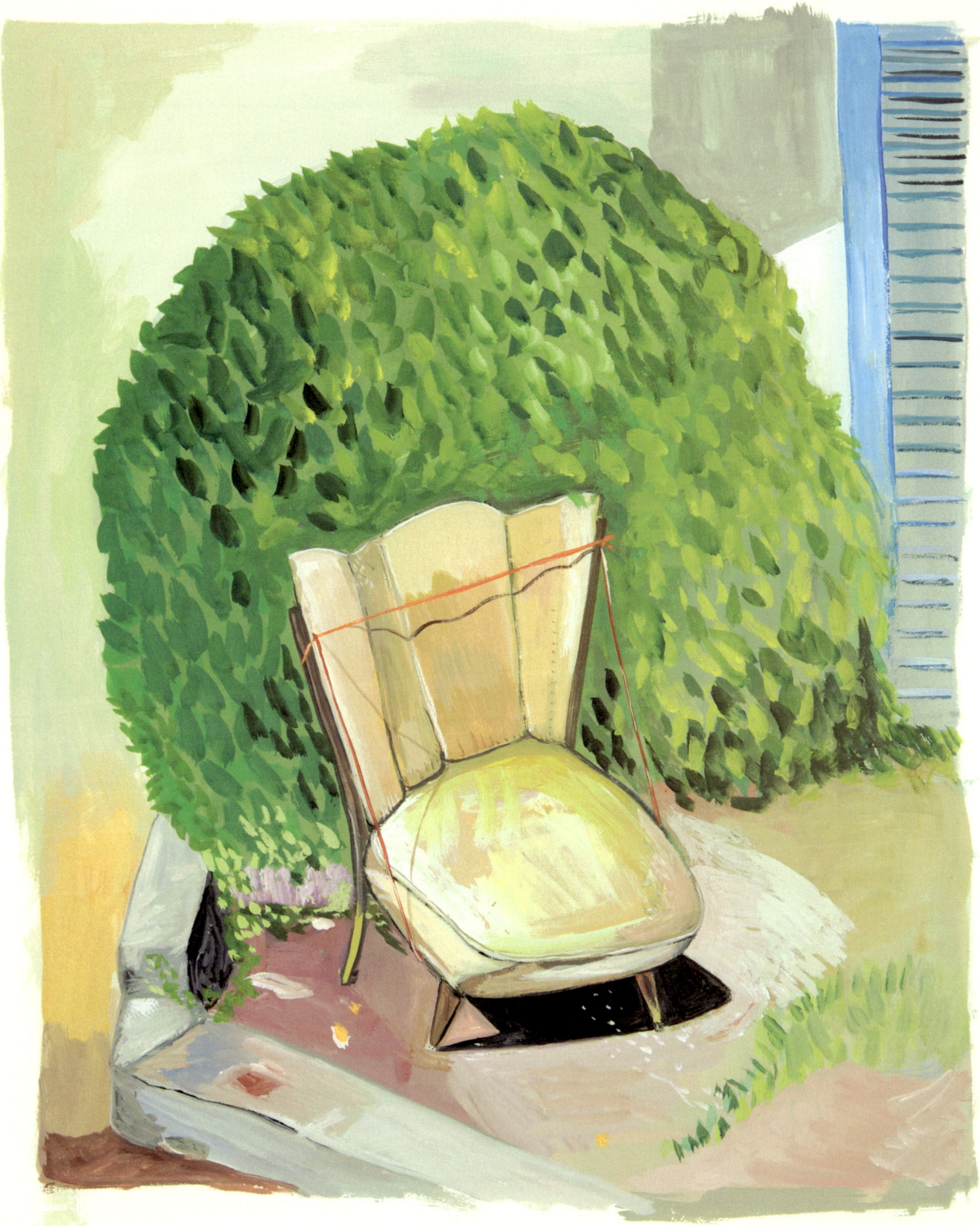

Broken Chair in Tel Aviv, 2008

Sofa, 2006

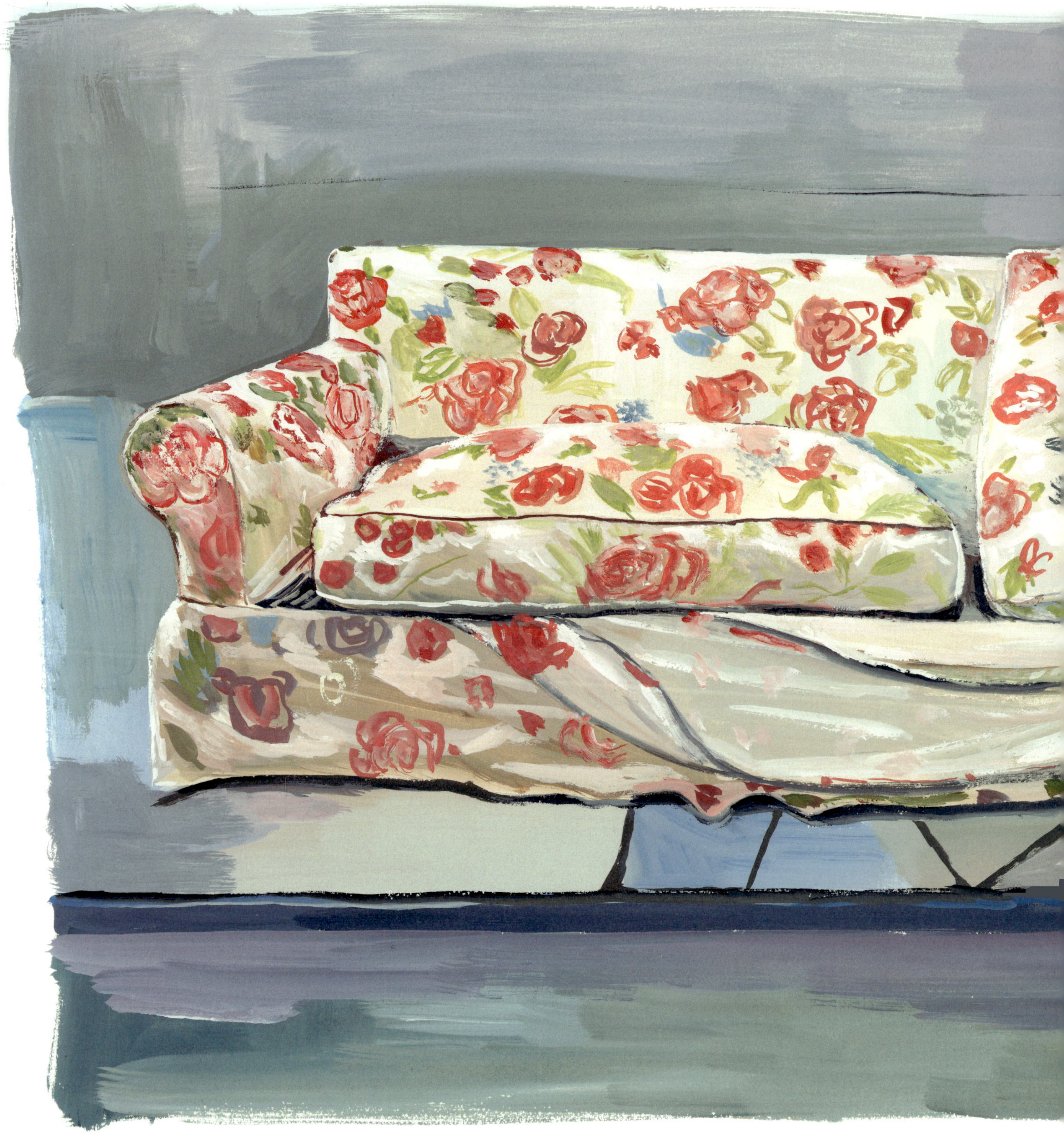

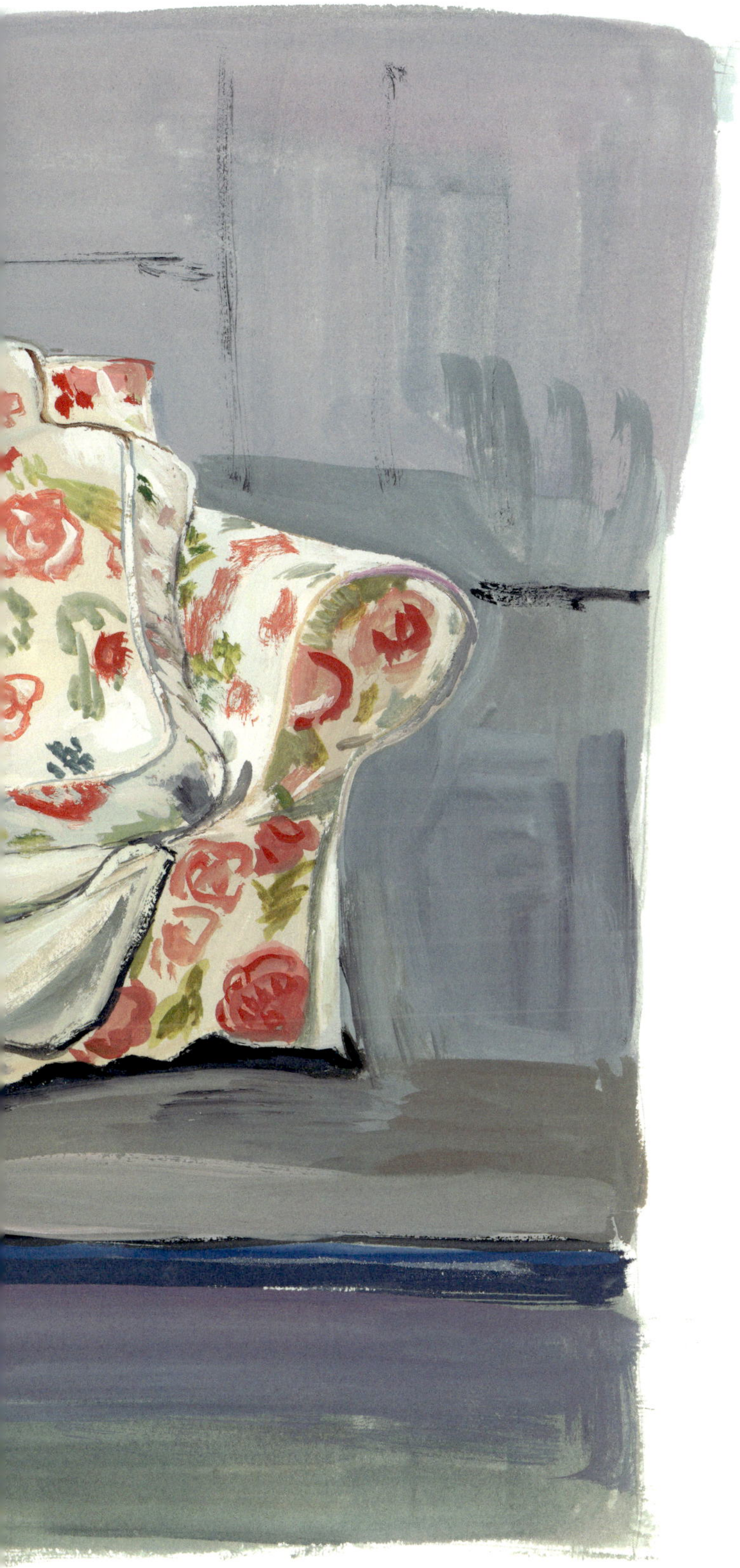

and rivers, which flow through Kalman's pictures, turning landscapes into lyrical dreamscapes and interiors into anxious states of mind. That woman hovering in sleep above her bed [page 62] might be less peaceful if she were aware of the creek running through the bedroom and that ominous suitcase on the shore/floor.[28] Finally, dreams are destinations. The Céleste Hotel in Algiers [page 63], for instance, frequently turns up as a haven, even though Kalman only knows the place from a treasured vintage postcard, where it appears, like the past, as a place one can only visit in dreams.

Dreamy since childhood, Kalman jokes that she dreamed her way into college. At the High School for Music and Art, she had focused on music. An accomplished classical pianist and so-so accordionist, Kalman says music remains a major distraction and source of solace.[29] Art had always been the domain of her sister Kika Schoenfeld, whose creativity was part of the family life Kalman considers formative, and whose inspiration is instrumental to this day. Enrolled at New York University, Maira was determined to become a writer and majored in English, briefly. "If I was there for eight minutes, that was a lot," she says of her college career.[30] Writing lots of bad poetry, she says, did teach her one thing: "that maybe if I drew what I was thinking, I would escape this horror of the word."[31] Not that drawing was necessarily an easier discipline, but what did work was merging the two into one fluid practice, a practice in which inscription, description, narrative, notation, quotation, painting, and poetry all flow from the same brush, the same pen, and occasionally from the typewriter. An IBM Selectric stands in her studio at the ready; she likes its conduciveness to "a lot of unexpected delightful mistakes."[32] Also at hand are needle and thread. Since 2005 Kalman has made embroidery on cloth an extension of her work on paper. (In her essay in this catalogue, Donna Ghelerter writes on these works in relation to embroidery traditions.)

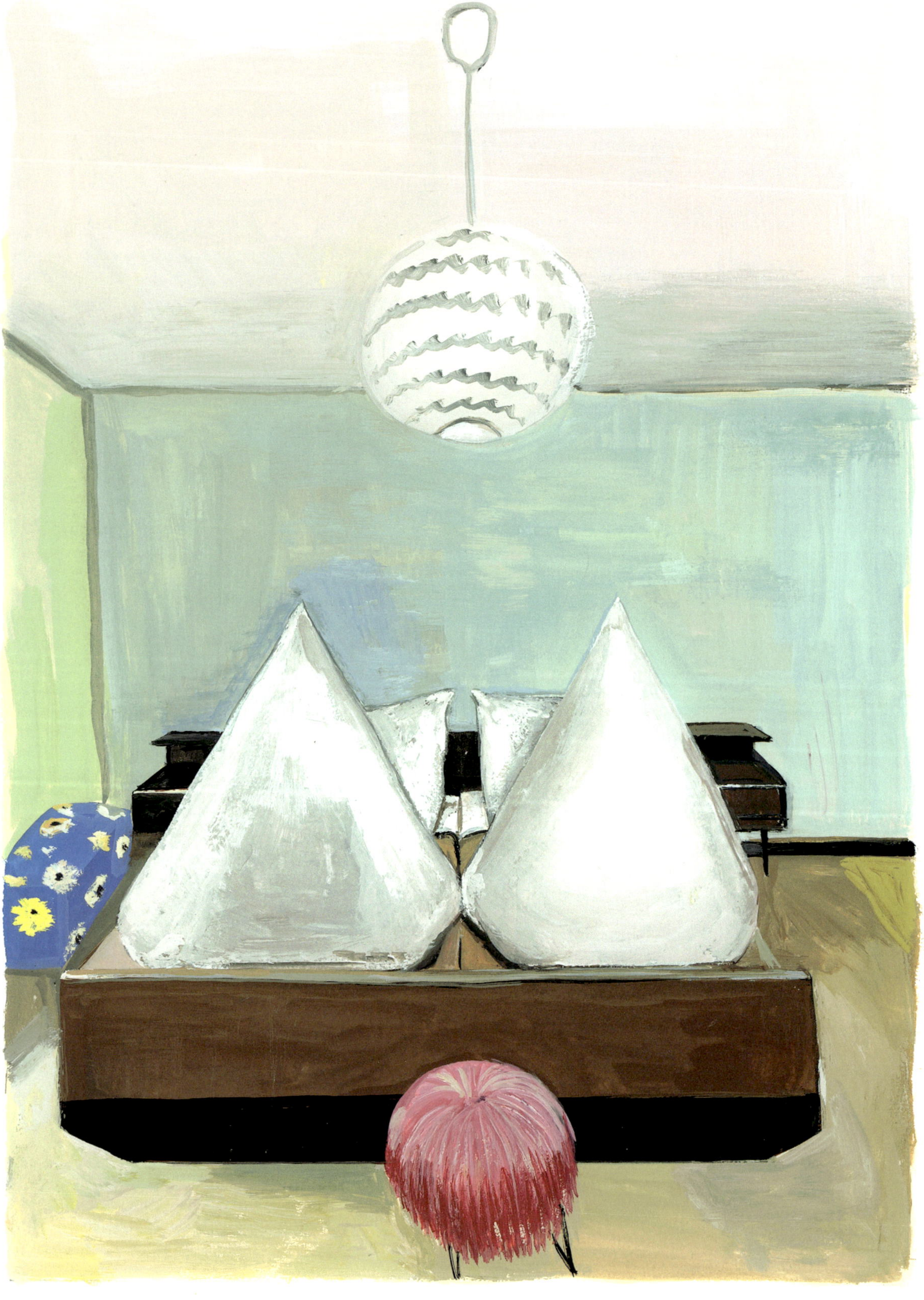

Schlafzimmer with Folded Quilts, 2007

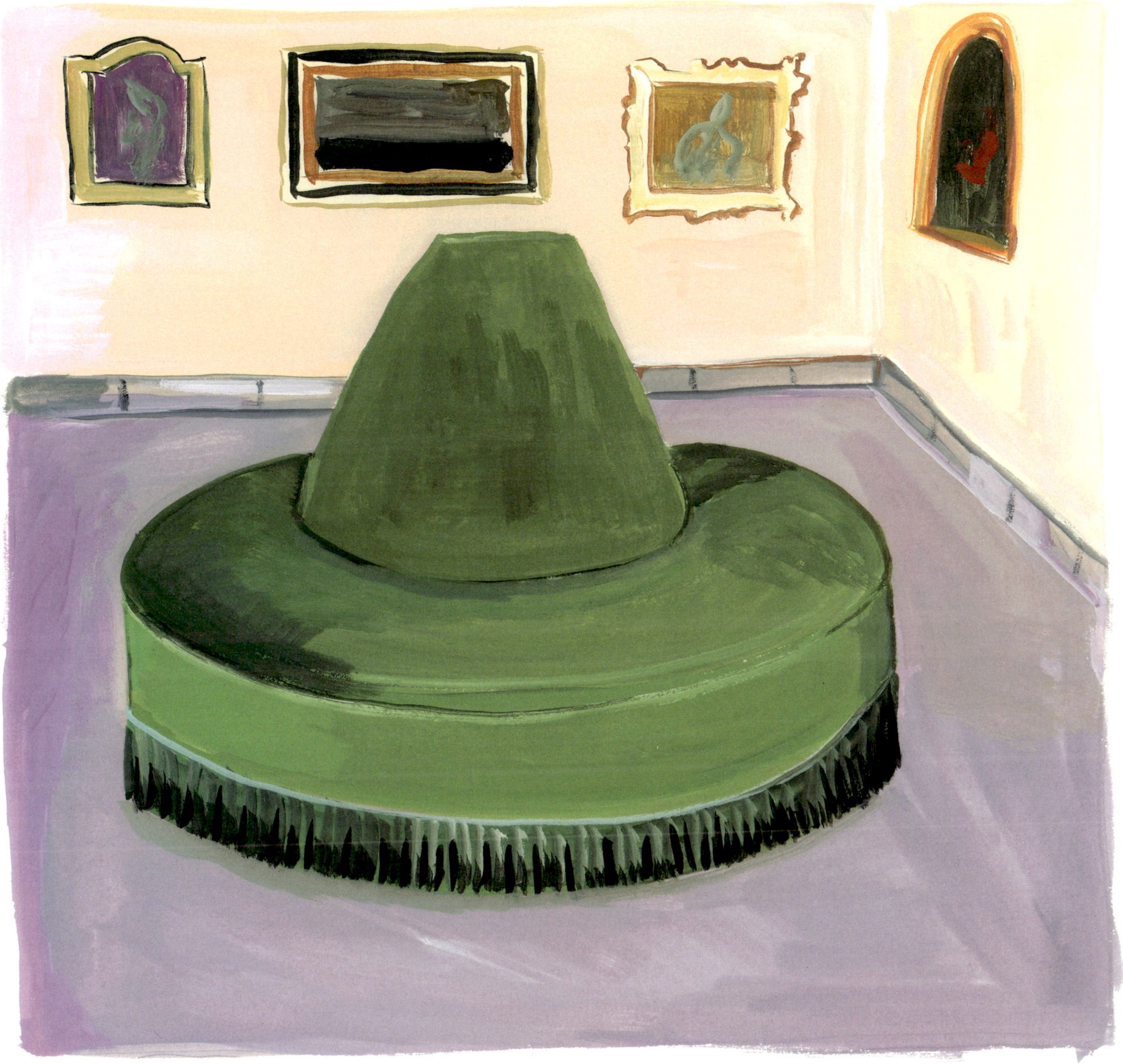

Outside the Proust Room, 2006

One might say that Kalman approaches writing like drawing and drawing like writing. One thing clearly does lead to the other in her work. Spindly drawn objects, organized in a grid, appear to have the look of a mysterious alphabet or grammar [page 21]. Kalman's fondness for the alphabet is expressed by a number of works, including children's books and a mural for P.S. 47 in the Bronx. In another ink drawing [page 24], columns of words and pictures create a kind of Rosetta Stone touchstone or index. A woman's elegant profile in a plumed hat, "Spinoza," what looks like a clown shoe (but is actually one of a pair Kalman owns, but has never worn, by the Japanese designer Junya Watanabe), "Cheeseburger," "polished étagère," and "Exaltations/ Observations" are among the citations. An actual coatroom claim check (number 1) and toothpick are collaged to the paper, this drawing of many things.

Words become pictures in the rebuslike illustration for this jingle: "He meant to blow the saxophone, but man, he blew his nose instead, and his glasses flew off his head onto the bed." And Kalman's own decorative handwriting – "an exaggerated version of my normal writing. I weep for the lost penmanship art"[33] – illuminates many a drawing.[34] Three of her favorite quotes – from Gustave Flaubert, Marcel Proust, and Sigmund Freud – appear penned on the gallery wall in this exhibition, turning its whiteness into a page. Printed words appear in her work as images in their own right [page 33]. The British wartime slogan "Keep Calm and Carry On" comes back usefully into the wartime picture today.[35]

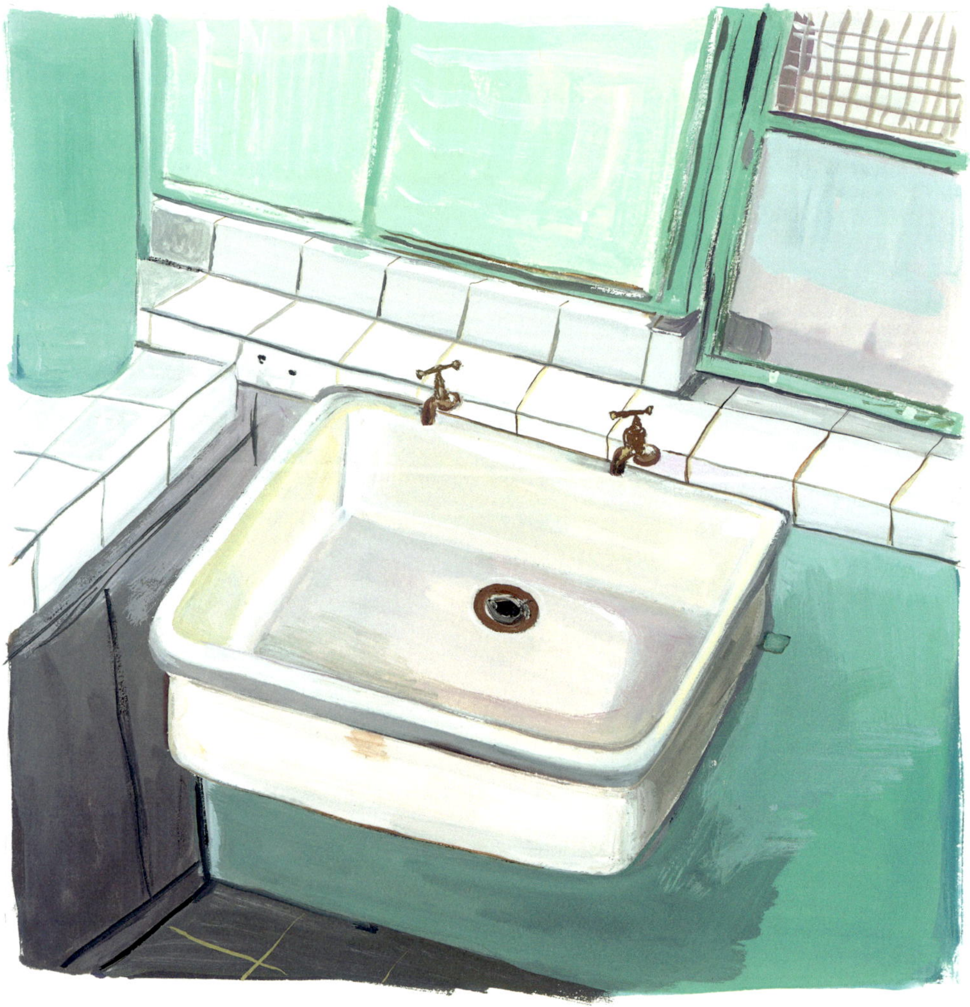

Le Corbusier Sink, 2006

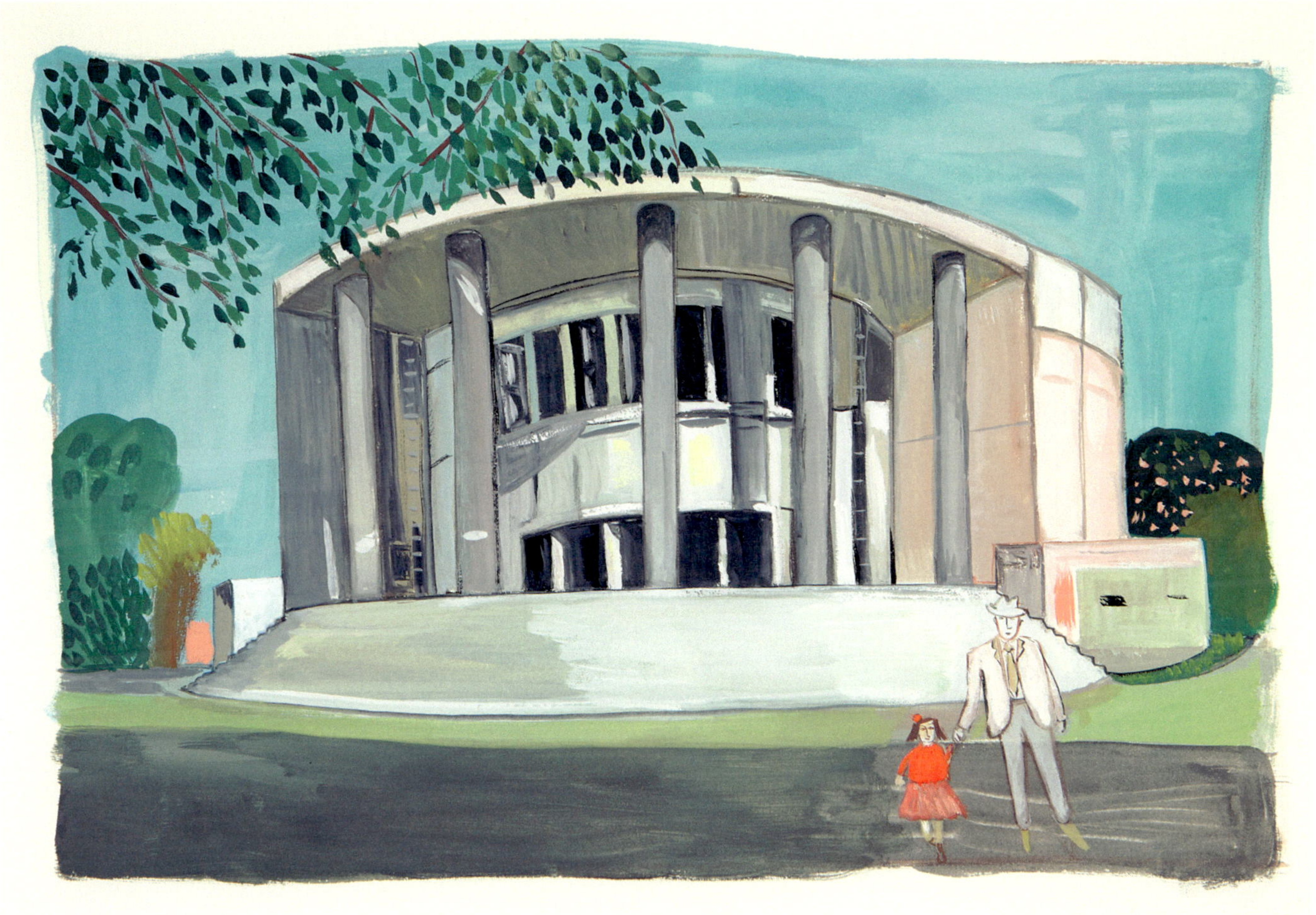

Tel Aviv Bauhaus Building, 2008

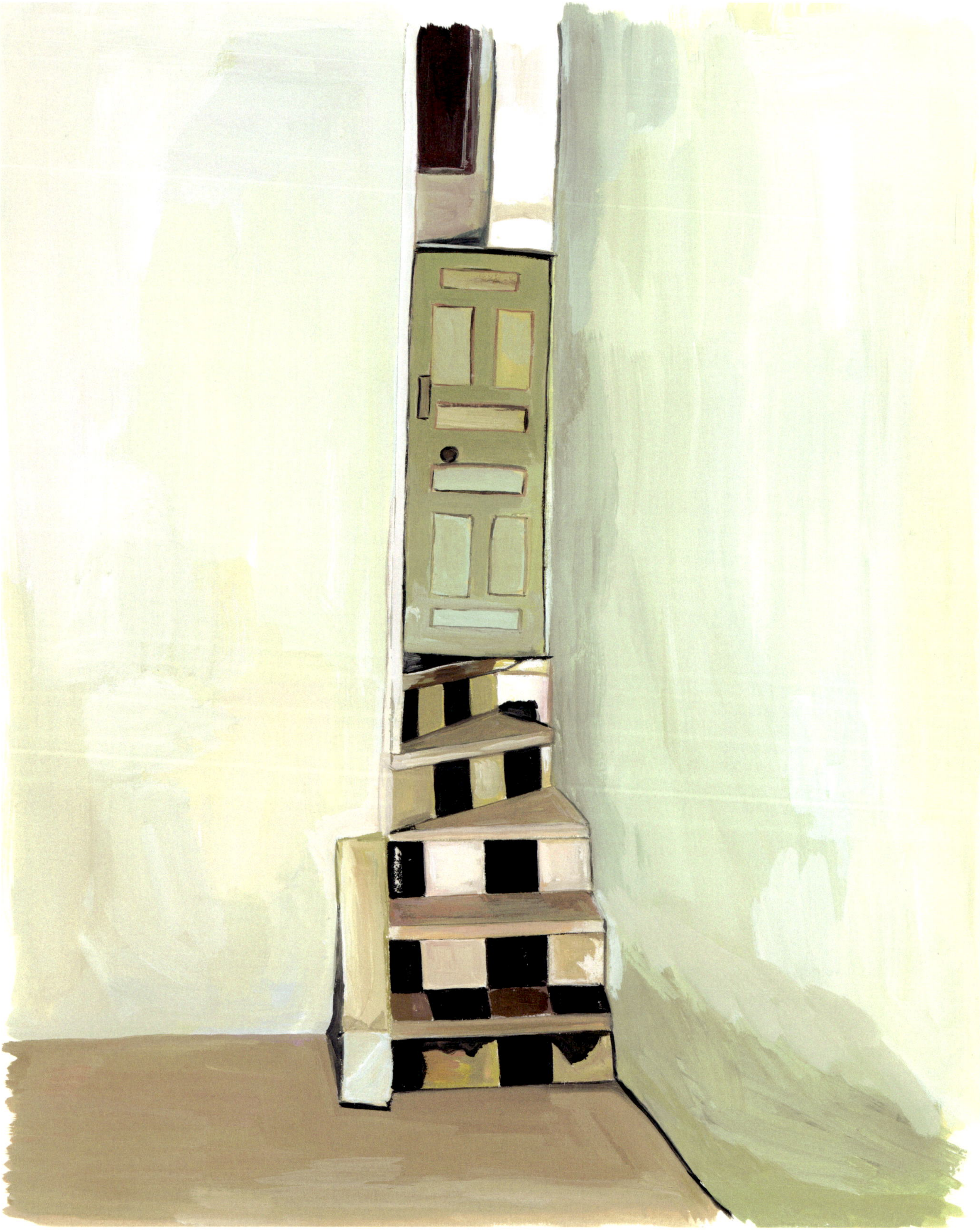

Sentence Fragment, 2004–5

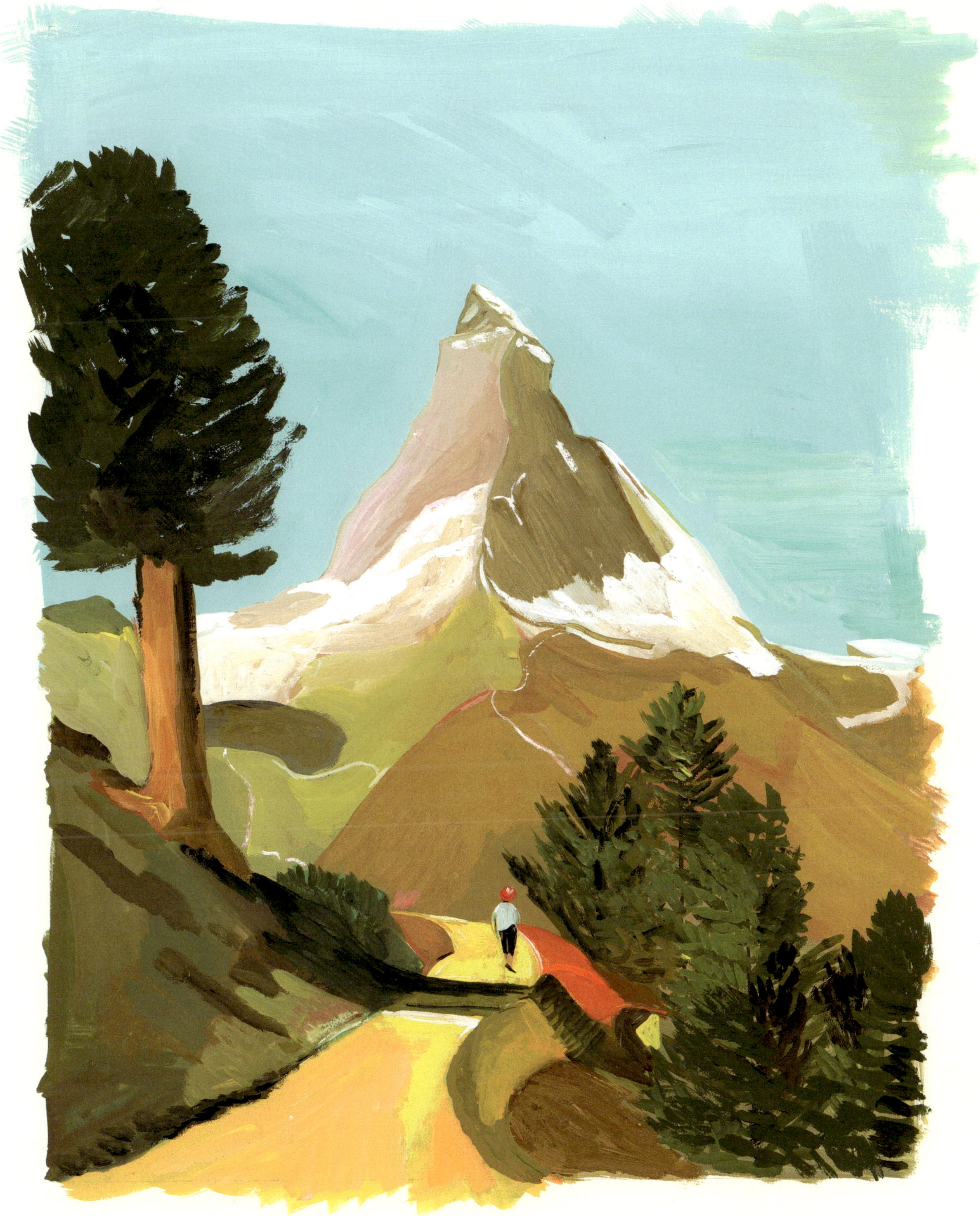

Zermatt, 2004–5

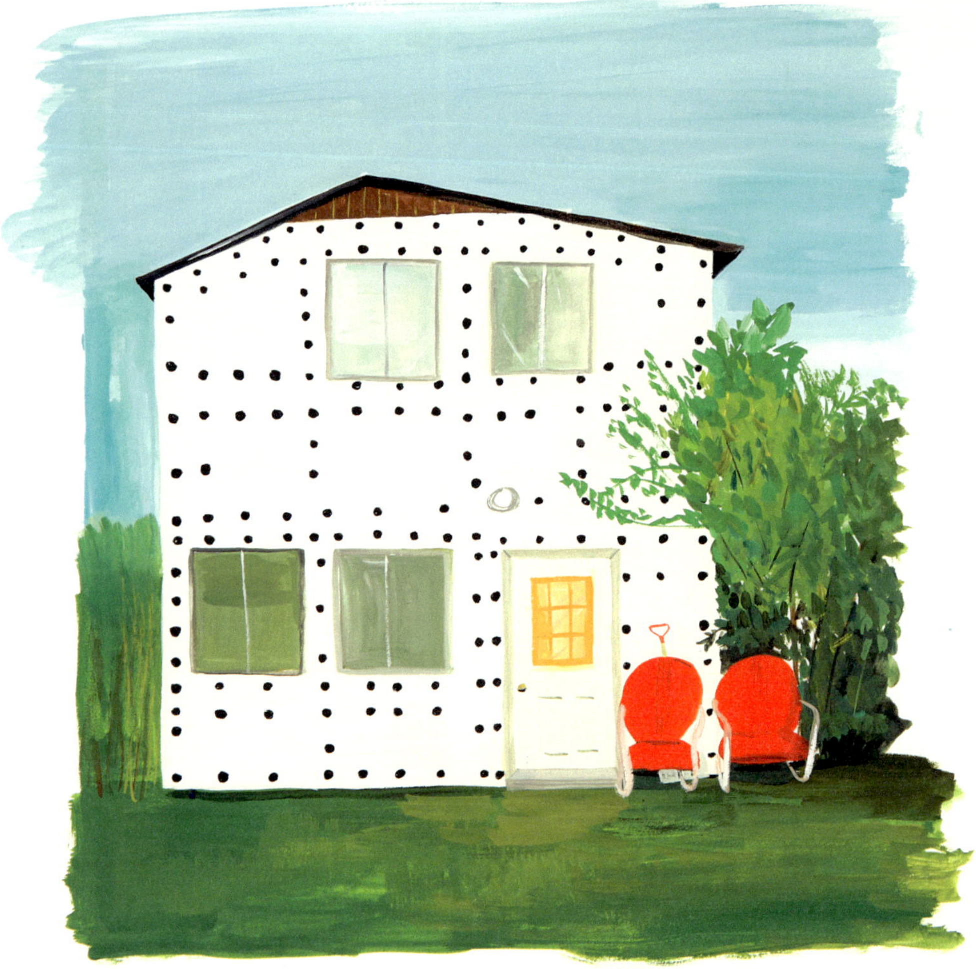

"In the droshky town of Lenin (named after the Princess Lenina) on the bank of the river Slootch... lived my wild and beautiful mother,"[36] begins a story that Kalman tells frequently through her work. Her mother, Sara Dolgin, grew up in a village in Russia and fled with her family to Israel to escape Jewish persecution. Kalman's own story picks up here in 1949 to her refrain, "I was born in sunny, sandy Tel Aviv"; in 1954 her family "moved to grey blue hard sizzling New York City."[37] Growing up in the Riverdale section of the Bronx, Maira and sister Kika enjoyed the benefits of their mother's serious love of distractions. Through culture: there were piano lessons, dance lessons, museums ("she took us to a million museums"), concerts. Through food: there were snacks in bed ("trays of little blintzes and fluffy mini sour-cream pancakes. Sliced apple and pears"[38]) and meals in Manhattan restaurants. Through shopping: trips to Lord & Taylor and the mall. And through storytelling: "About Masheh the idiot, who always forgot to put his pants on. About Rifke the deranged. . . . About Zispa, the thief . . . they made fun of EVERYONE. They were not mean, just sharp."[39] Her mother's childhood stories are the stuff of Kalman's work today. Masheh

Mapping

IN KALMAN'S WORK, THE CALLIGRAPHIC HAND TURNS readily to cartography. Of her many drawings of maps, the mother of them all is literally her mother's hand-drawn map of the United States, which Kalman has reproduced as a painting [page 25]. A blue blob with a little spigot (Long Island) holds a spattering of states, including "Pitzb." – short for the city of Pittsburgh, which appears to be the new abbreviation for the state of Pennsylvania (where Maira Kalman's exhibition is now taking place – in Philadelphia). The largest area is dedicated to "Sorry the rest unknown Thank you." Making space for "Jerusalem" and "Lenin," this map obviously charts personal terrain.

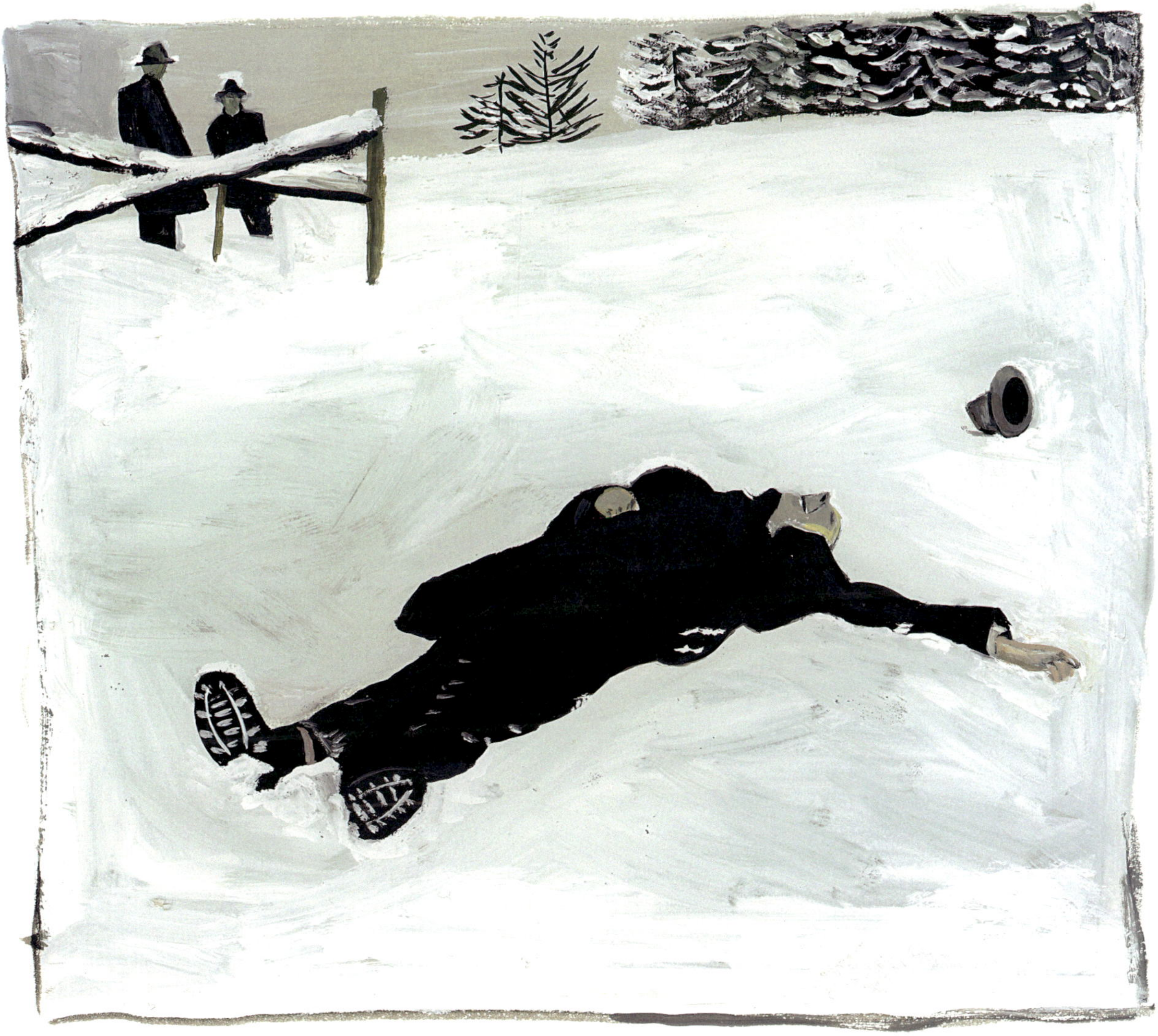

Dead Man, 2007

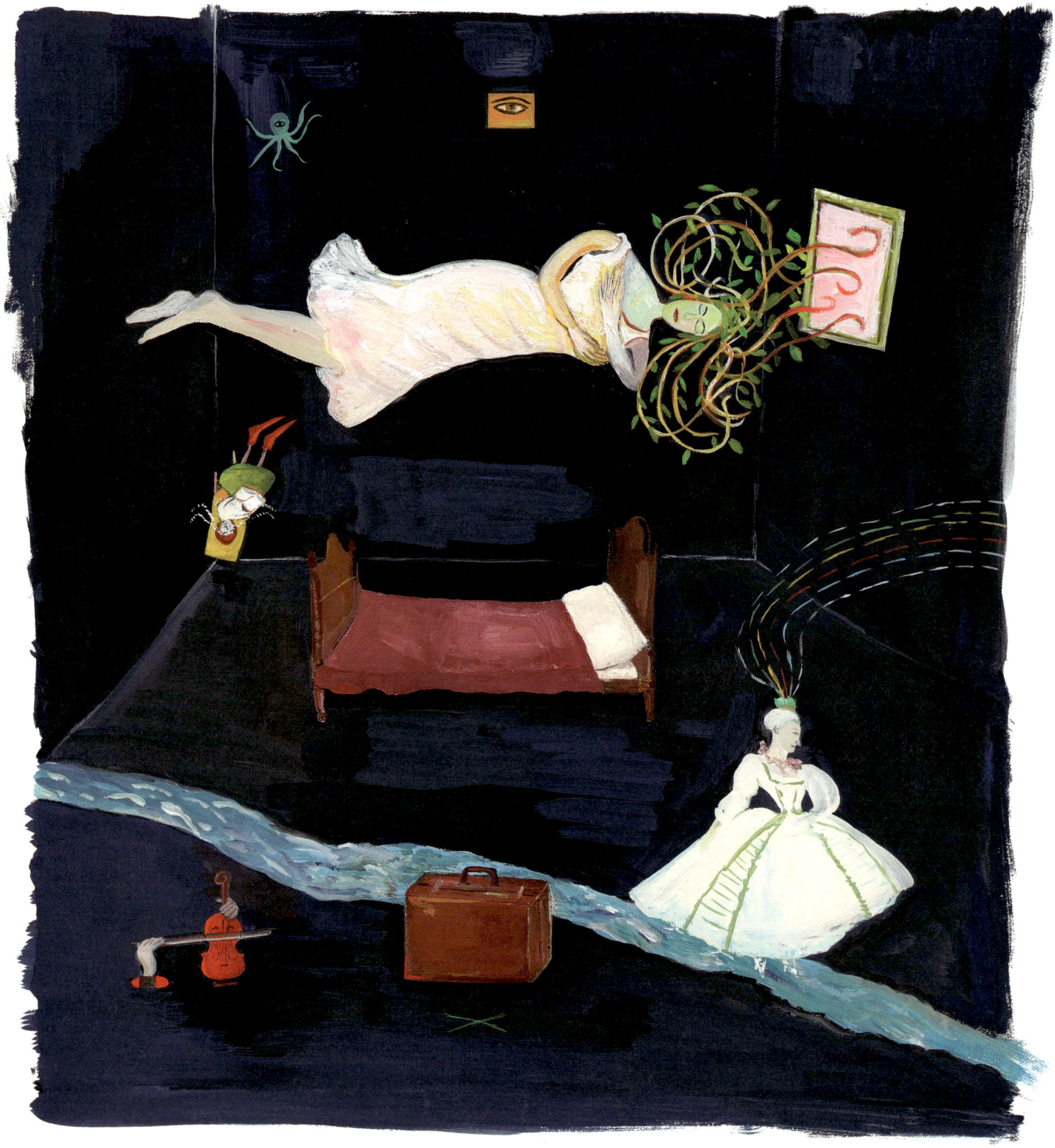

Her Story Is Strange, 2004

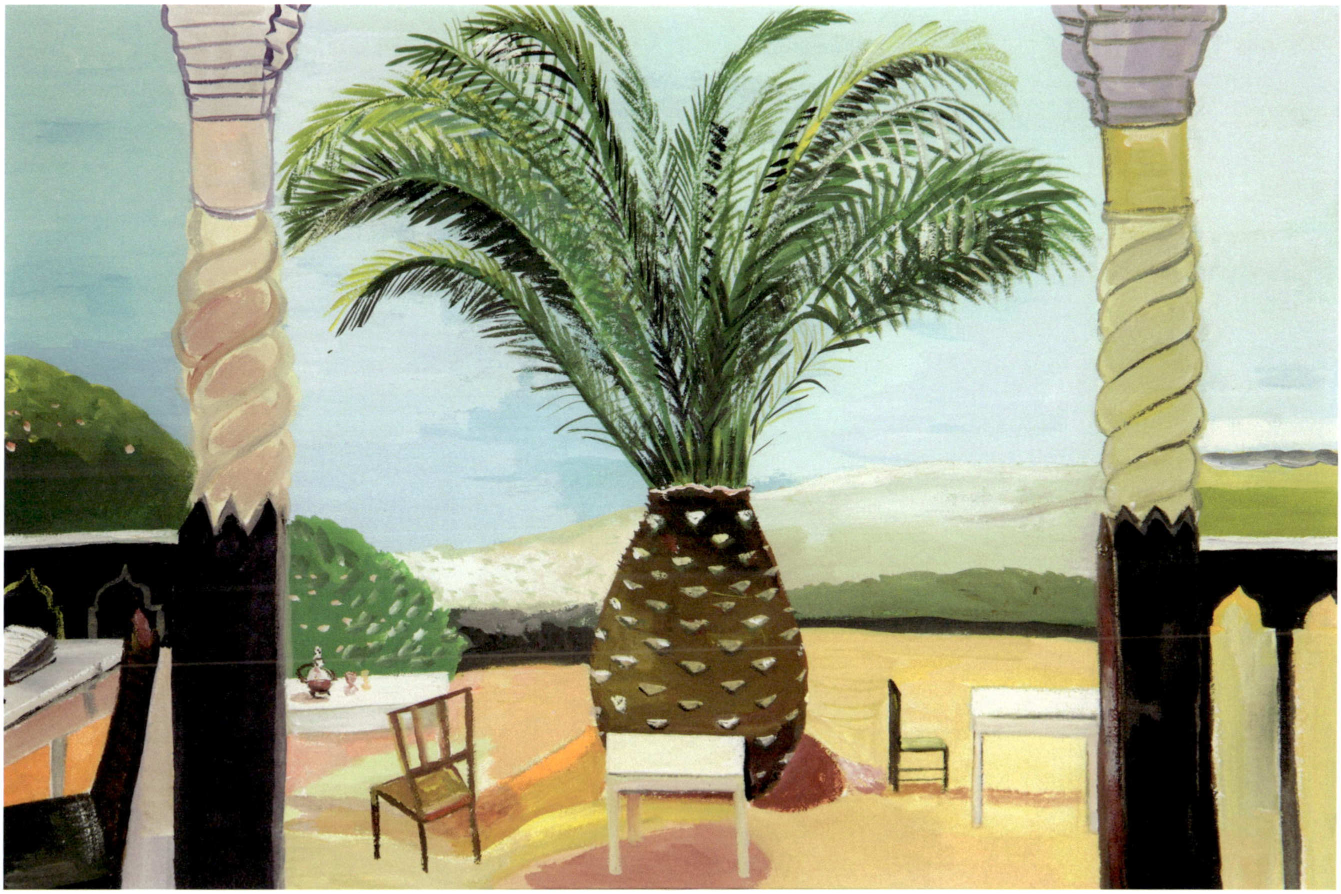

Celeste Hotel, 2006

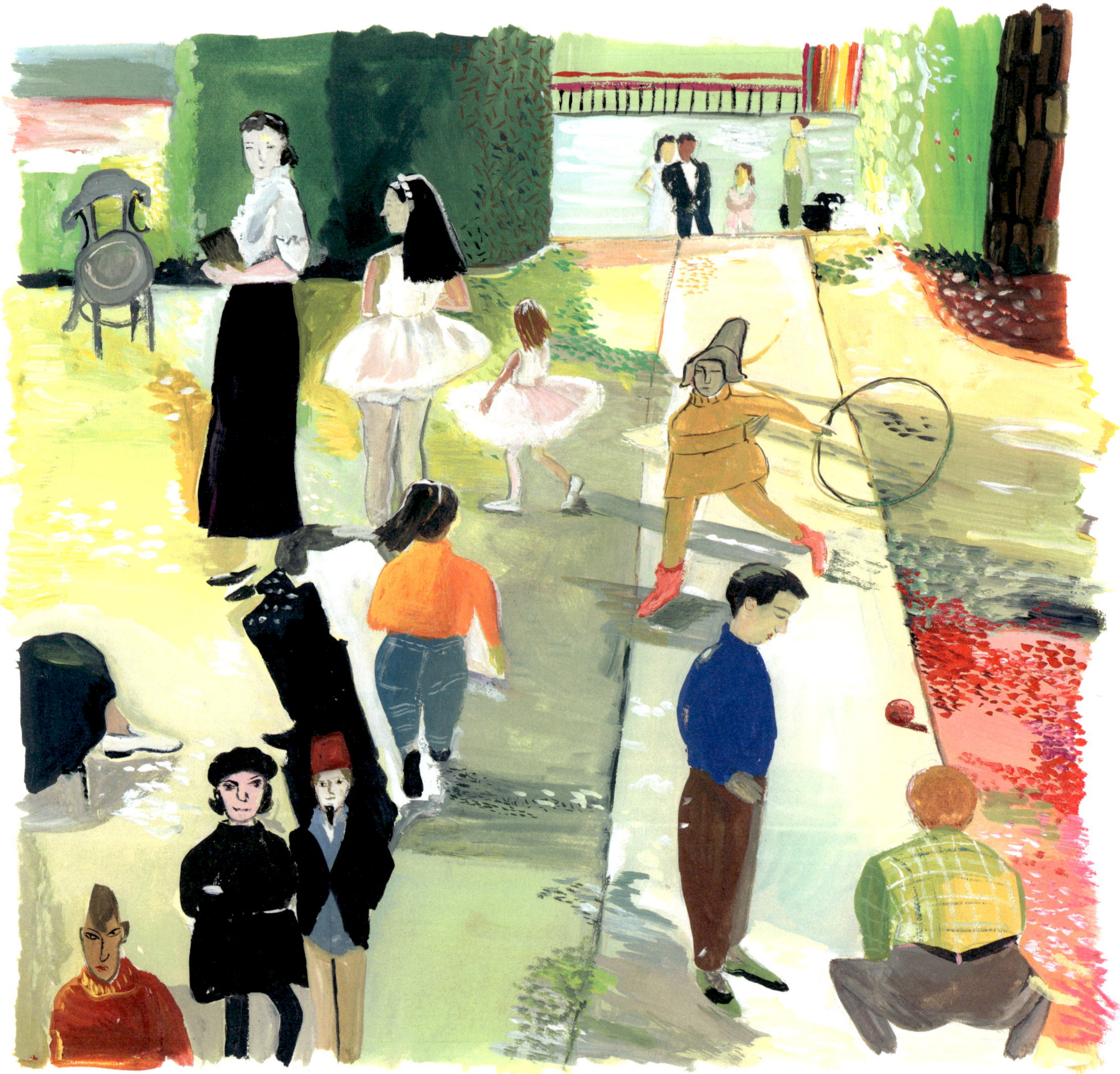

Sunny Day at Park, 2004

turns up as "Maisel Shmelkin" in **Hey Willy, See the Pyramids**. To spend time with Kalman's work is to connect with family bonds and history, to love her mother's nonjudgmental, free spirit and sense of humor, to mourn her death in 2004, and to appreciate her presence through Kalman's work today. "If my mother comes to my house and is frying schnitzel and telling me a story, that ends up in my work. I want everything I do to be connected in an absurd, funny way."[40]

Reflecting on her mother, Maira Kalman pauses to ask, "Where was her husband? My father, that is. Away, away, away. On business trips that lasted forever."[41] From Kalman's online column, we learn something more: his wife did not love him when they married. In 1952 he fell off a second-floor terrace in Tel Aviv, and though unharmed, he later went crazy. "Mein papi war verrukt," she writes elsewhere.[42] Pesach Berman's absence is a disturbing presence in his daughter's work. Only once in 2001 does she let it rip. It's in the midst of a newspaper interview. She is one of several New Yorkers asked to recollect how their day began on September 11: "You heard me right, pal. Nazi Germany. I think these thoughts every single day of my life. Why? Because my father survived the Holocaust and his family did not."[43] To back up, Kalman says she started the day making a painting of a pickle label followed by a walk in Central Park. In other words, the daily drill, a drill that involves her constantly thinking: "I am a lucky dog because 1. I am healthy and 2. I am not in a concentration camp in Nazi Germany. You heard me right, pal." These are heavy blessings to count.

Kalman's disclosure is a lightning flash onto the impenetrable darkness of a crazy world. It also illuminates a sense of personal urgency in images already fraught with history. Once we get the drift of meaning from her musings on an old leather suitcase – one of ten stacked in her living room, including one that belonged to a man who fled Danzig, Germany, in 1939 – now suddenly all images of suitcases in her work are slammed shut around the story of her father's family, their persecution by the Nazis, and their death in concentration camps. This story overwhelms everything, which is

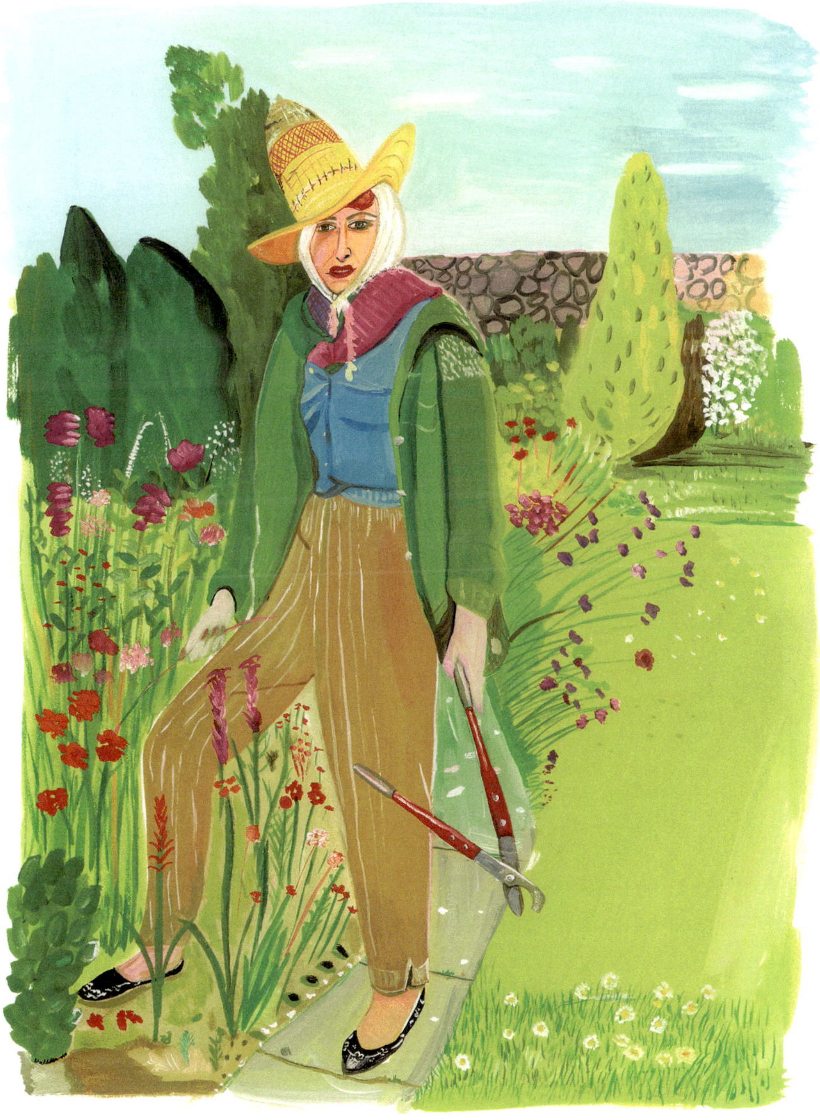

Lady Birley, 2000

perhaps why Kalman keeps it tamped down. We hardly need to know because it already informs and even obstructs what we see. I tell you that the dead man in the snow is the Swiss writer Robert Walser [page 61], who may have committed suicide in 1956 when he fell asleep outdoors. But in Kalman's picture, he falls before us, as if he had been shot while running across that snowy field. Following Kalman's points of connection, it's almost impossible not to see this fallen man figuring the fate of Walter Benjamin, the German-Jewish writer whose attempt to escape the Nazis ended with his suicide in a Spanish Pyrenees border town just short of reaching unoccupied territory.[44] In Kalman's portrait of him [below], we see Benjamin happy at his desk, where he wrote critical and illuminating essays about the modern conditions of mechanical reproduction, storytelling, collecting. The desk is graced with a vase of flowers.

Understanding the profound implications of Kalman's elusive father, we turn with some relief to a straightforward father figure in her art. Mere mention of the name Saul Steinberg gets us back onto maps. In his cartoon *View of the World from 9th Avenue*, Manhattan appears, then Los Angeles, right next to the end of the world, China. That map is as iconic to the twentieth century as Kalman and Meyerowitz's **New Yorkistan** is to the twenty-first. Steinberg's, too, first appeared as a *New Yorker* cover, on March 29, 1976. Since the 1950s, his illustrations have been synonymous with the magazine's sense of erudition and humor. One of Kalman's earliest drawings [page 20], a typewriter surrounded by animated pieces of handwriting, pays explicit homage to Steinberg's imagery of the desktop as a landscape, a creative terrain staked out by pencils, pens, bottles of ink, paper, postcards, stamps, and even pictures of his own drawings. And so does the exhibition installation of "many tables of many things" echo Steinberg's sculptural studioscapes, which were constructed from cardboard and rendered with surreal precision to hover between trompe l'oeil and drawing. While the harmony between Kalman and Steinberg begins as something self-consciously studied on her part, it becomes a genuine correspondence between the work of two illustrators who transcend artistic categories. In 1978 the critic Harold Rosenberg organized a major exhibition of Steinberg's work at the Whitney Museum of American Art. As he lauded Steinberg then, we laud Kalman now, as an "artist of the free imagination."[45]

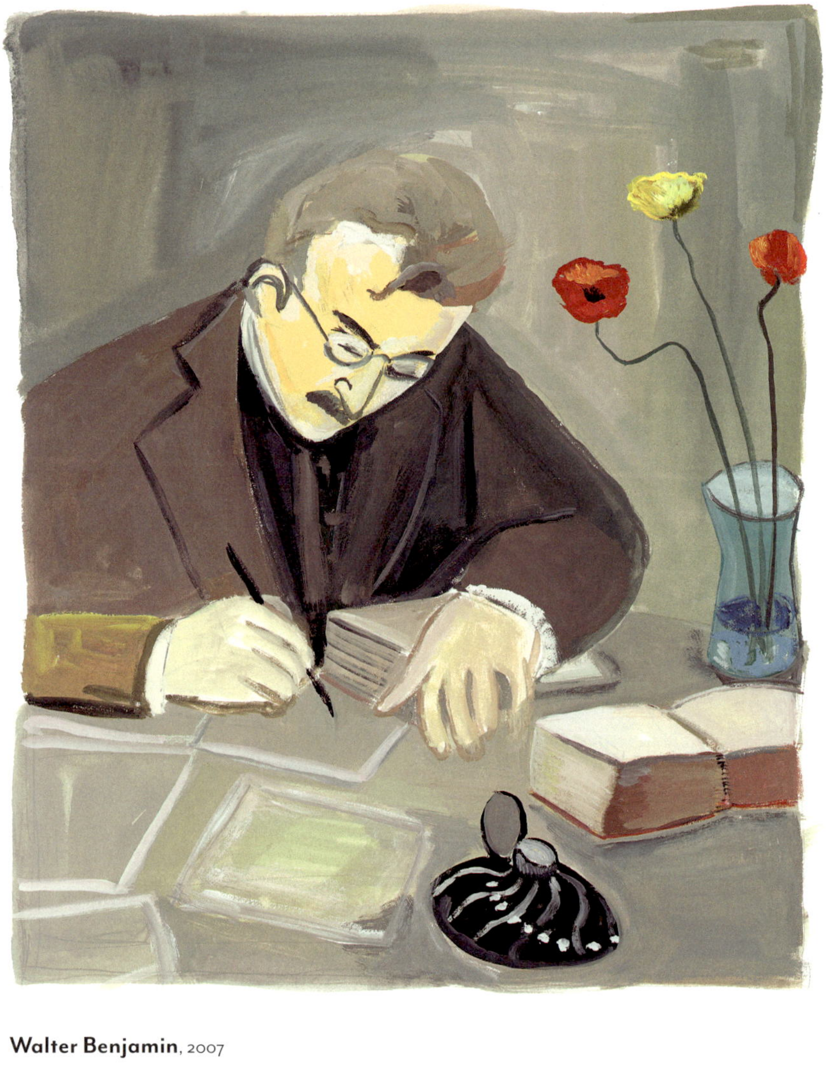

Walter Benjamin, 2007

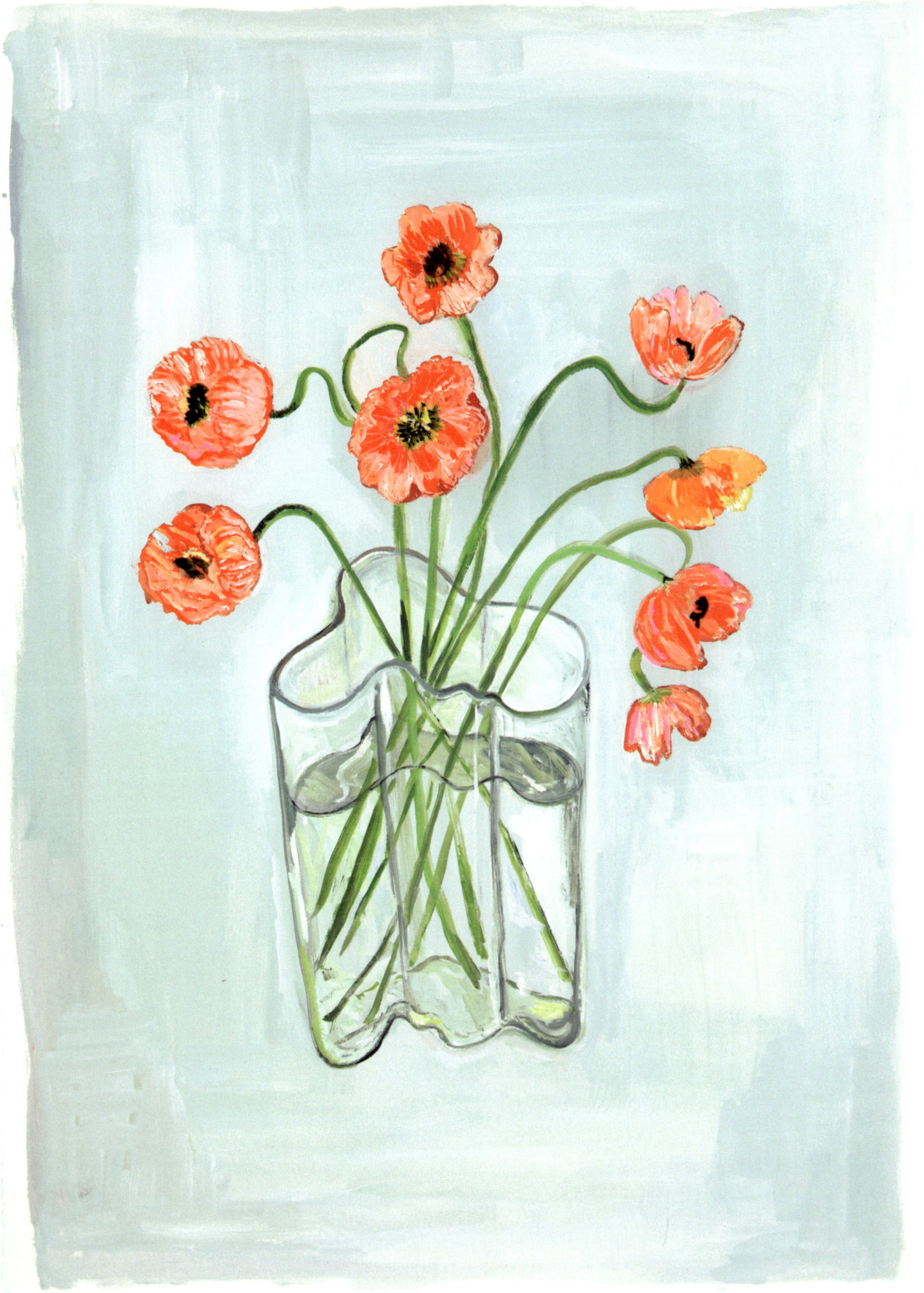

Aalto Vase with Poppies, 2008

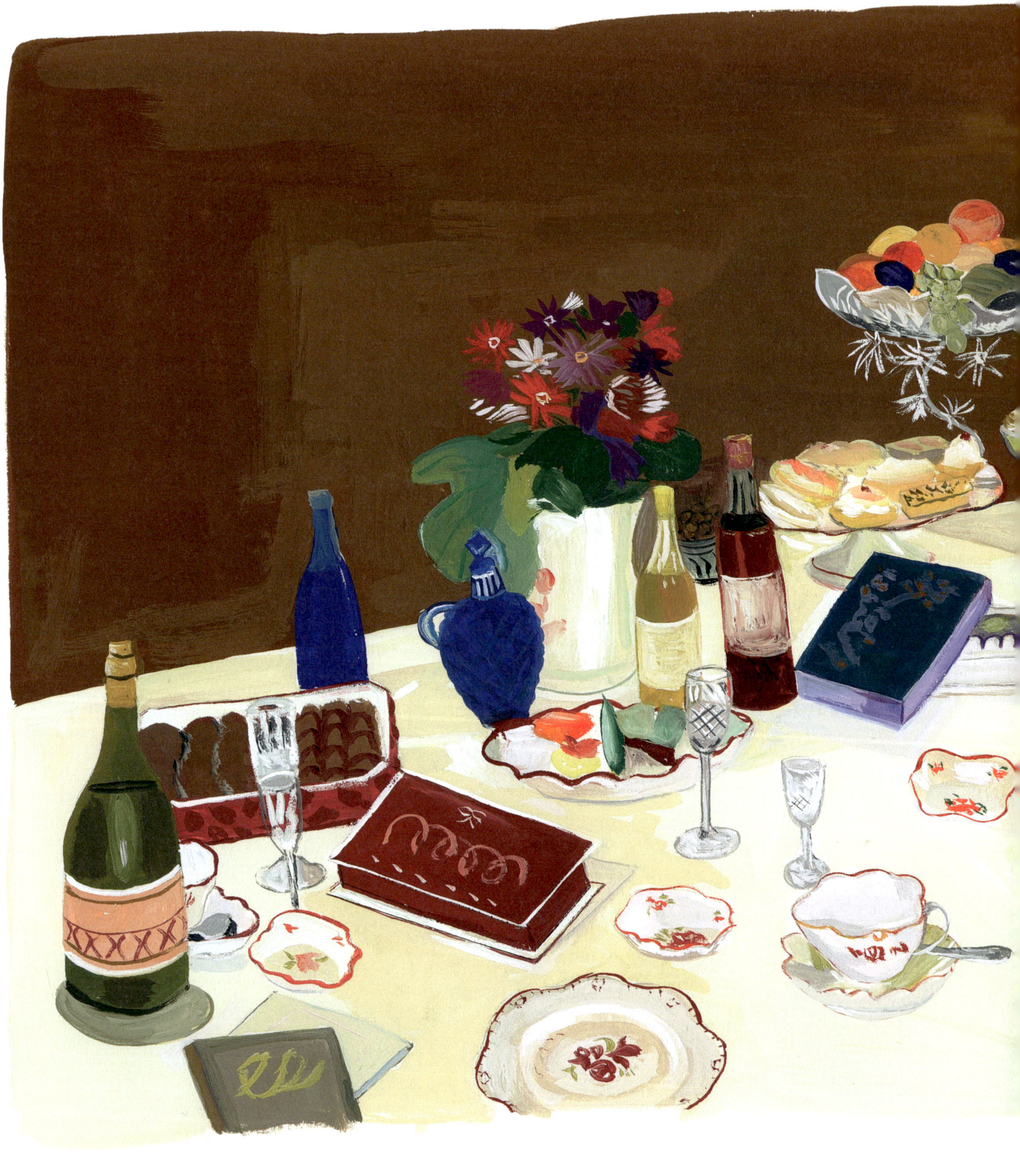

Chocolate and Champagne Party, 2004–5

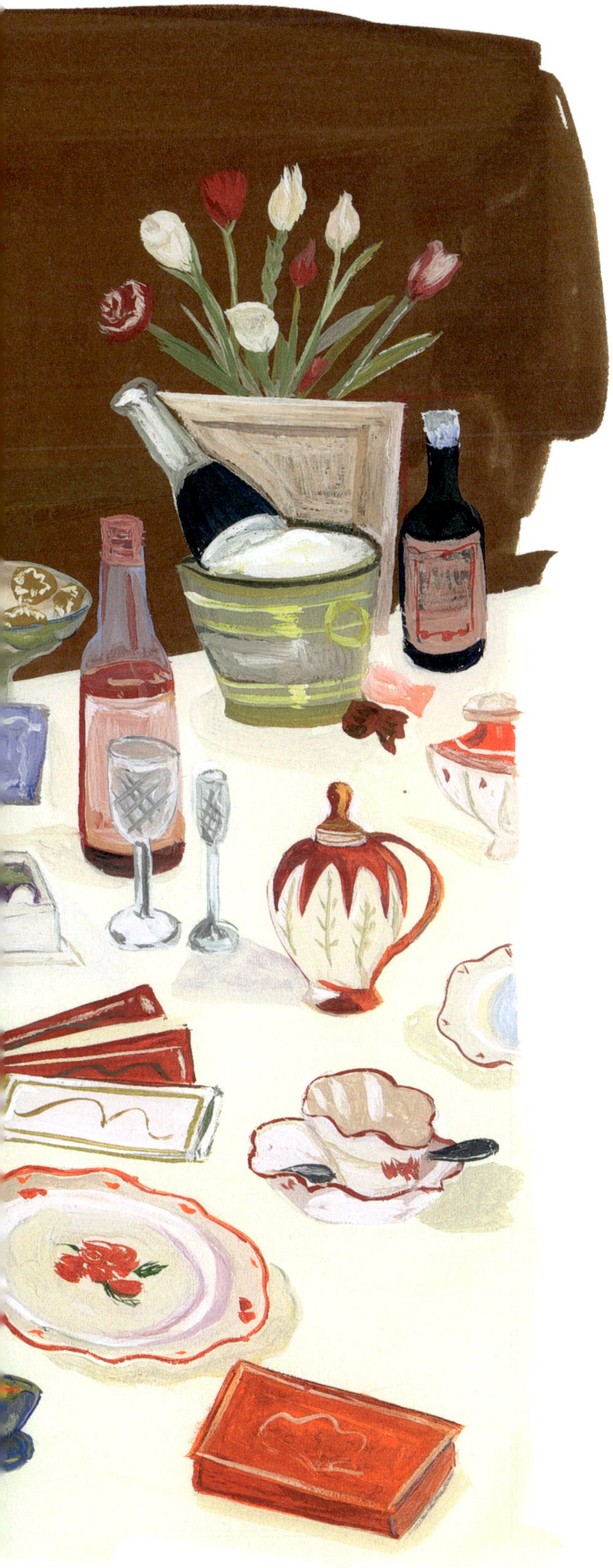

Freedom of Choice

THE FREEDOM NOT TO DIFFERENTIATE BETWEEN ART and illustration is assiduously exercised by Kalman. Especially over the past decade, the context for her work seems to keep expanding along with its sources and influences. Some have remained constant. Besides Steinberg, she has long been a fan of William Steig (of *Shrek* fame) and Ludwig Bemelmans, who besides creating Madeline for children was a prolific essayist.[46] Over the past decade, Kalman's work has become increasingly painterly in style and editorial in content. As she writes up front of being dispatched by *The New York Times*: "If someone asks you to go to the couture shows in Paris, you don't say 'I have to stay home and darn my socks.' You go."[47]

Kalman's editorial assignments have taken her into the worlds of fashion, travel, art, and architecture, and once there, she always makes time for her own pursuits. These pursuits take her off topic but they are tacitly understood to be part of the assignment. In Paris to cover the spring fashion shows for *The New York Times*, she painted the pink gown festooned with bells [page 78] that Viktor & Rolf showed in their collection, as well as the Maison de Verre, designed by Pierre Chareau and one of the most exquisitely decorative works of modern architecture. Dispatched by *Culture + Travel* for a piece on Sissinghurst Castle, she did more than due diligence by the gardens. "You will lose your mind with joy—a very desirable state," she writes of the White Garden, where all the flowers are white.[48] She also kept in sight more private devotions. Her love of Winston Churchill is witnessed by a painting of the slippers that once held "his dear little feet." The object of Vita Sackville-West's great love is observed in the portrait of Virginia Woolf that sits on the desk in the tower library [page 123].

Kalman's love of a particular thing or place sometimes appears to have delivered the assignment in the first place. For an online feature on Tel Aviv, her family ties and frequent visits inform an obvious affection for even the most vernacular Bauhaus-inspired architecture [page 57].[49] Dislike is also part of the bargain. When *The New Yorker* sent her to the Venice Biennale, the citywide exhibition of contemporary art, her

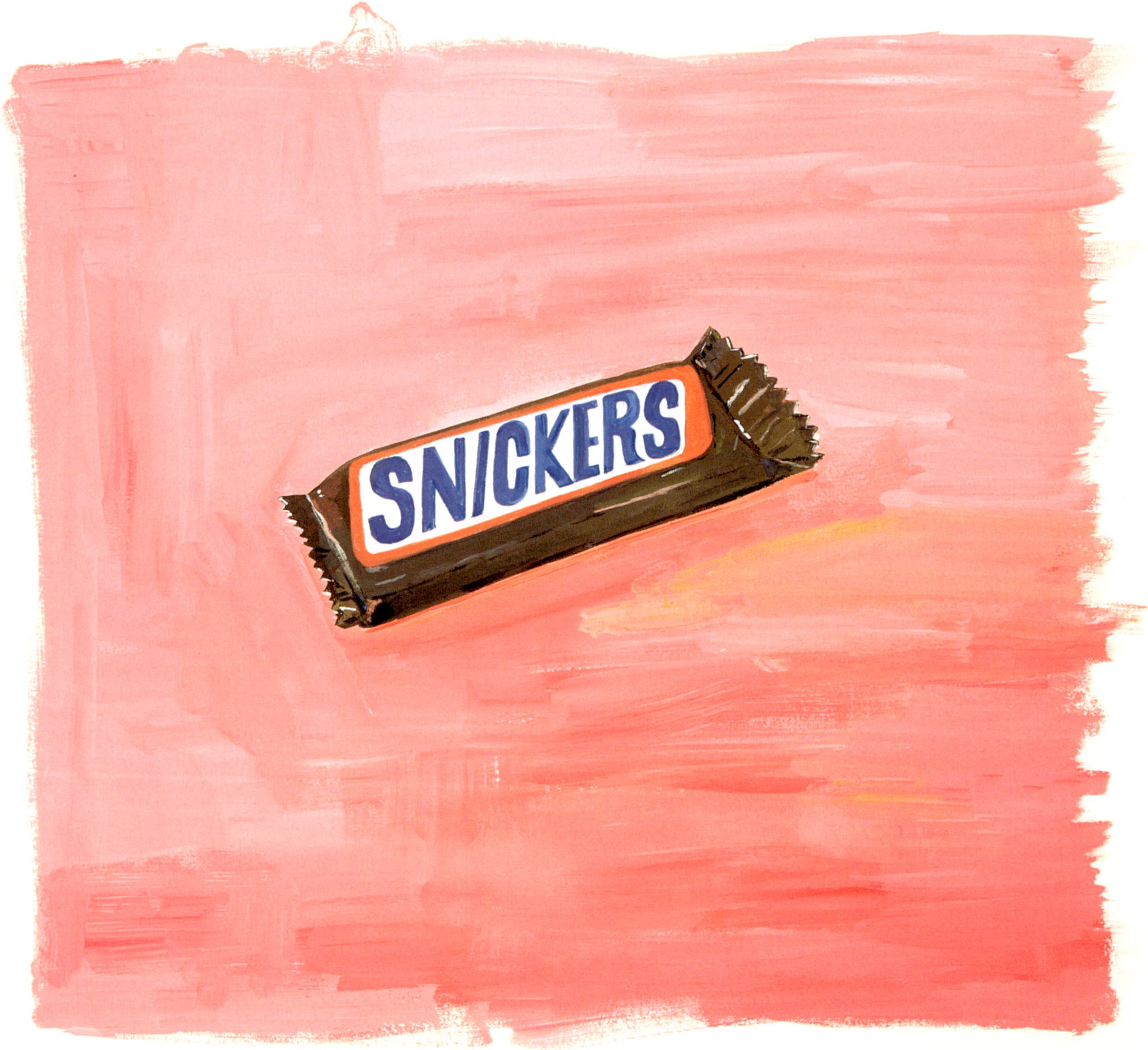

Snickers, 2002

Pickle Tag, 2010

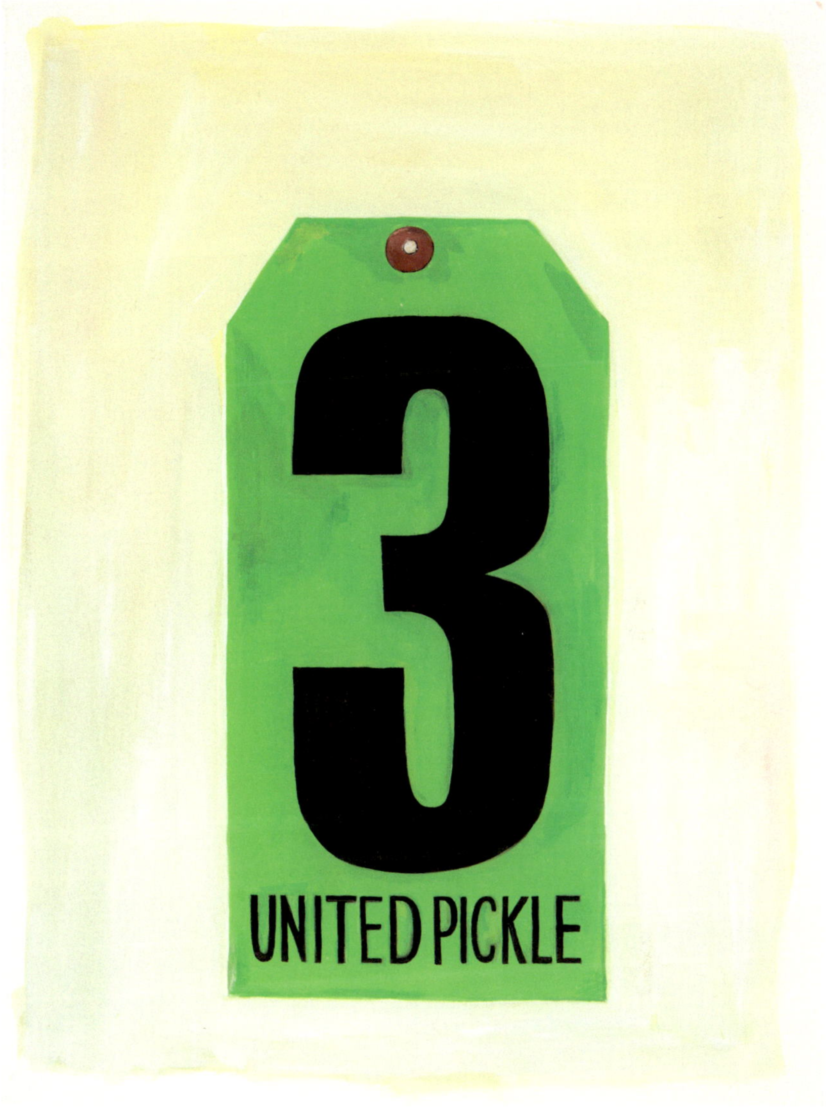

take was less than enthusiastic: "The ART. There was so much of it you found yourself (and everyone) muttering, 'I HATE ART.'"[50] Perhaps it was just the circumstances. Kalman's travel series for children presents a happy day of contemporary art with visits to see Walter de Maria's *New York Earth Room* and Richard Serra's spiraling sculptures [page 120]. A trip to Krispy Kreme for donuts rounds out the day.

When a magazine sends Maira Kalman out into the field, they want her to bring back the digressions and impressions that make her work so singular. "Basically I get paid to be myself – and for my imagination. My job is to be as creative and as eccentric as I can possibly be, and my job changes every day because I'm obsessed with changes."[51] Of course, this sounds like a dream occupation, and Kalman readily concurs it is. At the same time, being oneself isn't easy because it means figuring out who you are in the first place. Says Kalman, who has been at it for decades: "Not trying to be anything other than who you are. That's an absurdly difficult thing to do, and it takes many years."[52] For her, it all comes down to intuition and storytelling: "Telling a story makes sense to me. It allows for a benevolent relationship to the world."[53] Again, easy as that sounds, the work comes "painfully. I don't want to tell the story that I seem to be telling. I want to tell you the understory. The not-story."[54] And as often as not, the not-story is the courage it takes to be individual. When in the course of **And the Pursuit of Happiness** she visits the Supreme Court, ostensibly to report on democracy in America, we find ourselves sitting down with Ruth Bader Ginsburg [page 102]. Who knew that her favorite artist is Matisse? Or that her justice robes come from Paris [page 103]? Or that as the only woman on the Supreme Court, she feels lonely?

Kalman's online columns are monumental editorial projects that pitch into relief her process as a whole, in particular the role of photography. (In her essay in this catalogue, Stamatina Gregory discusses their significance within the blogosphere.) Like a reporter on the beat, Kalman develops each column from in-depth research on her elected topic. She does related travel, interviews, and copious amounts of note- and picture-taking. Her work these days is as much about street photography as it is journalism. A walker by habit, she appears ever on the lookout for eccentric outfits, broken chairs, discarded couches, the back of somebody walking in front of her, and other subjects that inspire her humanity. Back in the studio, she keeps these photographs on file to use like preparatory sketches for painting or to corroborate a story: "Sometimes the counterpoint of a painting followed by a photo makes an impact: this is actually what I saw, and not something I made up."[55] Indeed, there is something of a double-whammy in seeing a picture taken through Kalman's lens next to one rendered by her hand. It shows how intensely the world can be experienced through pictures.

All of Kalman's work comes from her focus on pictures. As much as she draws from life experience for her work's subject matter, the work itself is all drawn from reproductions. (In postmodern parlance, she is an illustrator of appropriated images.) And though she uses her own pictures a lot and often depicts works of art taken from reproductions, her art has always shown a marked affinity for seeing the world through iconic works of modern photography. Diane Arbus's grotesquely dignified portrait of a giant and his parents is echoed in Kalman's very early, very punk **The Guzelofkowitzes Visit Daughter Veronica Guzé (Know Your Roots)** [page 9]. Cecil Beaton's photo of a ballet dancer flying through a room gains an unflappable man, talking on the telephone [page 109]. Henri Cartier-Bresson's perfect day in the park, a photo from 1955 titled *France, Essonne, Near Juvisy-sur-Orge*, becomes for Kalman the emblematic painting of "what I want my life to feel like. Light, water, greenery, children at play, children in costumes, people caught in an utterly natural yet ethereal moment."[56] To complete the picture, she inserted her own children in it.

From the sound of it, what Kalman wants her life to

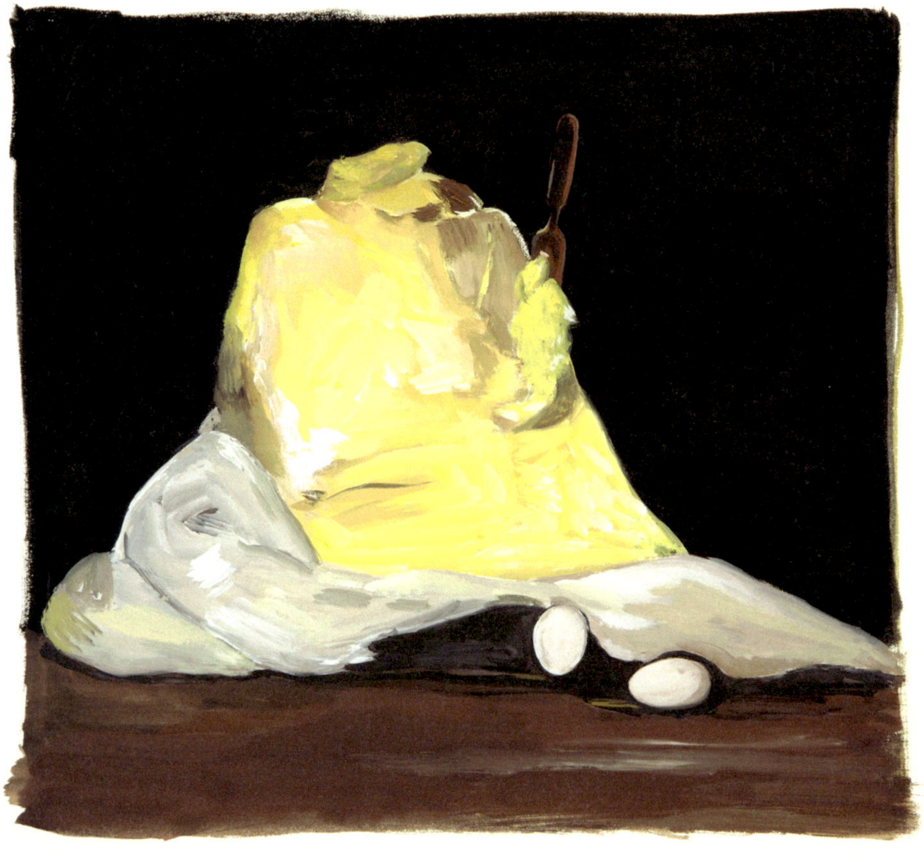

Butter and Eggs, 2009

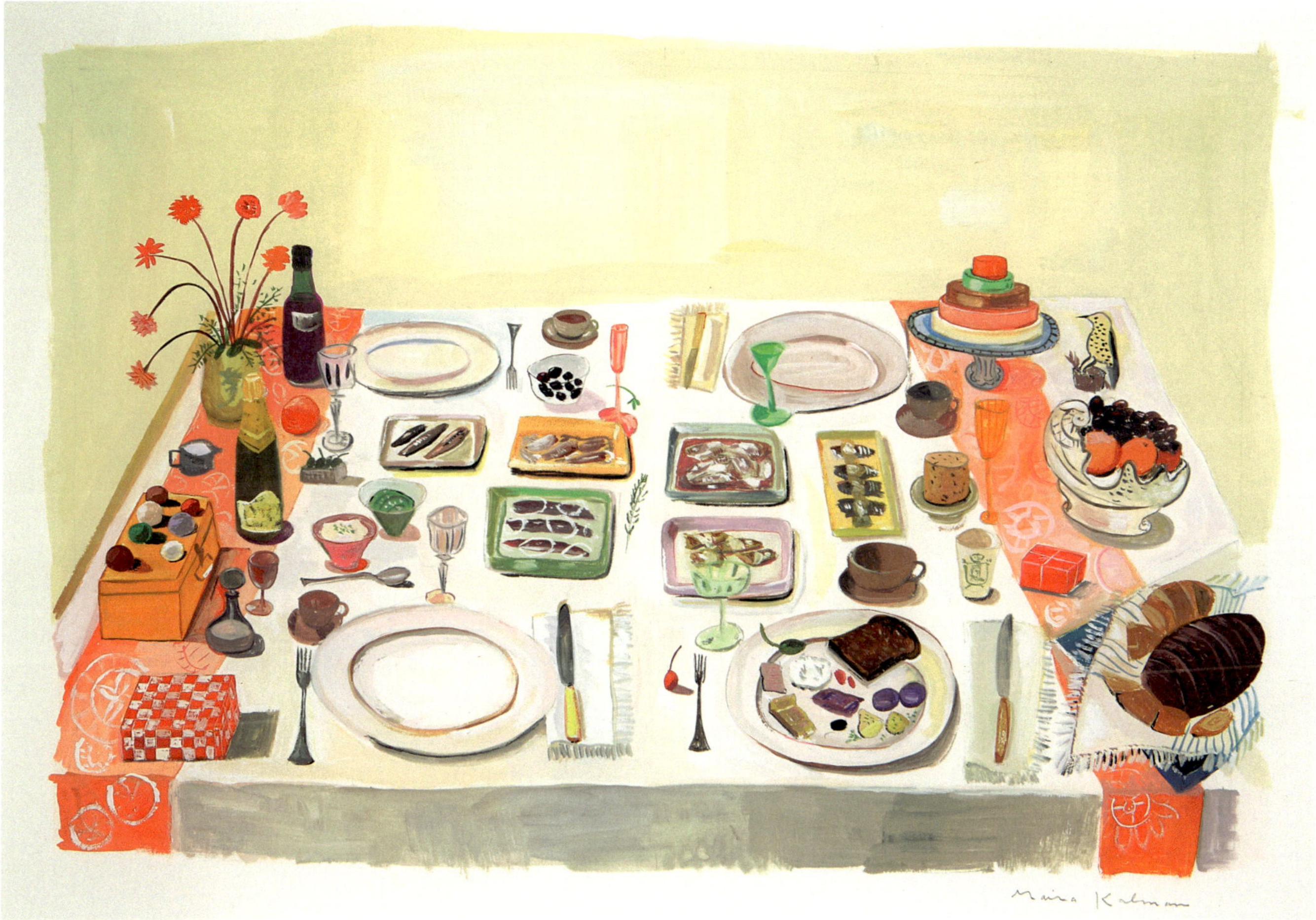

Herring and Philosophy Club, 2006

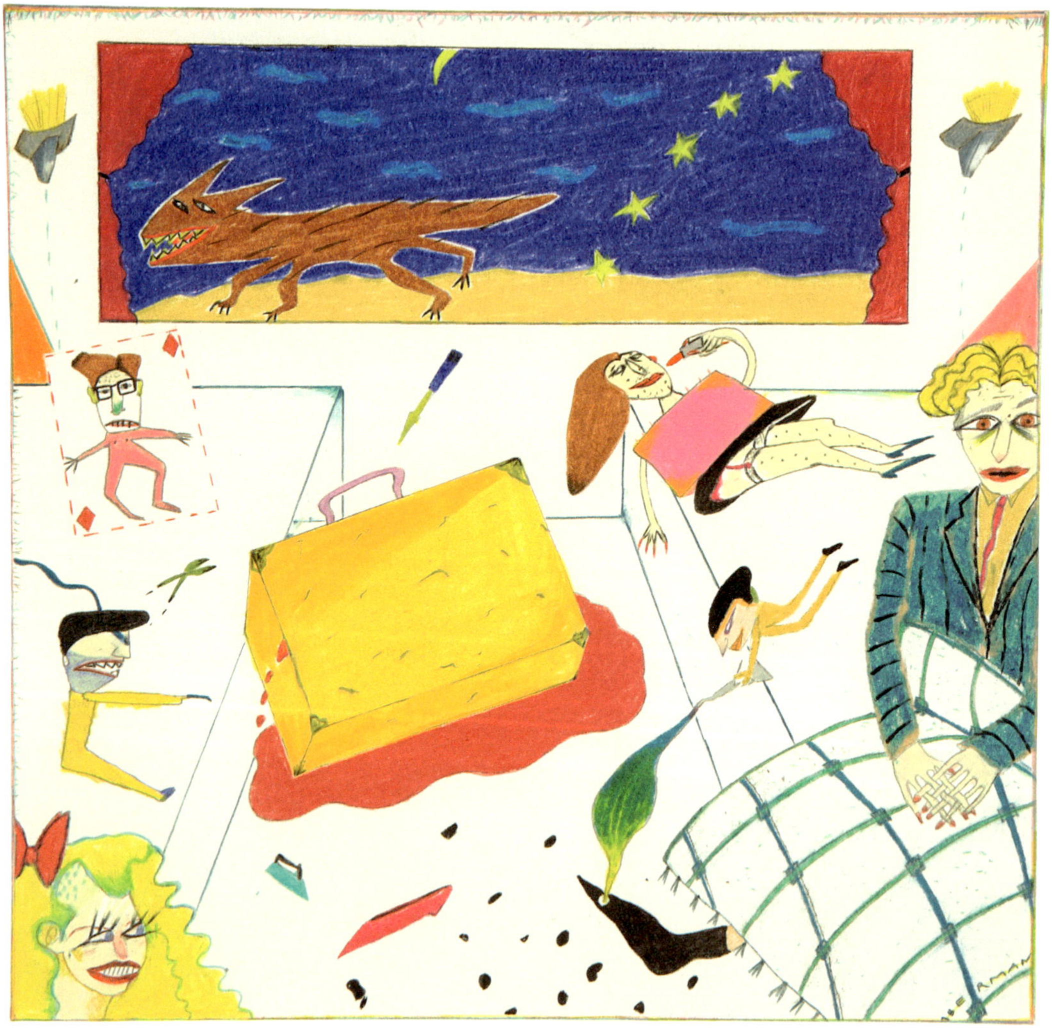

Suitcase, ca. 1982

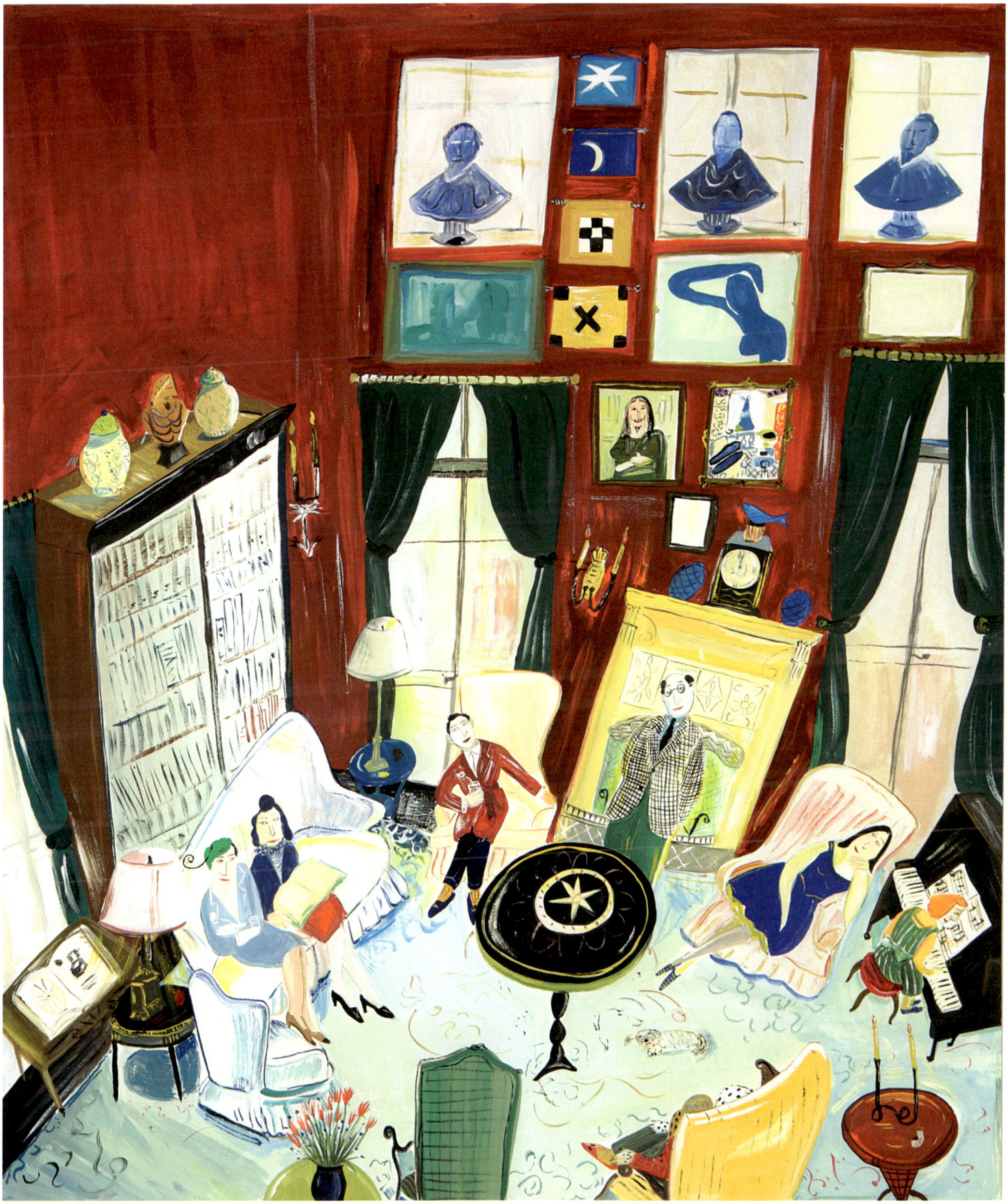

Red Room, 1992

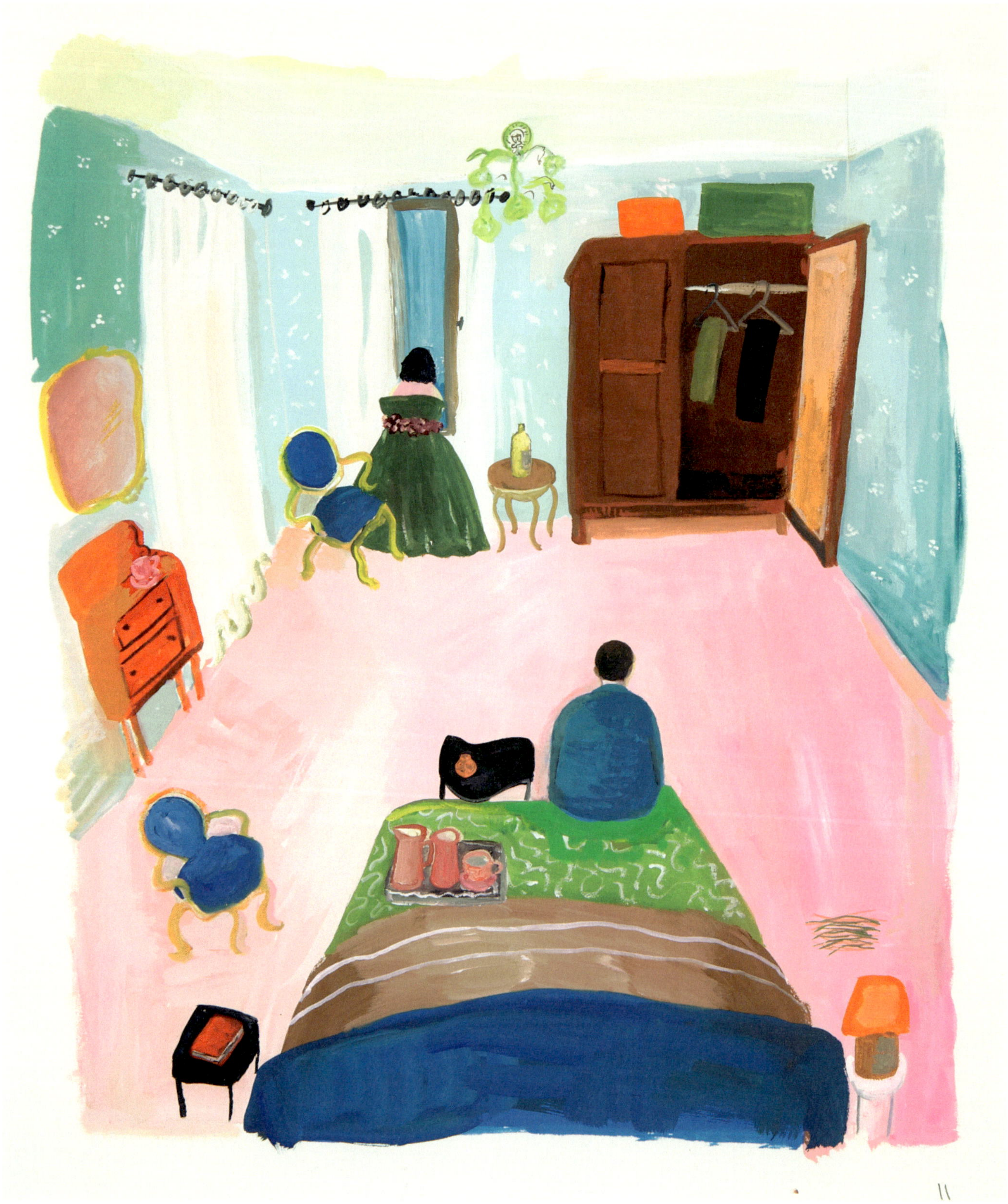

Dream in Venice, 2001

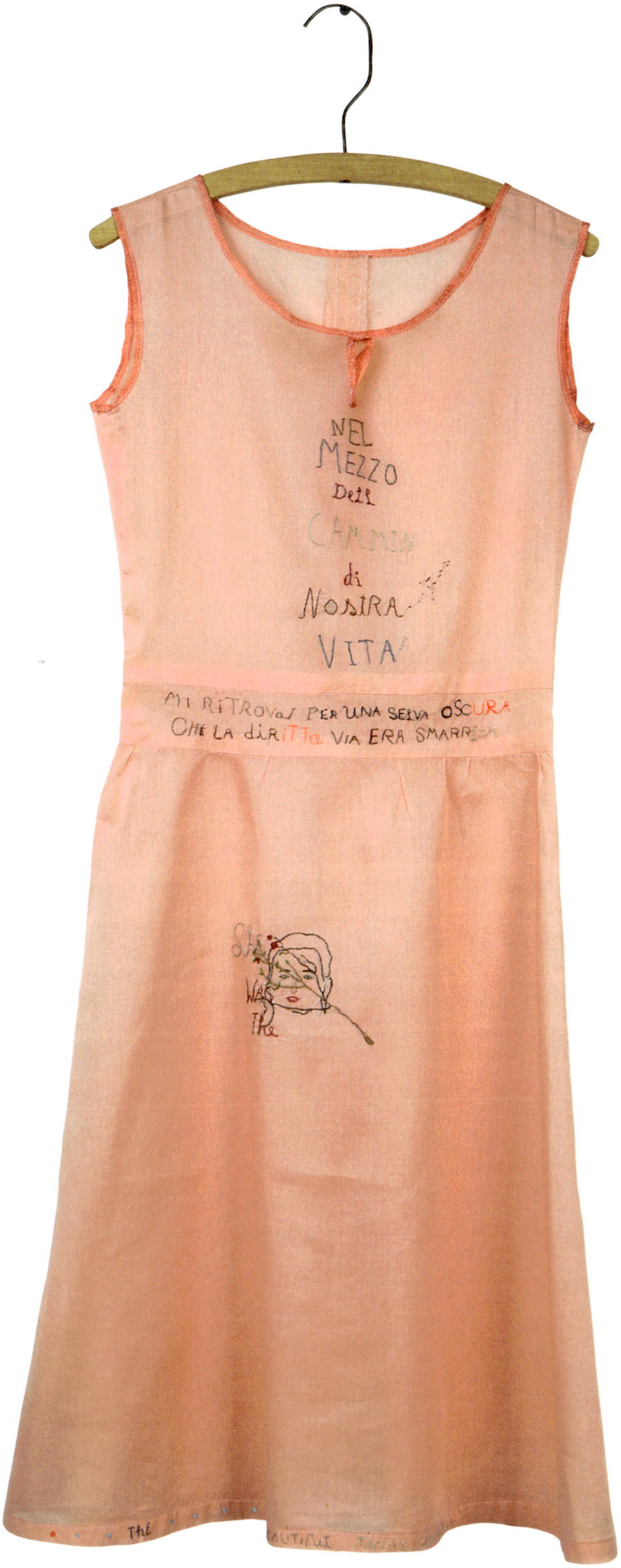

Pink Dress, 2005

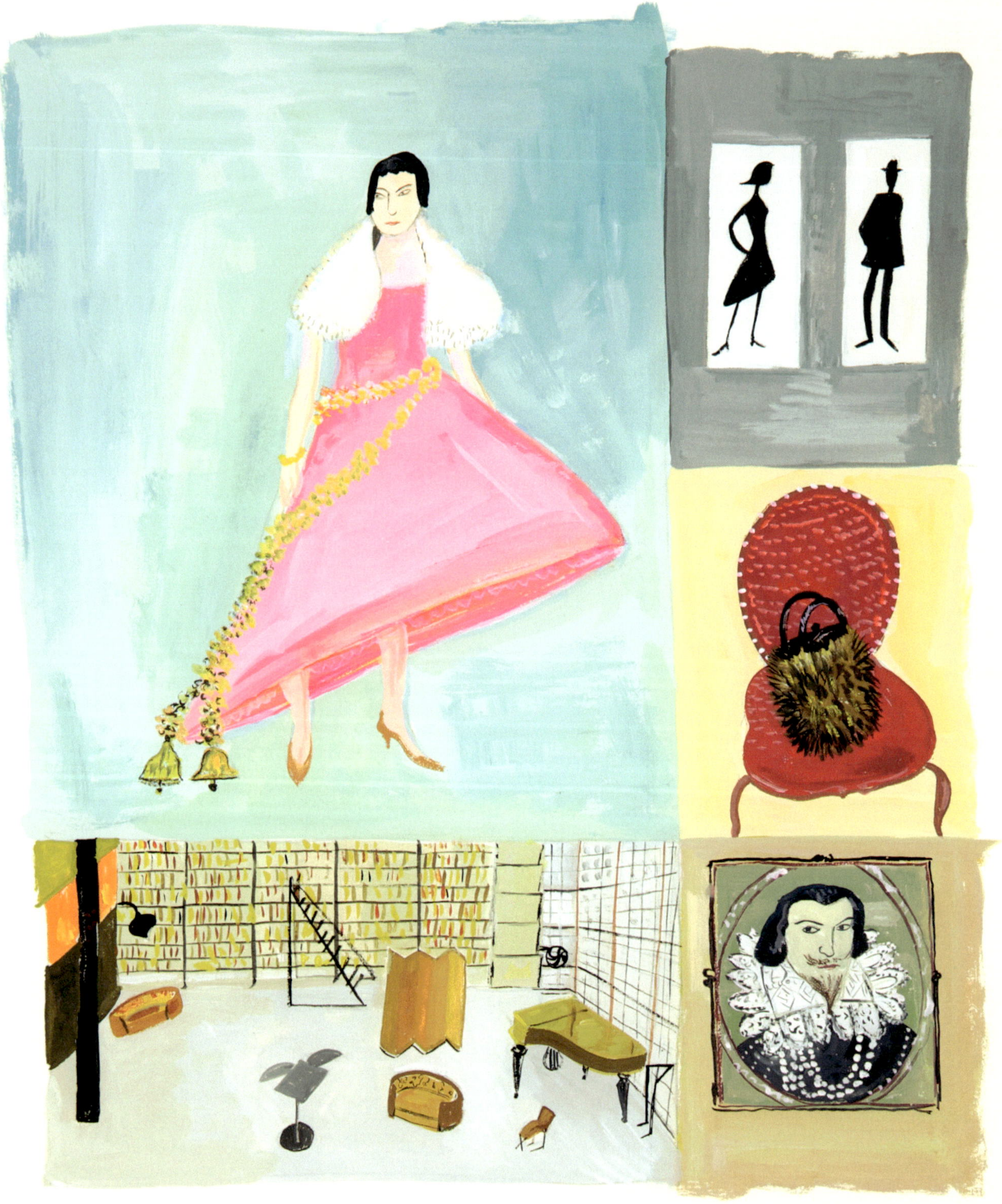

Viktor & Rolf, 2000

feel like is a Matisse painting. And so did Matisse, for that matter. The painter of *Luxe, calme et volupté* was an almost neurotically anxious man. He calmed himself by playing the violin and spent the rest of the time struggling hard to achieve the luxurious sense of relaxation, joy, and participation in life that music gave him. In Kalman's work, Matisse is a constant. There he is painting a voluptuous model in an armchair [page 112]. And there goes his painting *The Red Studio*, moved across a museum gallery, like a toy in pictorial pieces [pages 114–15].

Matisse is among a number of modern artists Kalman claims through her work. Obviously Marc Chagall, his figures floating dreamily and musically in spaces filled with reference to Russian folklore and Jewish culture, finds accord in Kalman's work. Charlotte Salomon is a less widely known reference, whose *Life? or Theater? A Play with Music* gives an ecstatic and visionary account of her life set to song through hundreds of gouache drawings. She began the work while living in exile as a German Jew in southern France and completed it in 1943 shortly before she was taken to Auschwitz and killed. The last lines urgently affirm: "And with dream-awakened eyes, she saw all the beauty around her."

Kalman's affinity for the widely known artist Marcel Duchamp may be less obvious, until you think of Duchamp's sense of humor and how at home any of his Readymades would be on one of Kalman's "many tables of many things." Moving into the present, the Chicago Imagist Jim Nutt, his cartoon style of abstracting the portrait down to a calm and crazy essence, makes sense. Maybe not Fred Sandback, the Minimalist sculptor, who drew with string in space [page 49], but then again, think about it. Simplicity and individuality are Kalman's modes of expression.

In literature, too, her work gravitates toward modern memoirists and collectors. A collector of butterflies, Vladimir Nabokov is practically part of the family. Kalman's portrait of him as a young boy [page 122], sitting in a rattan chair, wearing a tie, and looking up from the picture book on his lap, is presaged by a portrait of Max the dog in exactly the same picture.[57] That most parsing of poets Emily Dickinson is portrayed with her dog, Carlo [page 15]. Like an upholstered madeleine, an empty green ottoman stands in for Marcel Proust [page 55], who savored cakes and loved his mother, albeit to the extreme. And given that the most endearing term of affection in the Kalman family is "you idiot," it would be remiss not to mention Fyodor Dostoyevsky.[58] Look for Kalman's typed list of names from Part One of *The Idiot* amidst the things on view.

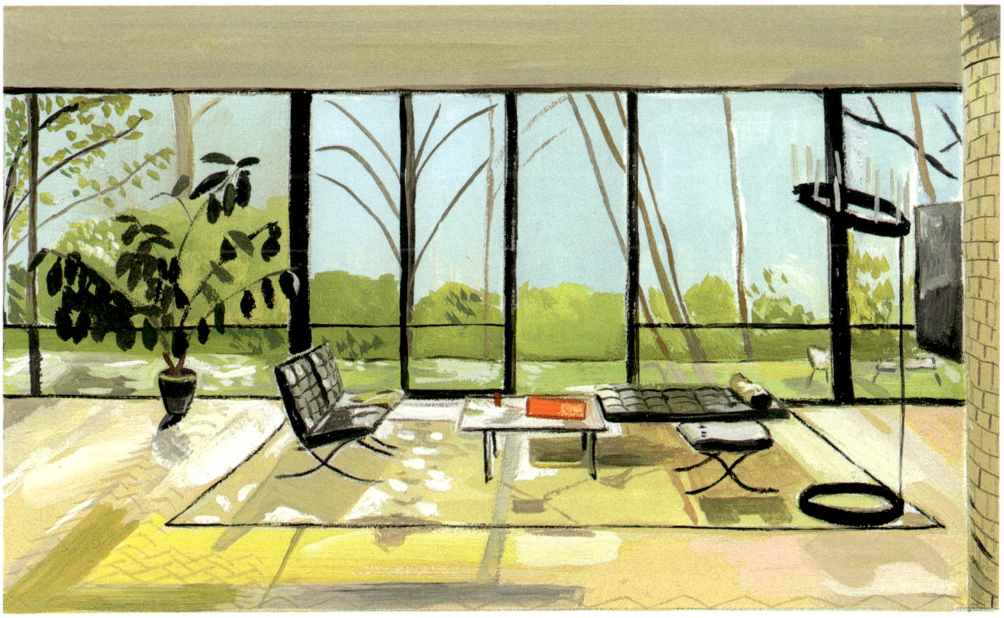

The Glass House, 2004–5

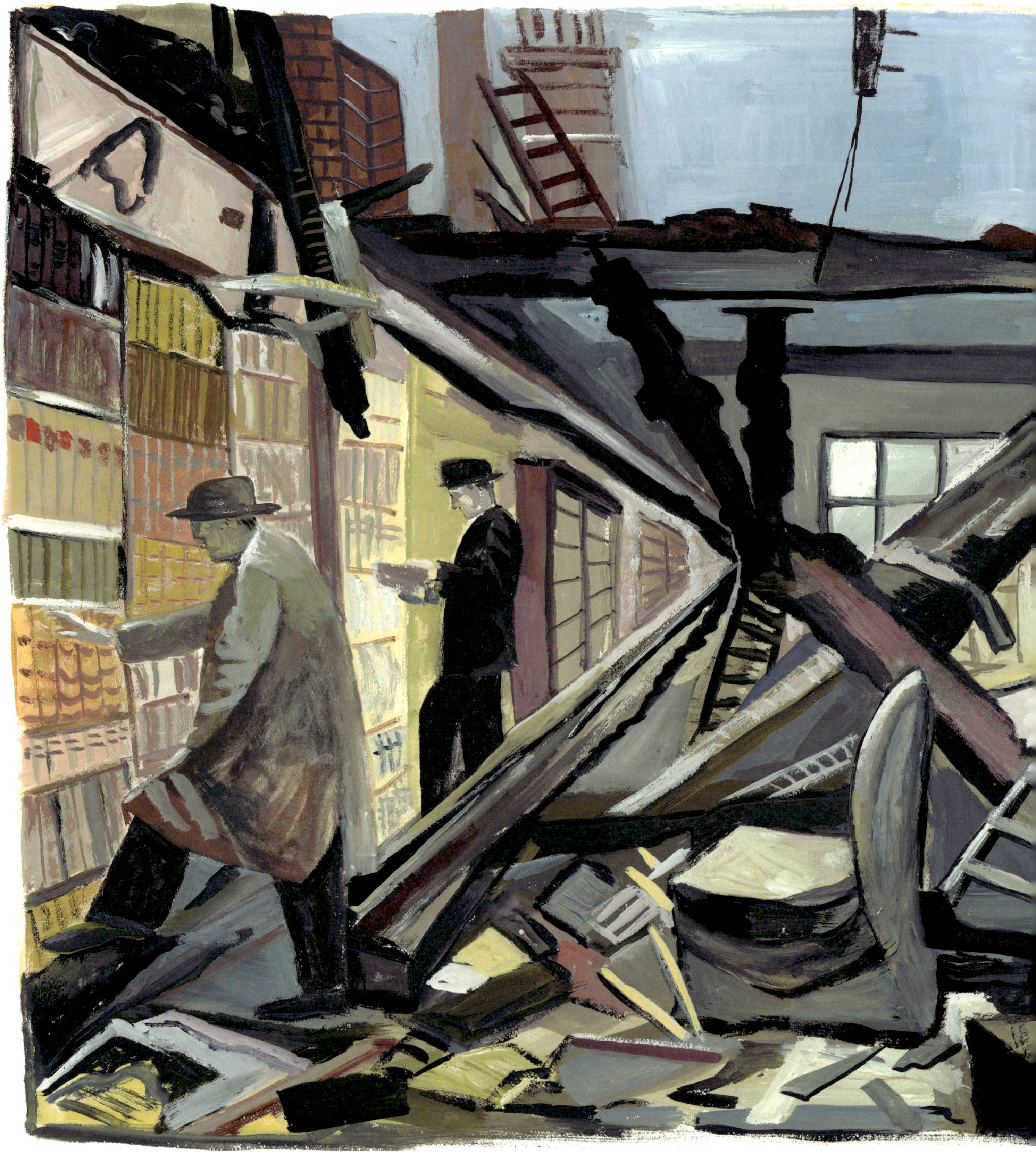

London Blitz, 2007

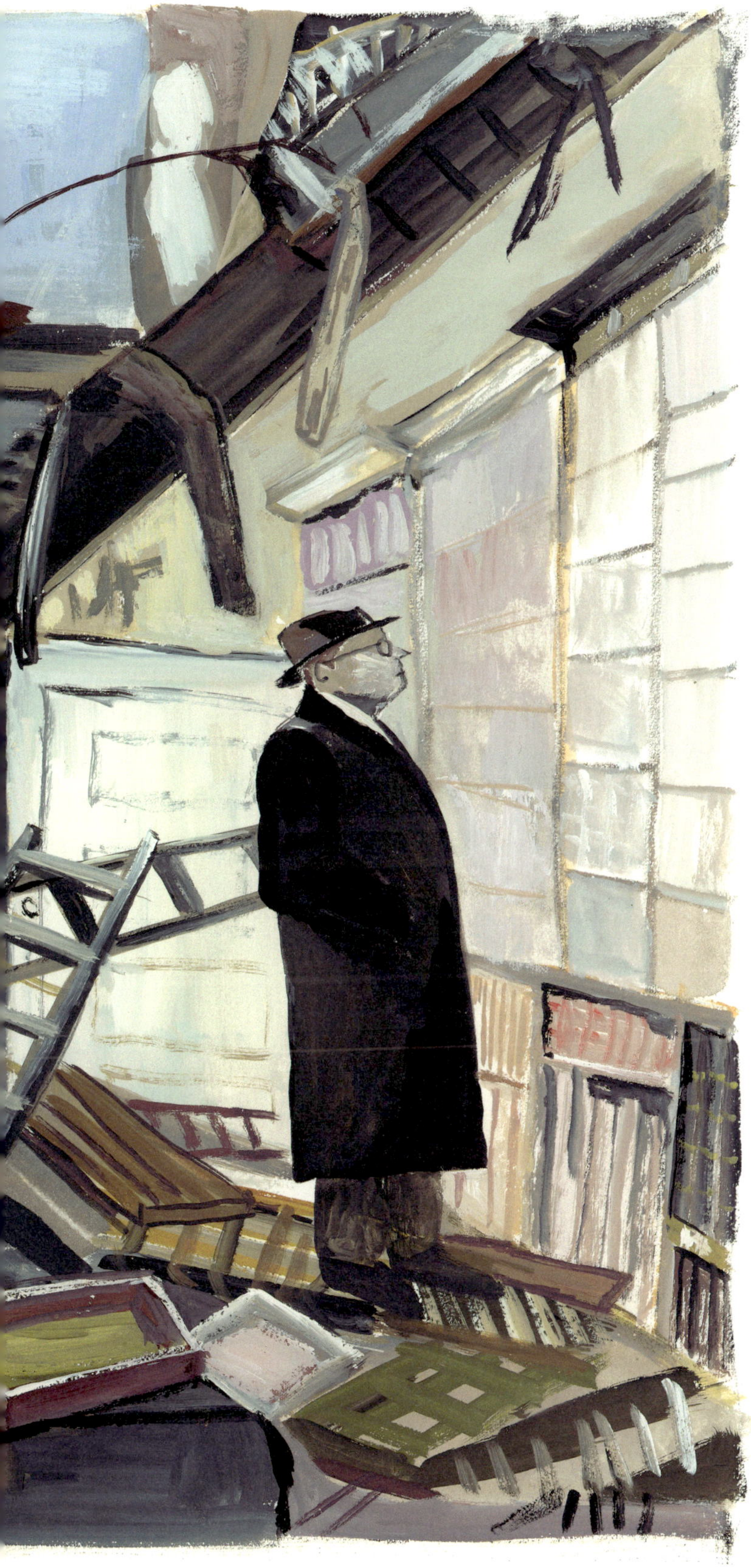

Milton

KALMAN'S WORK HAS CONTINUOUSLY MOVED OFF the page, taking its frame of reference with it. Imagine a world with men wearing the tapestry jacket [page 2] Kalman created with fashion designer Isaac Mizrahi in 1989, the first of their many collaborations. It would be furnished with sofas upholstered in the "Story of My Life" textile she designed for Maharam. And full of dogs sporting rainwear she created with Kate Spade. Kalman's work has entered the urban fabric, too, through her mural projects, which Kenneth E. Silver discusses in his essay in this catalogue. In 1995 she dressed the windows of the Sony Building with a diorama populated by the mannequins she designed for the display manufacturer Ralph Pucci. And in 2000 she created a spectacular theater curtain for choreographer Mark Morris's ballet *Four Saints, Three Acts*, based on the Gertrude Stein and Virgil Thomson opera.[59] Now envision all of these things merged into a great theater piece by Kalman, along the lines of how urbanist Jane Jacobs theorized the city as a public dance.

This is not as far-fetched as it sounds: there is a strong theatrical bent to Kalman's work – and to Kalman herself. In 1981 she appeared in *National Lampoon*'s "Unofficial Guide to Fort Lauderdale and Daytona Beach" as Terri Thompson from Asphaltville, Ohio, vacationing with her dentist husband, Timothy. The guide was designed by M&Co, as was the brochure for Kalman's 1989 Tokyo exhibition, announcing "An Evening with Maira Kalman in Nervous." And so she appears, dressed up in 1950s diva drag, complete with pillbox hat. Dressing up for pictures was the extent of her performance until recently. In 2005 Kalman appeared on stage (among other nonprofessionals on percussion, keeping time by spinning a Rolodex, typing, slamming a dictionary) with composer Nico Muhly, who created a song cycle based on her rendition of **The Elements of Style**. While there are no immediate plans for a theater piece, ideas have long been percolating. As Kalman envisions it, "The play will be a cacophonous musical *tanztheater* (with a touch of Pina Bausch [page 111]) that will tell the story of my family. . . . It will have Russian songs, and tangos, and other romantic evocative work."[60]

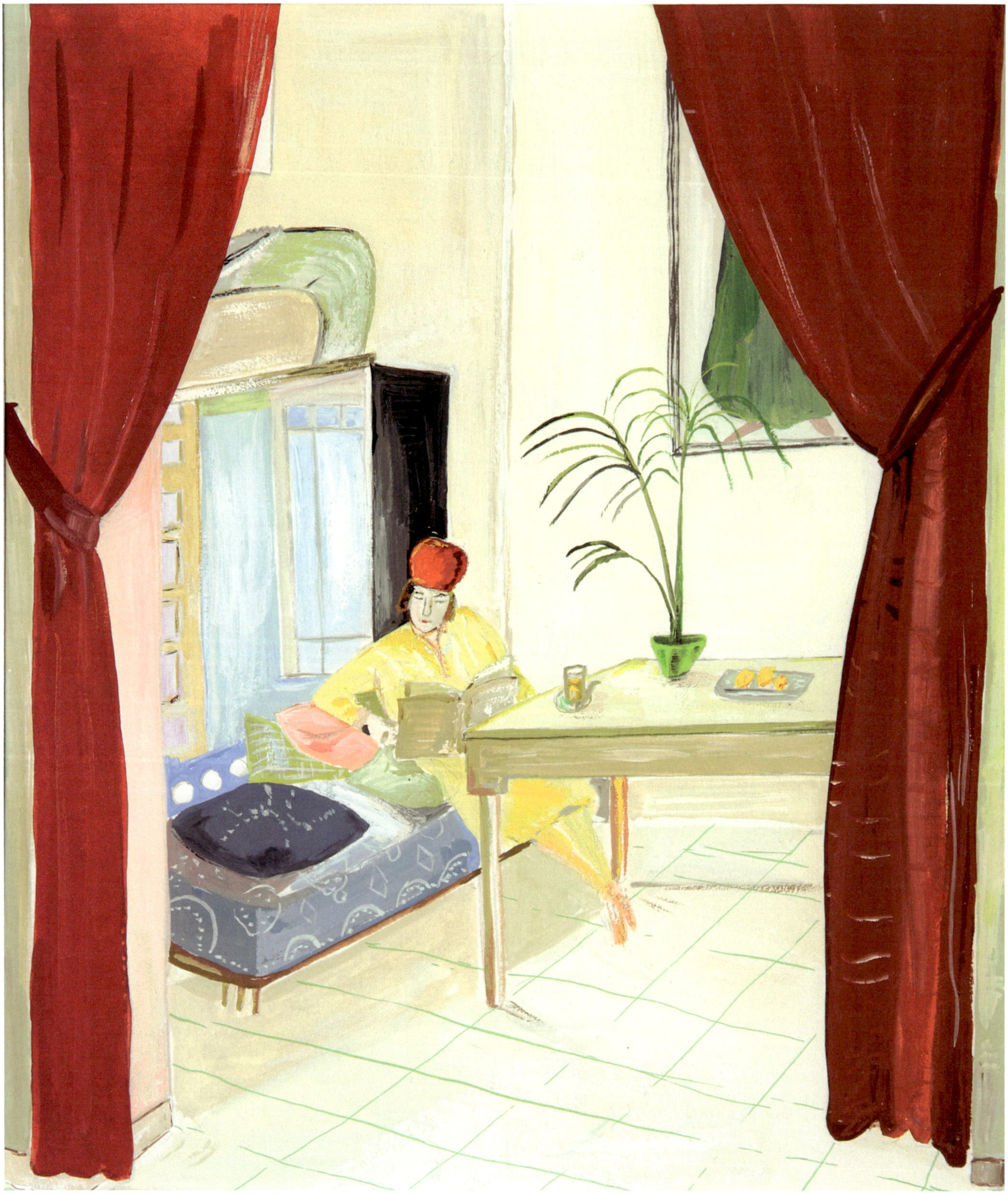

Celeste Hotel, Petit Salon, 2006

When asked by *The New York Times* what she would like to see someday in Times Square, Kalman responded with "Milton."[61] Essentially an alternative space without a director, Milton would run on a "PITTANCE . . . because we need small, eccentric places in the midst of the conglomerates." The program would "change with the proprietor. One week one hat is for sale. The next week someone is doing their ironing. The next someone is playing the violin." Within Kalman's work, a number of conceptual, Miltonian events have already been performed. For instance, one afternoon during her first exhibition at the Julie Saul Gallery in New York visitors were invited to stop by and "have a button sewn on any article of clothing." In the background, there was ironing.[62]

Matisse would have approved! Art should be "a soothing, calming influence on the mind, something like a good armchair that provides relaxation from fatigue," he famously said.[63] What could be more soothing than the draw of the needle, the press of the iron, domestic tasks quietly abstracted? Like Matisse, Kalman is a connoisseur of decorative distractions and bourgeois pleasures, ostensibly the very things the avant-garde set out to destroy, or at least mock. As late as 1945, an interviewer said to Matisse, "People still have not given up reproaching your art for being extremely decorative, meaning that in the pejorative sense of *superficial*." And Matisse shot back, "The decorative for a work of art is an extremely precious thing. It is an essential quality."[64]

While Postmodernism has done a fair job of making the decorative safe for critical discussion, charm has yet to be recuperated. Or even really touched, since *charm* is essentially a term of dismissal, denoting something not to be taken seriously. Andy Warhol's graphic art is charming; his mechanically reproduced silkscreen paintings are not. The polemics of charm quickly rev up to questions of gender and other polarizing issues. But for now let's slow down and look at moving the compass in a different direction.

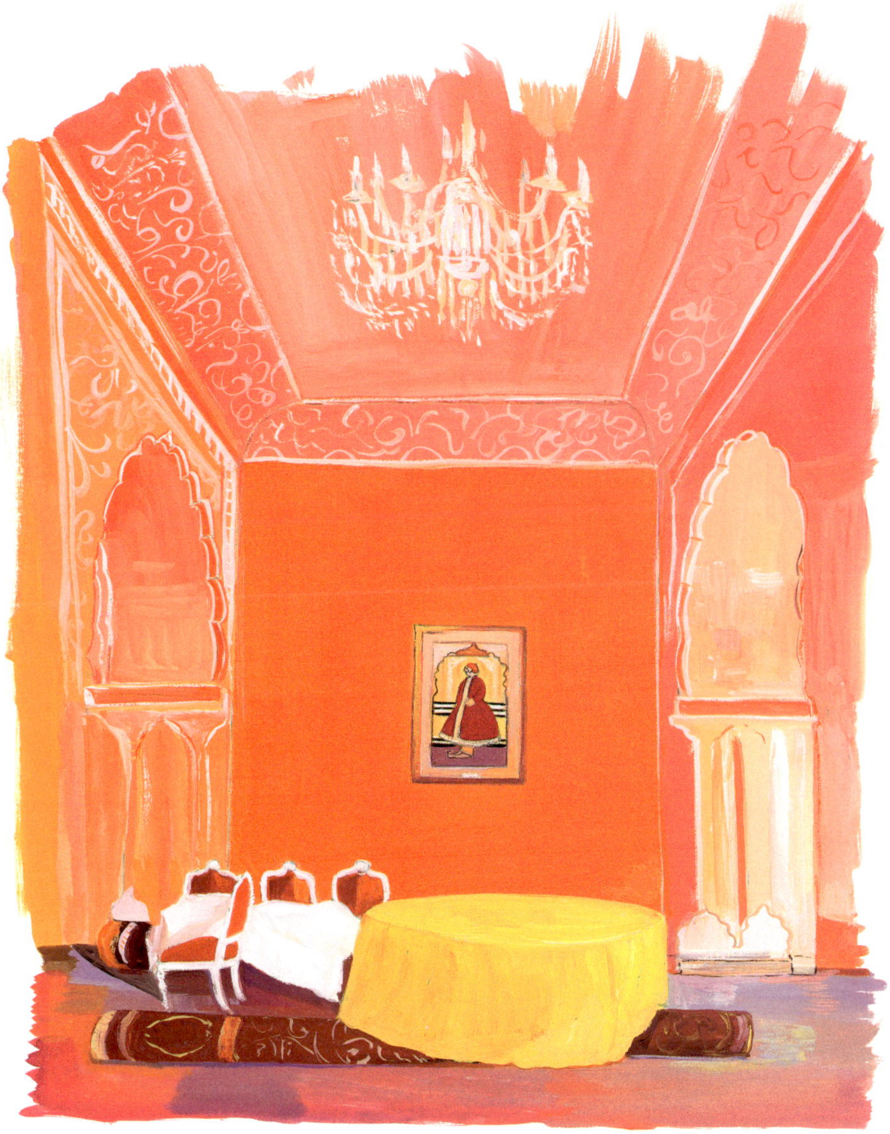

Rajastani Room, 2004–5

Maira Kalman's work is certainly charming, even powerfully so, given how loaded a term *charm* seems to be. So why not take this opportunity to accept it at face value? Like a gift. In his captivating and widely read book *The Gift: Imagination and the Erotic Life of Property*, Lewis Hyde reckons that art is a gift that cannot be bought or sold, only received. And, as any reader of anthropology knows, gift giving and getting is no passive act but more or less a test of one's own humanity. Hyde writes: "That art which matters to us – which moves the heart, or revives the soul, or delights the senses, or offers courage for living, however we choose to describe the experience – that work is received to us as a gift is received."[65] How can it be said any better? Maira Kalman's gift is to illuminate that which matters, affirming our own capacity for joy, sadness, humor – and even charm – along with our hunger for those very things, and some snacks.

Presidents, 1978

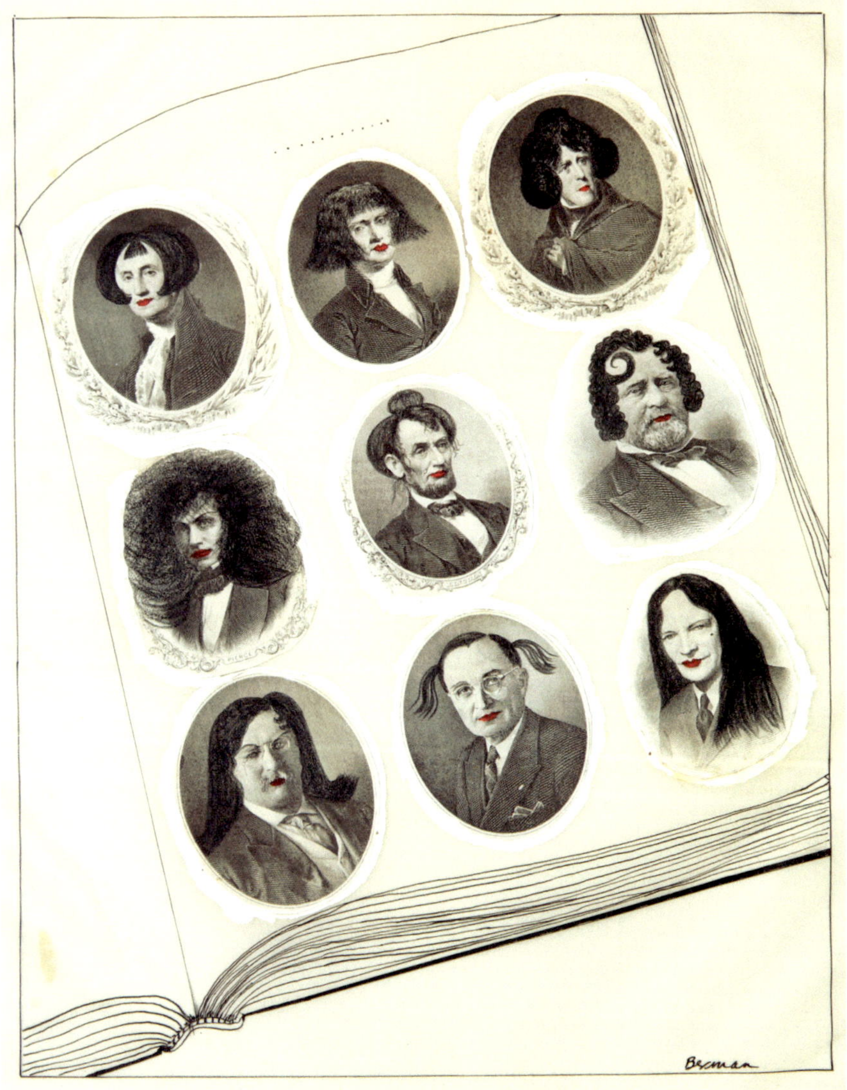

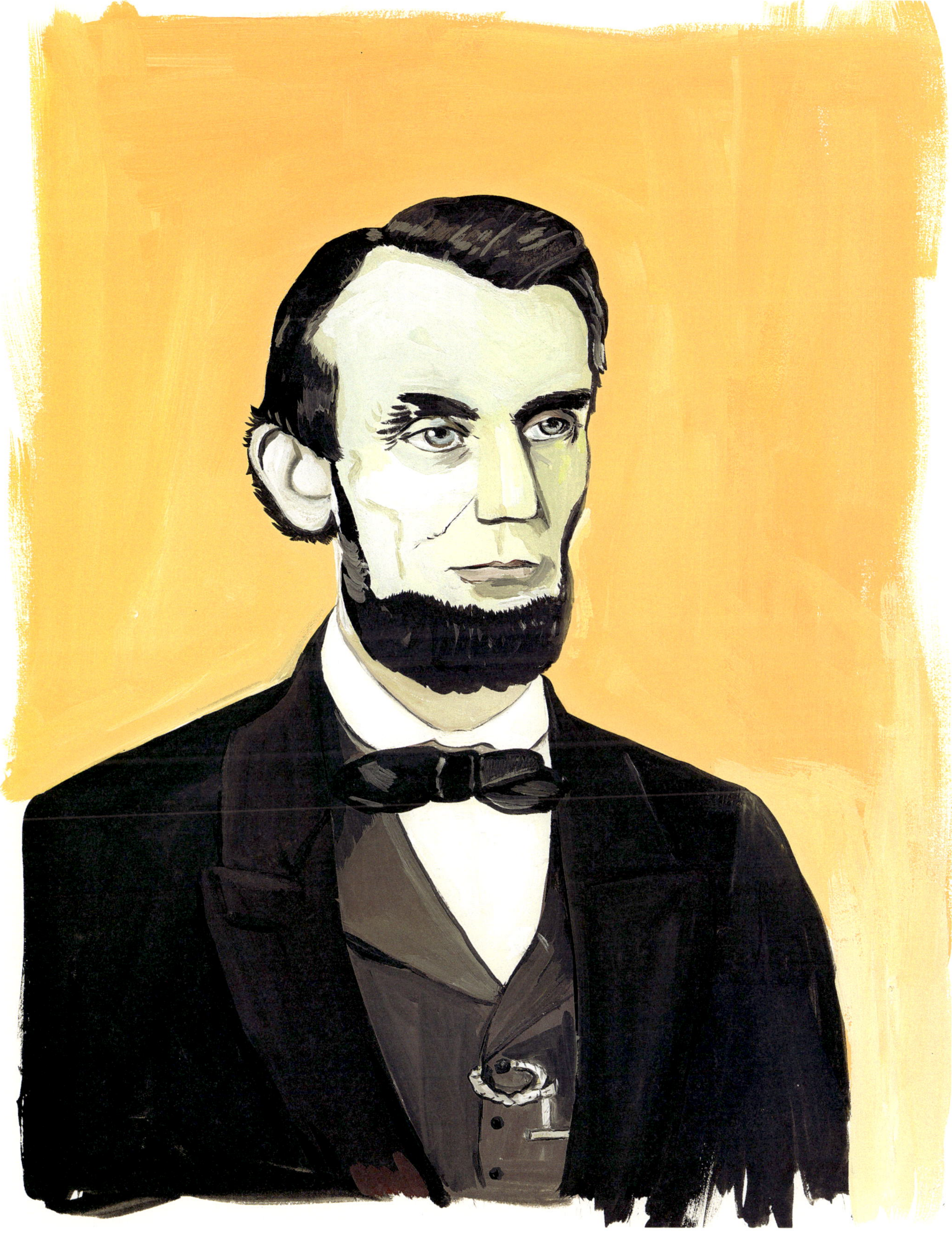

Abraham Lincoln, 2004–5

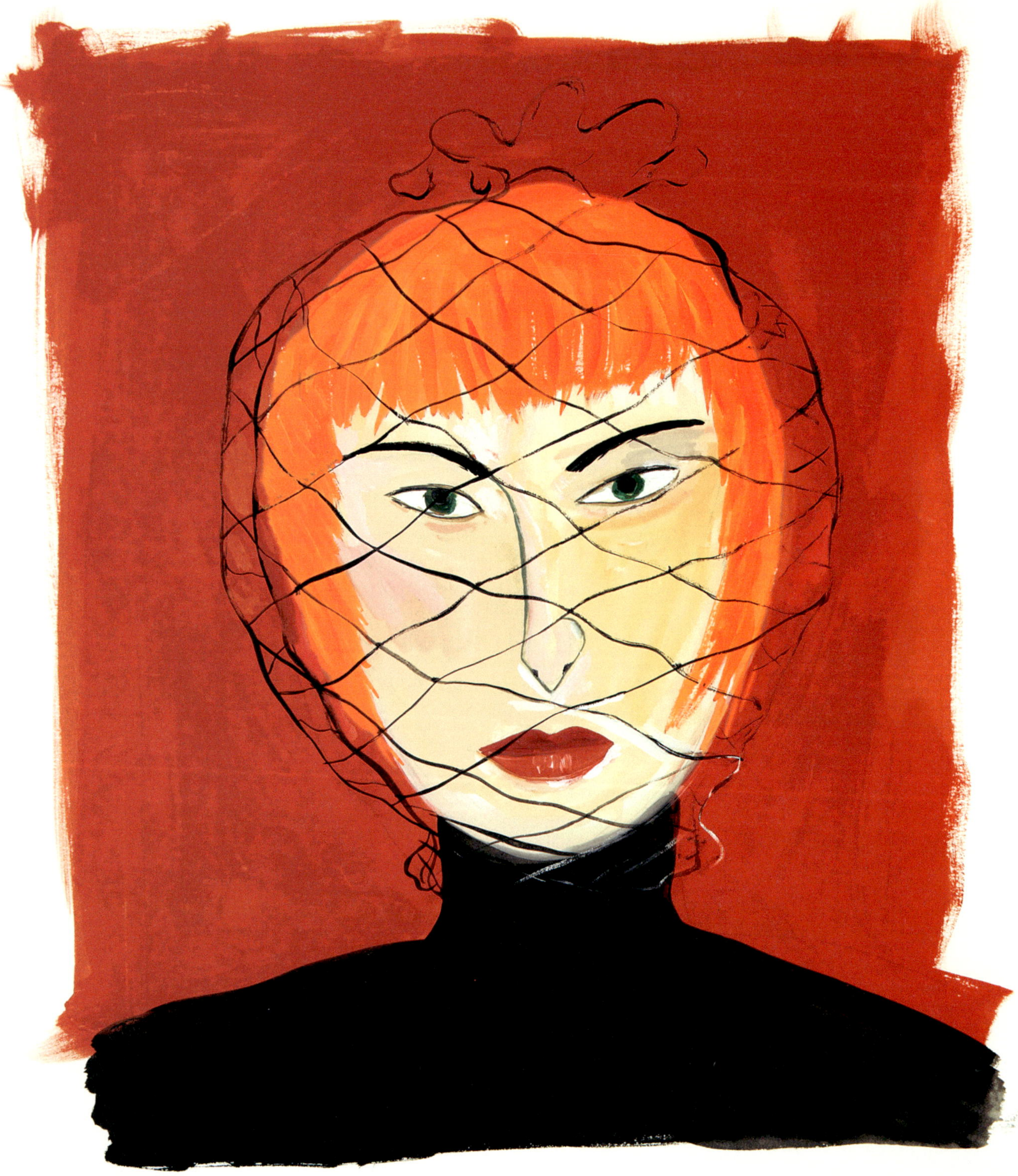

Woman with Face Net, 2000

Notes

I would like to thank Donna Ghelerter for her careful critical reading—essential to bringing this essay into the pink!

1 Although published by *The New York Times* as a "blog," Kalman prefers to call it an "online column," which seems to her truer to the process of research and reportage these pieces entail.

2 Sarah Boxer, "A Funny New Yorker Map is Again the Best Defense," *The New York Times*, December 8, 2001, 13. I would like to thank Laura Holzman, in the graduate program at the University of California, Irvine, for the insightful exchange about her writing on Maira Kalman's online columns as a "public panacea."

3 Maira Kalman and Rick Meyerowitz, "Things to Do on Valentine's Day," *Los Angeles Times*, February 14, 2003, B17.

4 As they drove, what precipitated Kalman's shout-out was Meyerowitz's comment on how tribal the Democratic Party was becoming as the city approached the mayoral election. For the full account see "New Yorkistan" on rickmeyerowitz.com.

5 Maira Kalman, "One on One: In-Depth Interviews with Host Katherine Lanpher," Barnes & Noble Studio, 2007, http://downloads.feedroom.com/podcasts/t_assests/20071108/776a1931ff2ef46a44ea91af30c7b6cb5c6187d6.mp3.

6 Kim Hastreiter, "What They Do," *Paper Magazine* (May 2004): 84.

7 As Kalman describes them: "A group that according to its mission statement is 'bound together by our love of rubber bands.'" Maira Kalman, "How-to Dept.: Art, a Crash Course," *The New Yorker*, January 15, 2001, 35.

8 Quoted from Maira Kalman's lecture on simplicity for the 2007 TED conference; TED is a small nonprofit devoted to "ideas worth spreading." Kalman's talk can be accessed through its website: http://www.ted.com/speakers/maira_kalman.html.

9 James Kaplan, "(T&)M&Co," *New York Magazine*, November 23, 1998, 40. An invaluable profile of Maira and Tibor Kalman: individually and as a couple. I am also grateful to those who spoke to me informally, including Bethany Johns and Douglas Riccardi among others, about their M&Co days.

10 As CEO Maira Kalman maintains M&Co, not as a studio but as a licensing enterprise and venue for new design projects, including the "Zupa" rubber ball clock, the "Prozac" paperweight, and, in 2000, the book *(un)FASHION* by Tibor and Maira Kalman.

11 Published in 1973, *Our Town! An Insider's Guide to New York Brought to You by the People of Barnes & Noble Bookstores* was a promotional publication created by the innovative "book supermarket" founded by Leonard Riggio in the 1970s, with Tibor Kalman as director of planning and development.

12 Kaplan, "(T&)M&Co," 44.

13 Undated early artworks and publication tear sheets at Kalman's studio.

14 "New York File 1: Maira Berman," *Illustration* [translated from Japanese] (February 1983): 123.

15 Quoted in Chee Pearlman, "Unleashing Her Inner Child," *The New York Times*, November 1, 2001, 8.

16 Hiroko Tanaka in *The Collection of Women Illustrators Presents an Evening with Maira Kalman in Nervous* (Tokyo: The Ginza Art Space, 1989), unpaginated. Hugging is not off the table when it came to Max, whose likeness was made into a plush toy to promote the series in 1995.

17 Trisha Hall, "For Young Readers, Picasso Not Bunnies," *The New York Times*, January 9, 1992, C2.

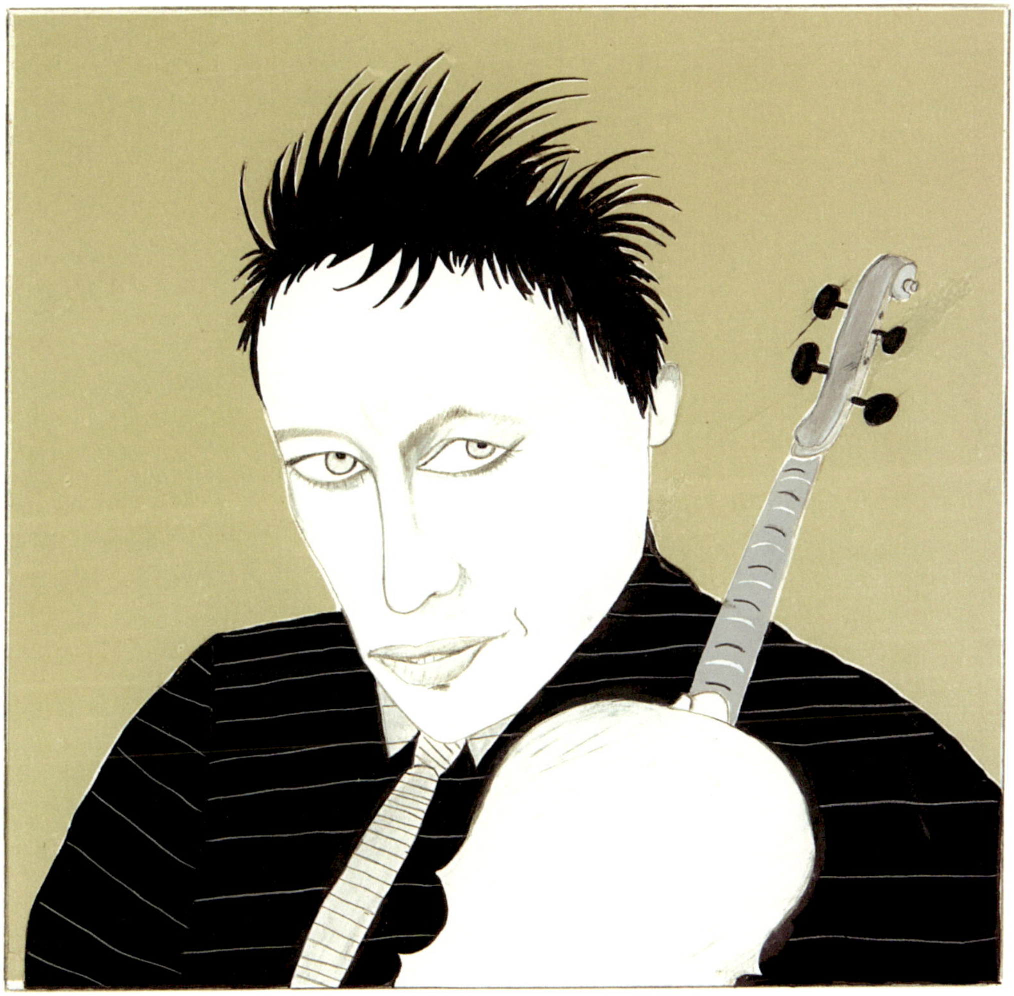

Laurie Anderson, 1982

18 Liz Farrelly, *Tibor Kalman: design and undesign* (New York: The Ivy Press, 1998), 22.

19 Steven Heller, "Interview: Maira Kalman," *Eye* 47 (Spring 2003): 61–62.

20 Published by the Whitney Museum of American Art, *Roarr: Calder's Circus* (1991) brings Alexander Calder's toy masterpiece (1926–31) to life with text by Maira Kalman, photographs by Donatella Brun, and design by M&Co.

21 The book-in-process is mentioned in a number of publications, including *Tibor Kalman: Perverse Optimist*, ed. Peter Hall and Michael Bierut (New York: Princeton Architectural Press, 1998), 160. One gets a sense of how the city might have appeared in Max the dog's eye view from "Piccolo Mondo," Kalman's editorial on children's fashions in the March 6, 1994, issue of *The New York Times Magazine*.

22 Kalman, "One on One."

23 Maira Kalman, "Tibor Swimming in the Ocean," *The New York Times Magazine*, January 2, 2000, 66.

24 Kalman, TED lecture.

25 Kaplan, "(T&)M&Co," 42.

26 Maira Kalman, "Mad about the Met," *Departures Magazine* (May–June 2008): 232.

27 Kalman, TED lecture.

28 Interesting to note is the reference to Frida Kahlo's painting *The Dream* (1940), in which Kahlo appears, encircled in foliage, asleep in a bed floating in the sky. (A skeleton slumbers on top of the bed canopy.)

29 "Music had the power to take me out of my despair," Kalman says of the period during Tibor's illness. More recently she took accordion lessons, finding "merriment" in the one tune she has mastered: "It's transporting." See Elaine Louie, "Bellows and Barks to Soothe the Soul," *The New York Times*, April 20, 2003, sect. 9, 9.

30 Hall, "For Young Readers," C2.

31 Kaplan, "(T&)M&Co," 43.

32 Jesse Nathan, "'I Want to tell you the understory. The Not-story.' An Interview with Maira Kalman," in *More Things Like This* (San Francisco: Chronicle Books, 2009), 184.

33 Ibid.

34 Combined in print, Kalman's words and pictures often exist on two separate sheets of paper, with the writing on a sheet of vellum.

35 Kalman isn't the only one to put the slogan back into circulation; there is a "Keep Calm" trend in Britain. According to historian Bex Lewis, "the 'Keep Calm' poster, meant to be distributed in the event of a German invasion, was extremely obscure for many decades." Lewis traces it's recent revival to a bookshop in northern England, where one of the original posters turned up "in a box of old books." See Bob Walker, "Remixed Message," *The New York Times Magazine*, July 5, 2009, 19.

36 Maira Kalman, "The Family Way," *The Book* (Neiman Marcus), December 2001, 62.

37 Some variation on these lines comes up, it seems, whenever Kalman is asked about her early biography. See, for instance, her website.

38 Maira Kalman, "Bedtime Story," *O! At Home* (Spring 2006): 32.

39 Kalman, "The Family Way," 62.

40 Hastreiter, "What They Do," 84.

41 Kalman, "Bedtime Story," 32.

42 Maira Kalman, "Martin Fell Down," *The Ganzfeld*, no. 2 (2002): 96.

43 Maira Kalman, "Sept. 10, 2001 . . . The Day Before," *The New York Observer*, December 17, 2001, 12.

44 Benjamin's suicide isn't literally represented by this snowy scene but is evoked as emblematic of the deaths of so many Europeans who attempted to elude the Gestapo in the 1930s and 1940s.

45 Harold Rosenberg, *Saul Steinberg* (New York: Whitney Museum of American Art, 1978), 12. More recently, Joel Smith's excellent 2006 exhibition and catalogue (organized by the Vassar College Frances Lehman Loeb Art Center), *Saul Steinberg: Illuminations*, finds an echo in the title of this show of Kalman's work.

46 Bemelmans wrote, among other things, a yearlong series of editorials on the state of tourist destinations throughout postwar Europe. The assignment from *Holiday* magazine proved less than congenial to his otherwise charmed outlook on life.

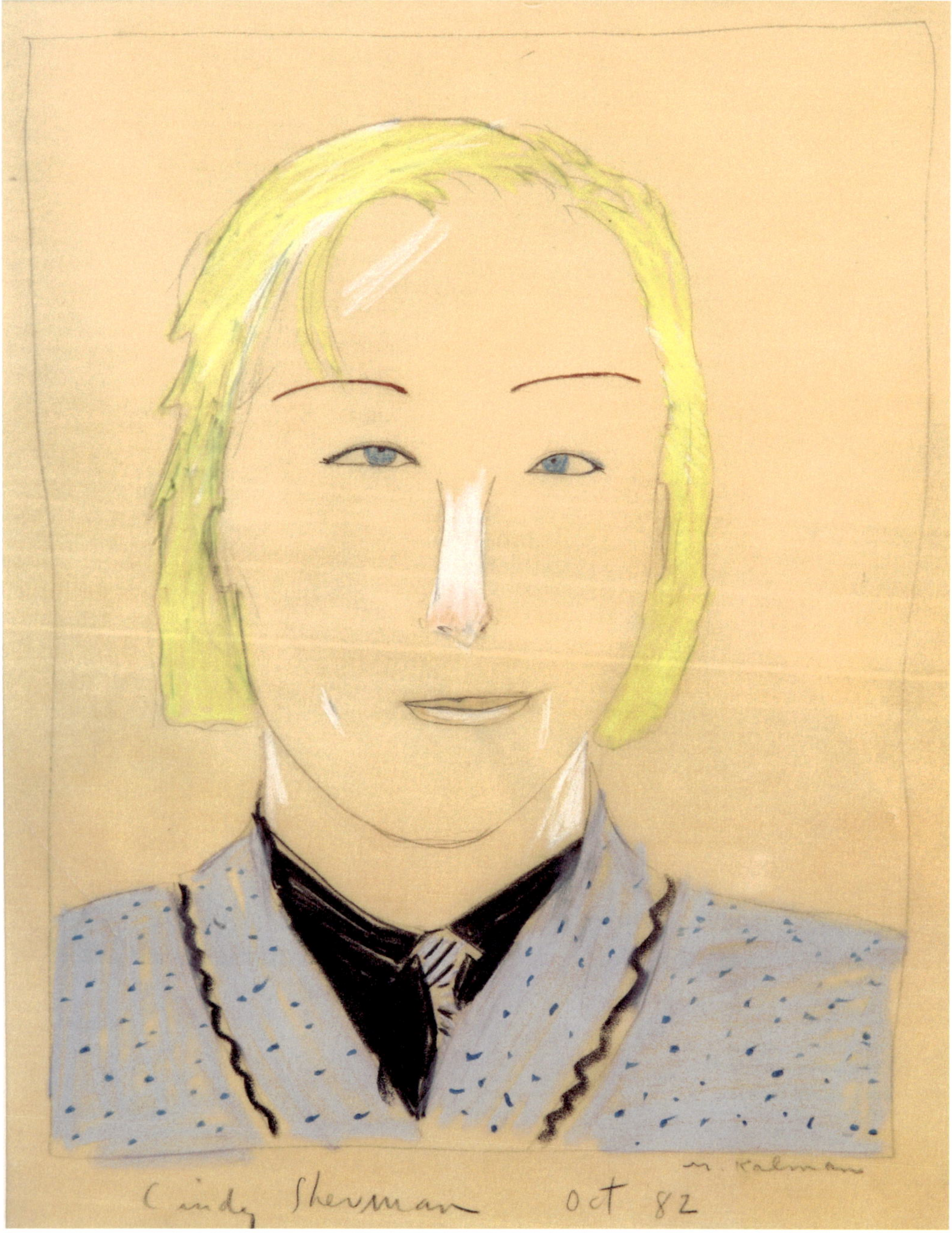

Cindy Sherman, 1982

47 Maira Kalman, "Couture Voyeur," *The New York Times Magazine*, November 5, 2000, 70.

48 Maira Kalman, "The Splendid Garden(er)," *Culture + Travel* (Winter 2007): 108.

49 Maira Kalman, "My Tel Aviv: A Stroll through the City," *Tablet*, September 5, 2008, http://www.tabletmag.com/arts-and-culture/737/my-tel-aviv.

50 Maira Kalman, "Vis-à-vis the Venice Biennale," *The New Yorker*, August 22, 2005, 49.

51 Maira Kalman, "Fun Work If You Can Get It," *O!* (May 2002): 231.

52 Holly Davis, "Guileless and Gutsy," *The Artist's Magazine* (October 2009): 46.

53 Nathan, "I want to tell you the understory," 182.

54 Ibid.

55 Francine Prose, "The World According to Maira," *Aperture* 197 (Winter 2009): 62.

56 Maira Kalman, "Mind's Eye," *Aperture* 189 (Winter 2007): 88.

57 Maira Kalman, *Swami on Rye* (New York: Viking, 1995), 1.

58 Kalman, "The Family Way," 62. "And I have to say, that the term of endearment most often used in my family is 'you idiot.'"

59 The opera was originally performed in 1934 with costumes and decor by Florine Stettheimer, who's confectionary style of painting makes her another modernist icon in Kalman's personal pantheon.

60 Heller, "Interview," 61. "And Einstein may be mentioned. You can't go wrong if you bring in Einstein."

61 Maira Kalman, "Through a Glass, Brightly," *The New York Times*, June 13, 2004, sect. 15, 5.

62 During the course of the exhibition at the Institute of Contemporary Art, University of Pennsylvania, plans are underway for a weeklong program called "Milton," organized by Penn students in Kenneth Goldsmith's "Writing through Art and Literature: Transforming the Wor(l)d" seminar.

63 Henri Matisse, "Notes of a Painter (1918)," in Jack Flam, *Matisse on Art* (Berkeley: University of California Press, 1995), 42.

64 "Interview with Léon Degand (1945)," in Flam, *Matisse on Art*, 164–65.

65 Lewis Hyde, *The Gift: Imagination and the Erotic Life of Property* (New York: Vintage Books, 1979), xii.

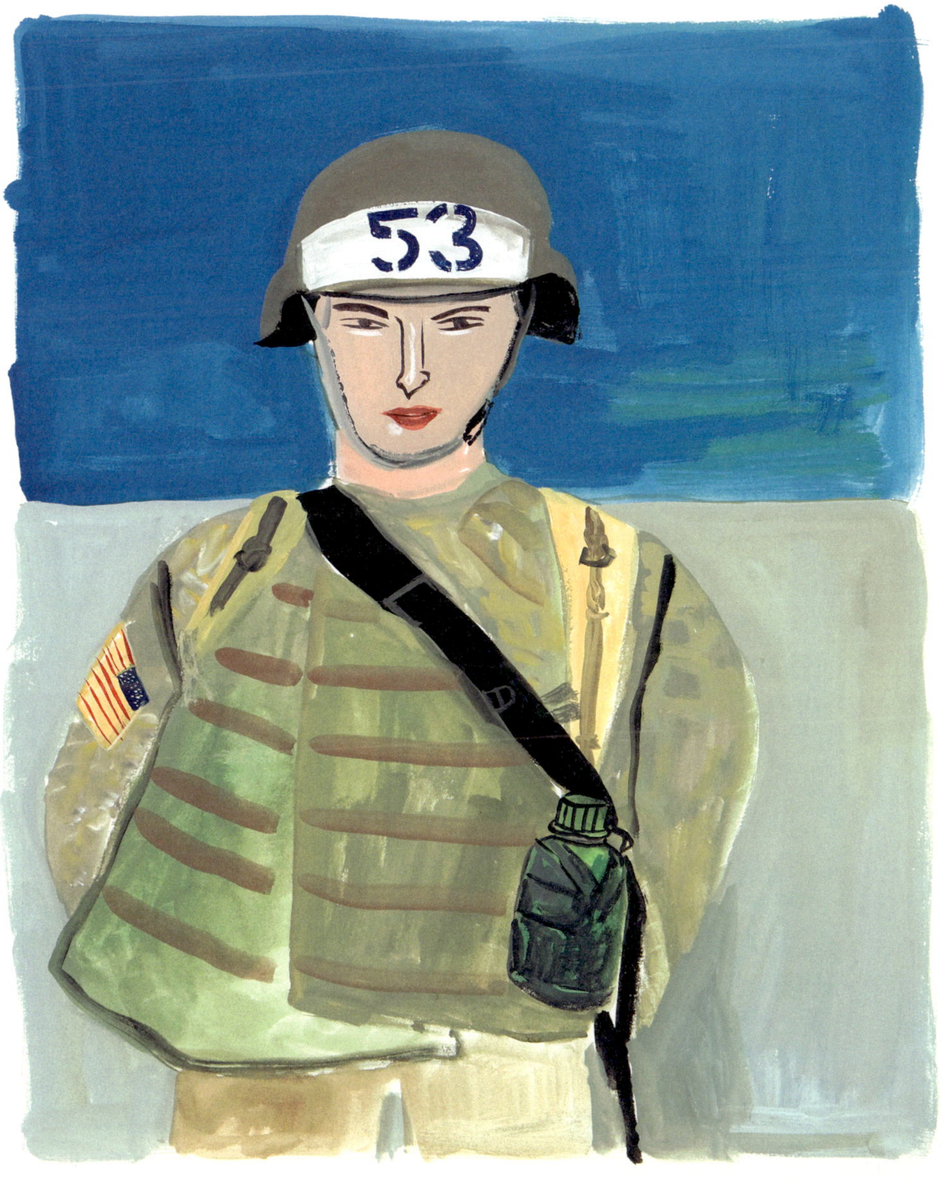

Soldier, 2009

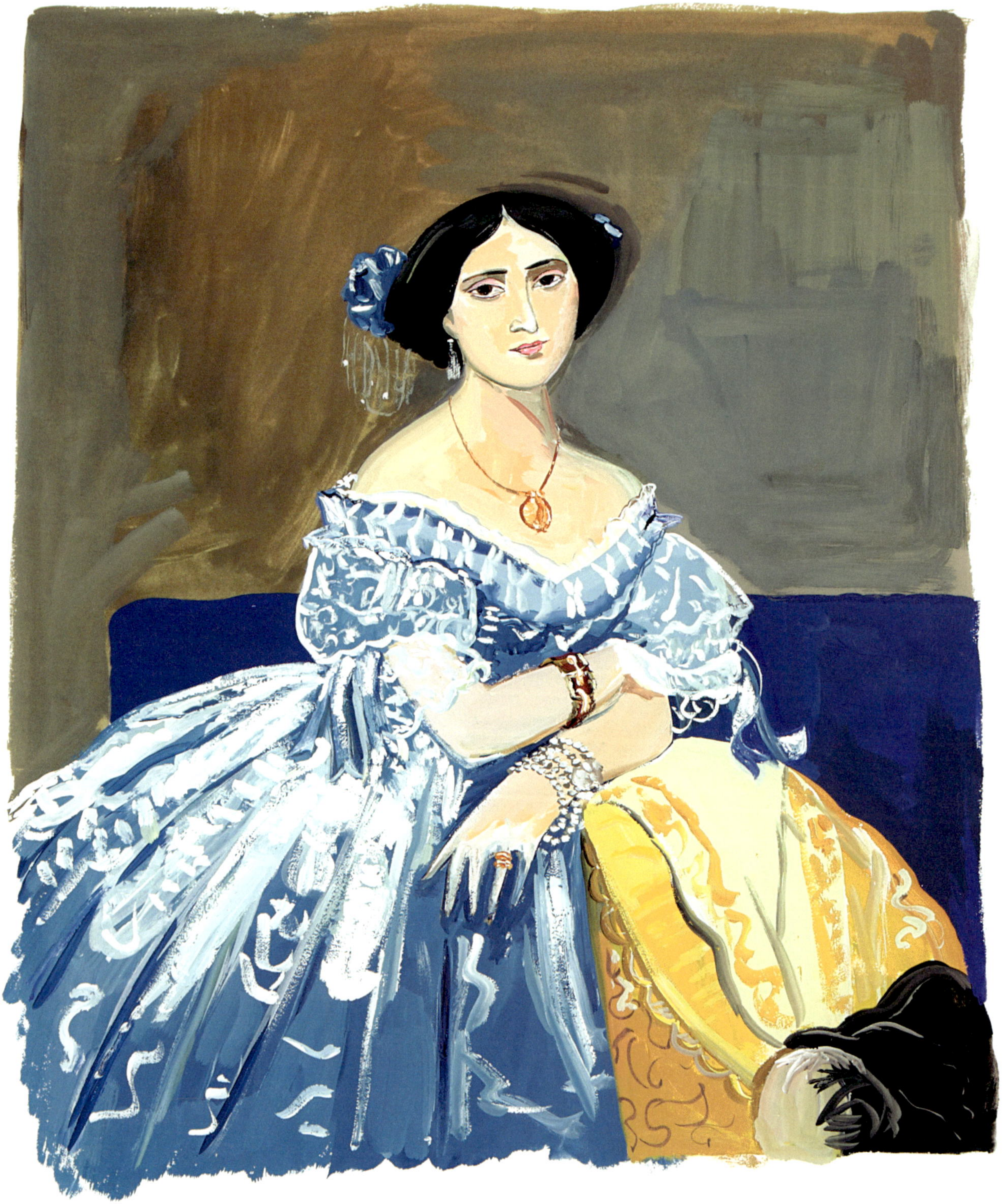

After Ingres, 2008

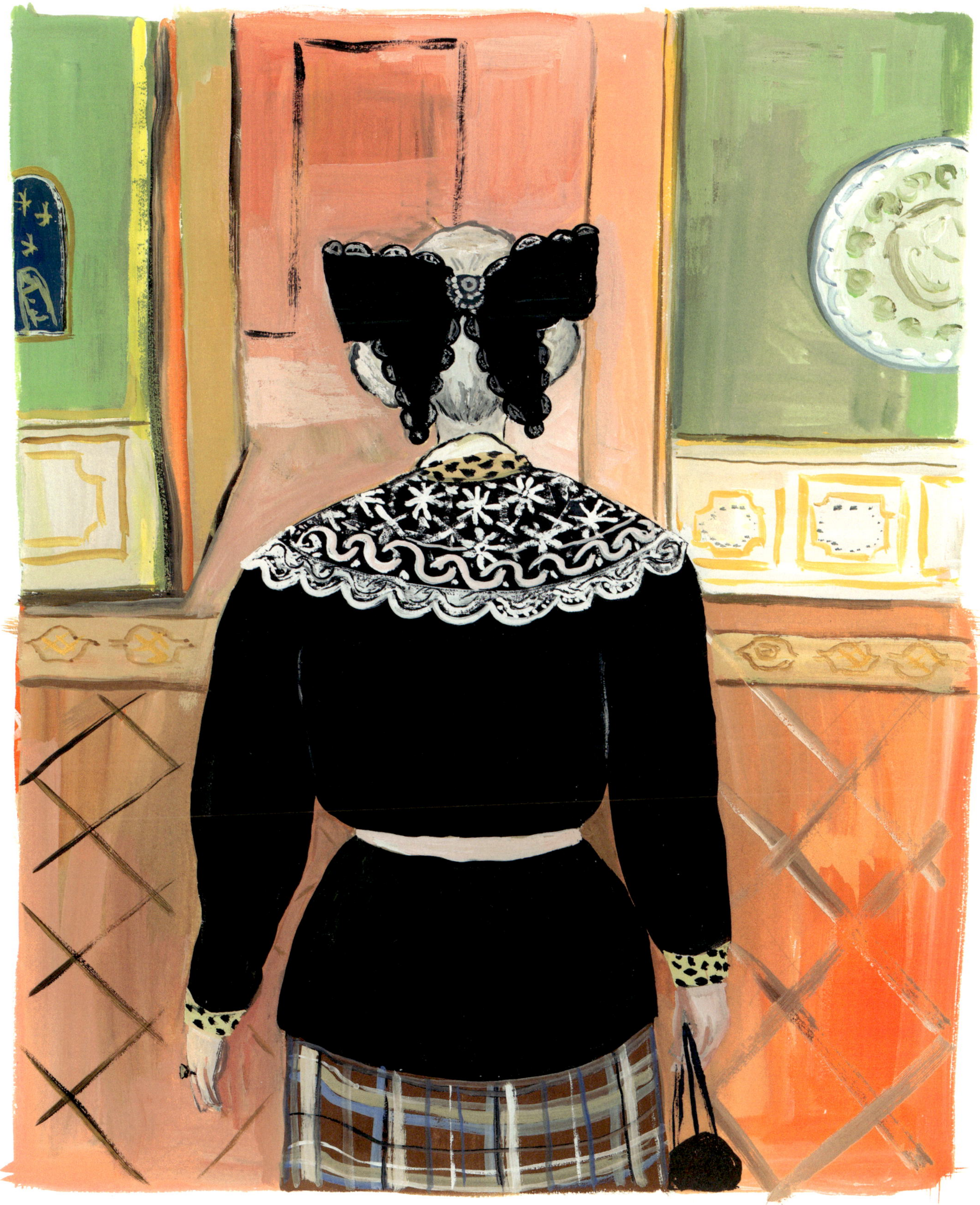

Museum Guard with Bow, 2007

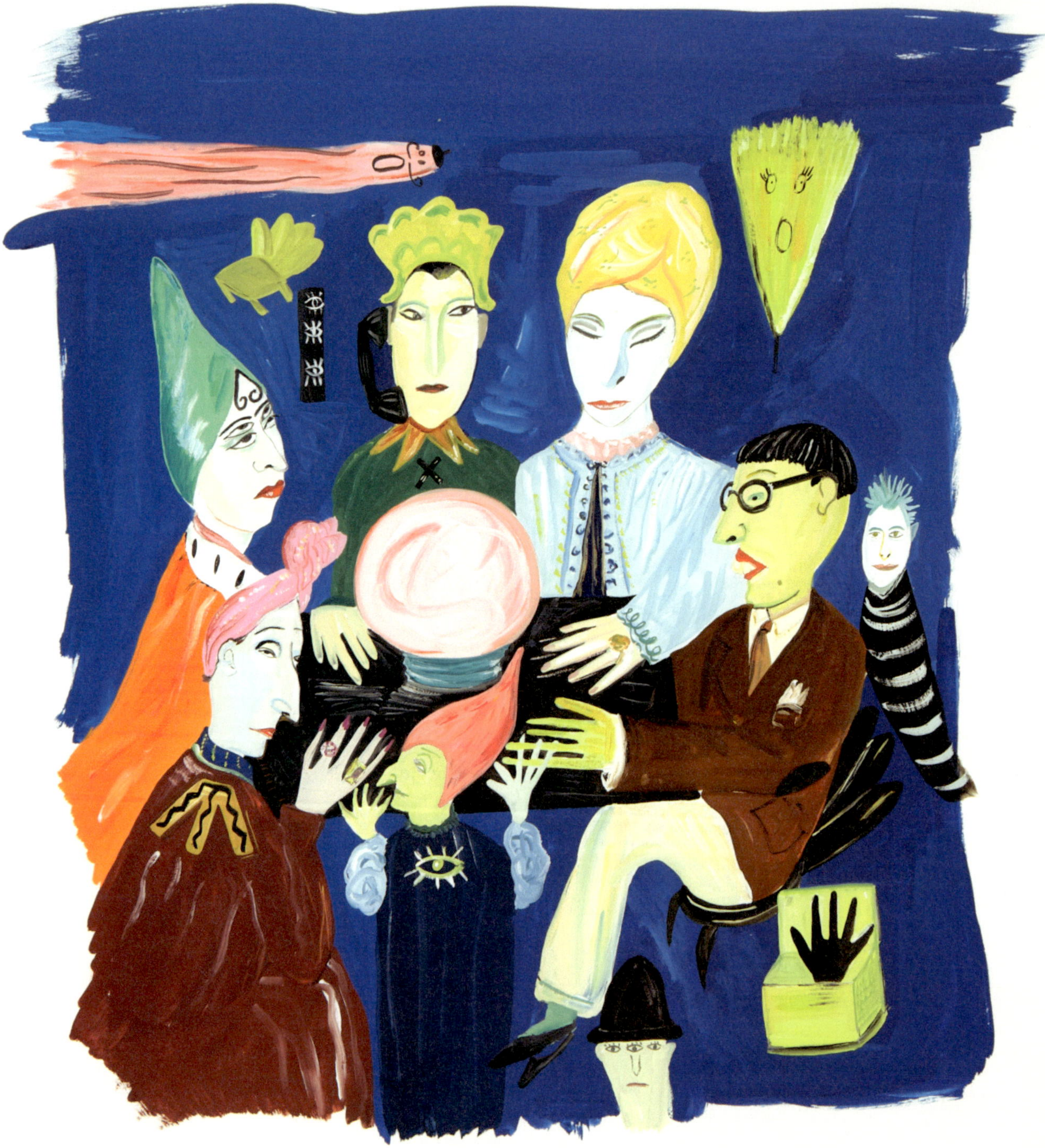

Séance, 1991

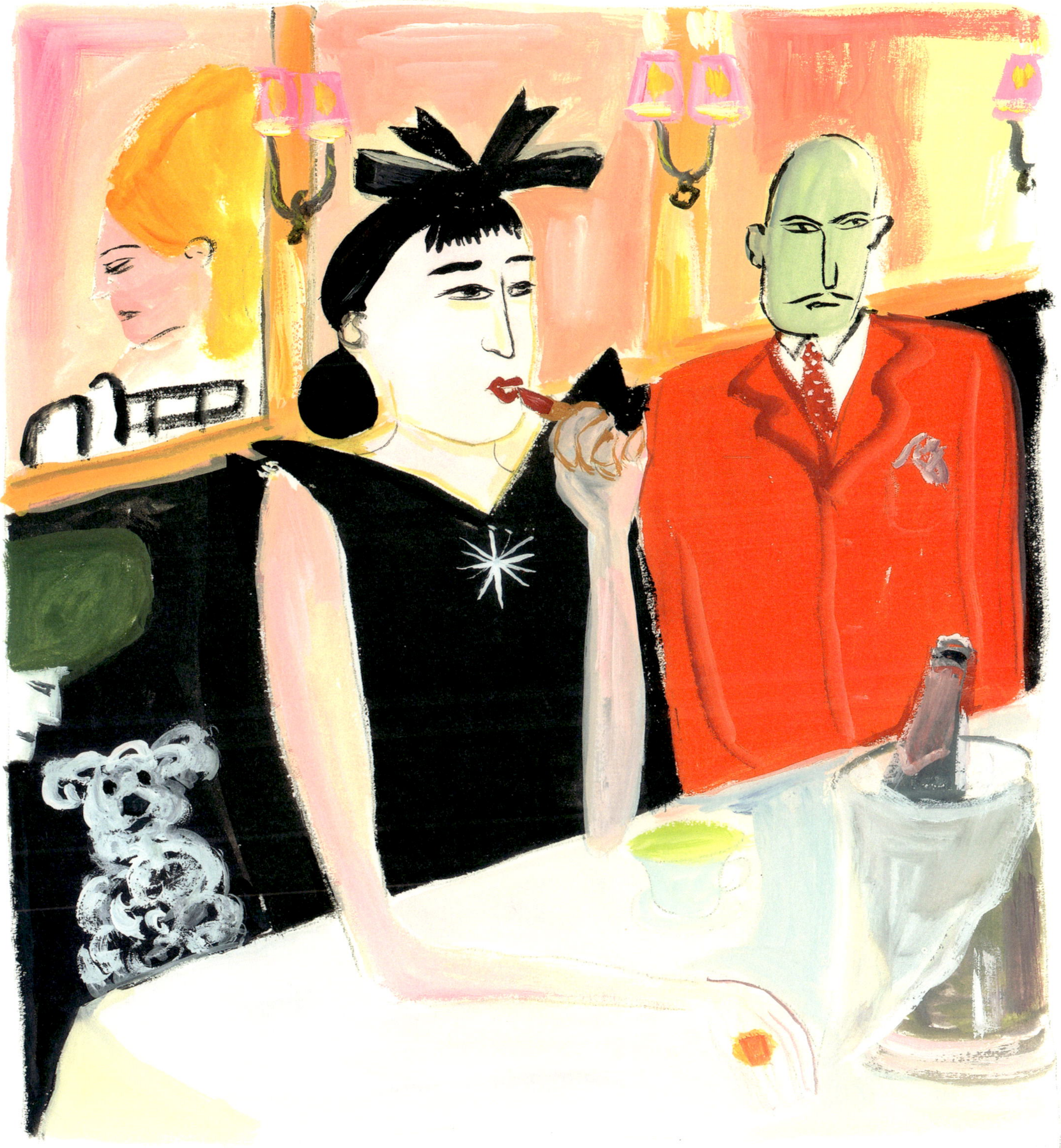

Woman with Bow, 2006

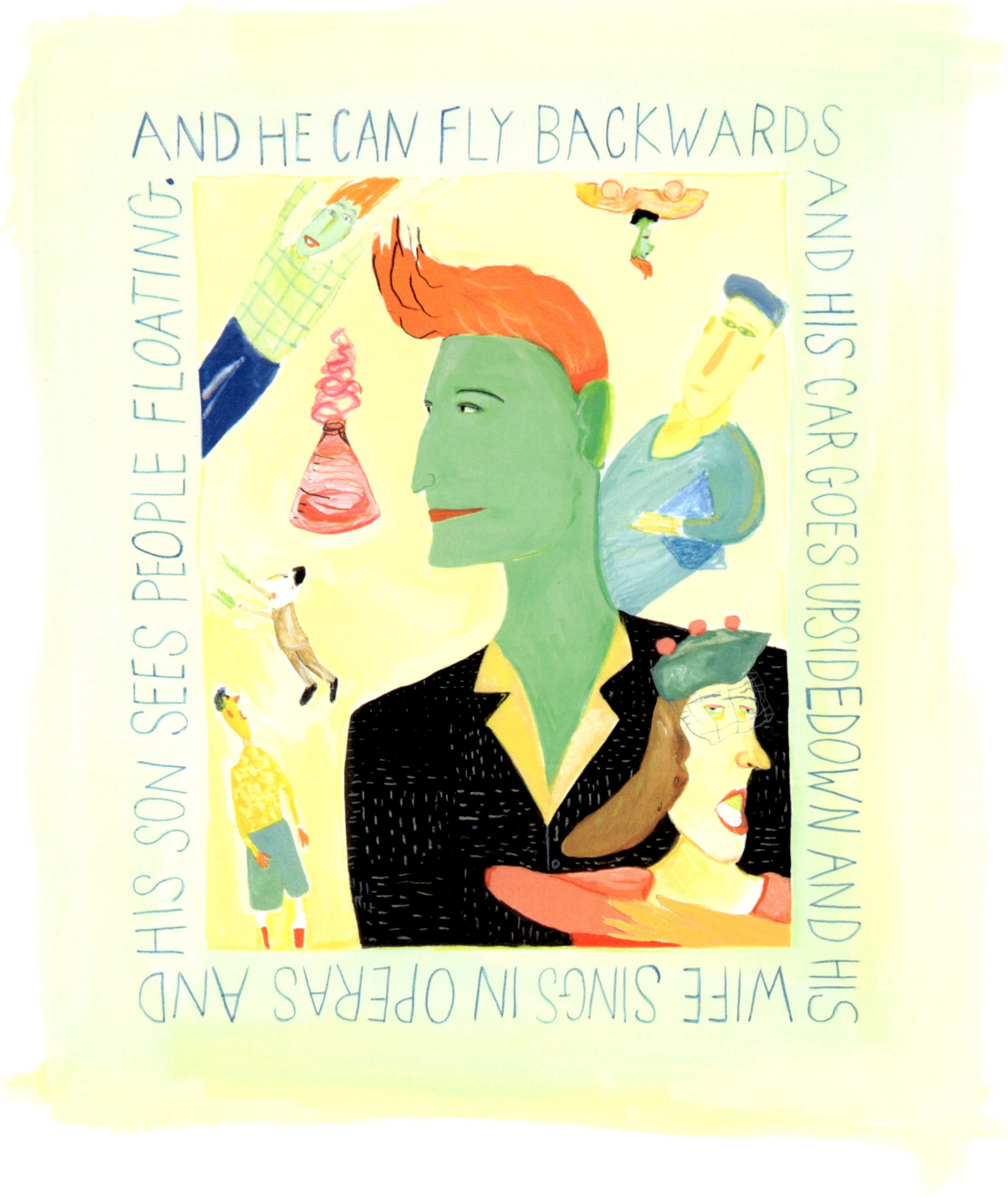

My Cousin Ervin, 1988

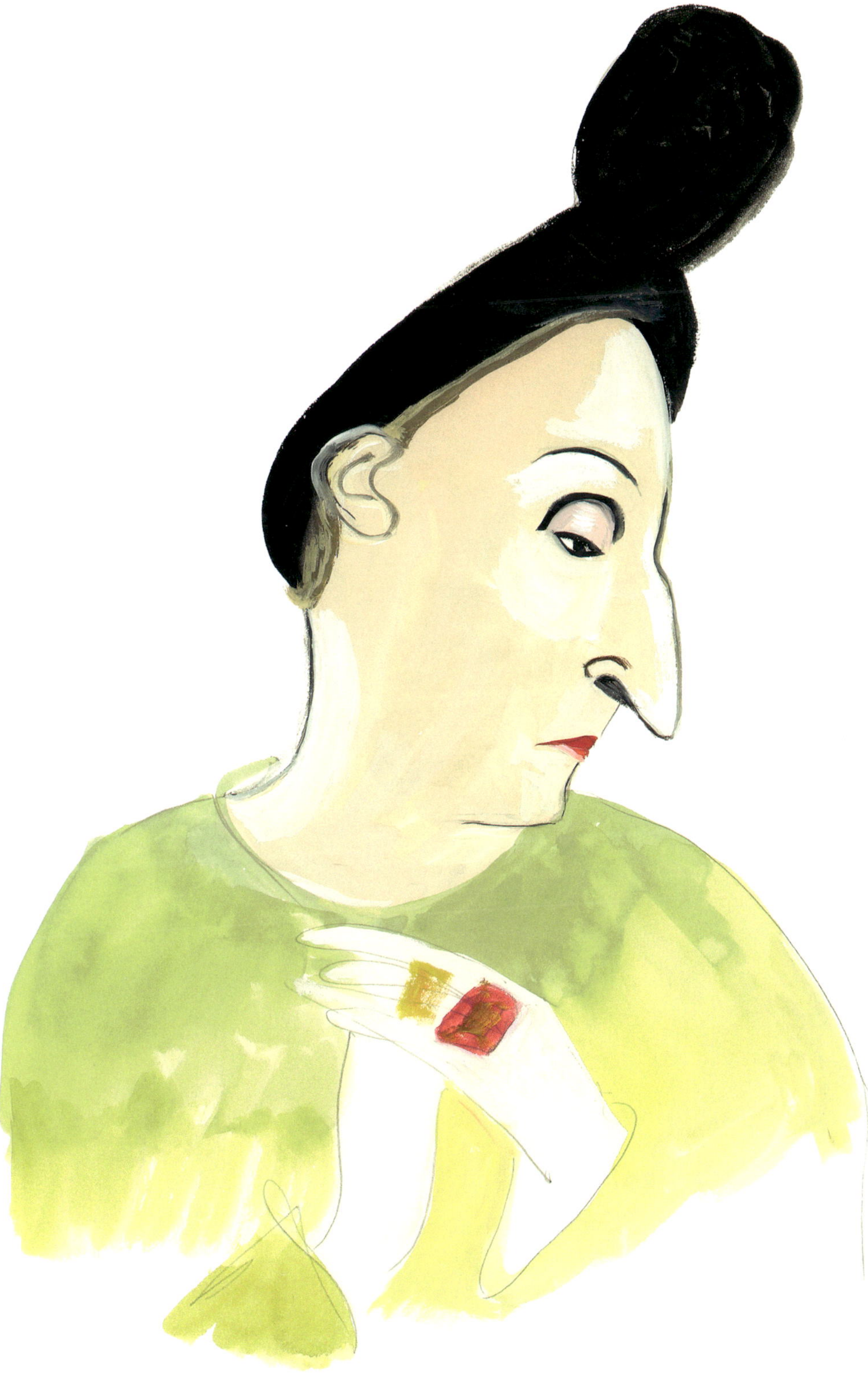

Edith Sitwell, 2006

Marking Cloth

Donna Ghelerter

MAIRA KALMAN WOULD LIKELY SHARE GERTRUDE Stein's notion of a handkerchief in a drawer – "It might be like having a handkerchief in a drawer and never taking it out but always knowing it was there. It would always be new and nobody ever would be through with having it there."[1] But fortunately Kalman sometimes does take cloth out of its drawer, or closet, or wherever she keeps her collection of linens, and embroiders it with words and images. In doing so she follows a tradition of needlework made by young girls. But Kalman is not a schoolgirl and rote learning is not her endgame.

For both schoolgirls and Kalman, the recording of information on cloth serves as an *aide-mémoire*. The act of embroidery, passing the needle and thread through the cloth, reinforces the retention of information. Embroiderers of the past learned to stitch the alphabet in numerous typefaces, from simple linear letters to extremely ornate and formal styles of lettering, for marking personal and household linens. Darning samplers, composed of modern-looking, overlapping geometric motifs,[2] taught the useful skill of how to repair worn-out cloth. And British samplers embroidered with maps of the United Kingdom, or the world, were intended to teach geography.[3]

Texts found in historical needlework are most often didactic verses, worked on samplers from the seventeenth through the nineteenth centuries, or more mundane platitudes, stitched on twentieth-century examples. Moralistic texts were selected from the bible and other sources such as Isaac Watts's *Divine and Moral Songs for Children* (first published in 1715). The Lord's Prayer occurs often. Concise directives for behavior also appear: "shun idleness"[4] and "be not weary in well doing."[5]

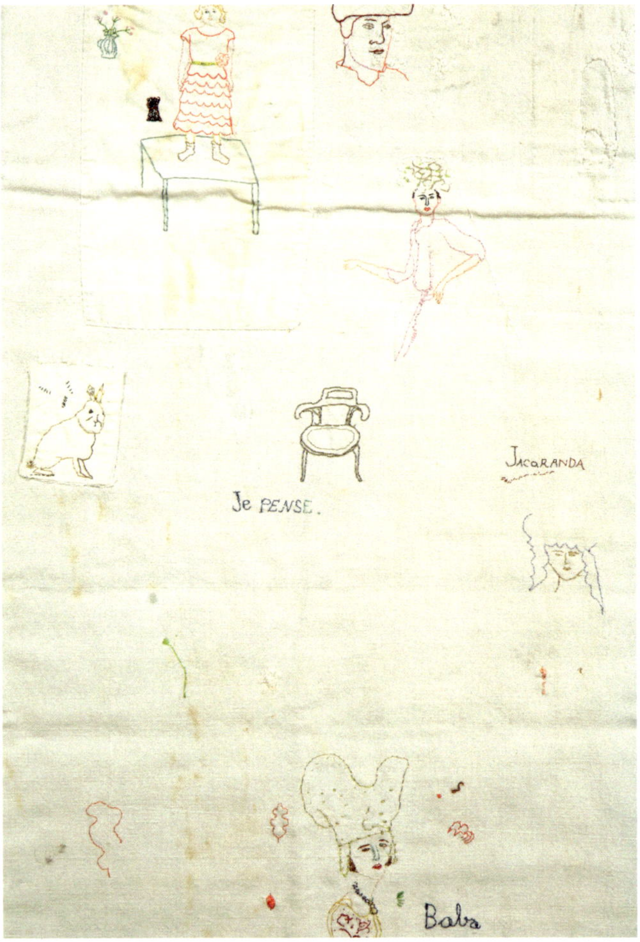

To the Stars (detail), 2005

Kalman's cloths are marked with words from Johan Wolfgang von Goethe, Dante Alighieri, and Abraham Lincoln, and their words also instruct.

Kalman's first embroideries express common clichés, but these were not chosen because they are particularly worthy texts. She incorporated trite sayings into her art after she visited a fortune-teller in the spiritualist community of Lily Dale, in upstate New York, who told her, "Don't cry over spilled milk." (This was not exactly the insight she had hoped for.) So she worked that saying into an embroidery, as well as others such as "Alls [*sic*] well that ends well," "Good things come to those who wait," and "Time will tell"—each accompanied by ponderous-looking animals and women with various types of headdresses [page 40].

Some unusual embroideries from past centuries record historical events that were of interest, for some reason, to the girls who made them. An English sampler worked in 1694 states, "There was an earthquake on 8 of September 1692 in the city of London but no hurt tho it caused most part of England to tremble."[6] A sampler worked by Elizabeth Gerrish when she was eight documents in great detail the death and burial of England's fattest man, Daniel Lambert, who died in 1809.[7] From this cloth, completely covered in words, we learn how much Lambert weighed ("52 stone, 11 pounds") and the dimensions of his oversized coffin ("6 feet 4 inches long 4 feet 4 inches wide 2 feet 4 inches deep being 112 superficial feet of elm"). Kalman considers, and embroiders, lines spoken by Lincoln at his Annual Message to Congress in 1862, covering a cloth entirely with words memorialized in American history.

Kalman's later embroideries, worked following the death of her mother, serve primarily as memorials. Nineteenth-century embroidered mourning pictures, common in American needlework, typically feature an inscribed tombstone beneath a weeping willow tree.[8] When Kalman's mother died, she embroidered these lamenting lines from Goethe's *Faust*:

> I feel a sense of dread, tear after tear is falling,
> My rigid heart is tenderly unmanned—
> What I possess seems something far away
> And what had disappeared proves real.
> (29–32)

Interspersed with the Goethe text are repeated images of her mother as a young woman, based on a particular family photograph [pages 30–31]. This icon of her mother also appears embroidered on a pink silk dress inscribed with lines from Dante's *Inferno* [page 77].

In Kalman's embroideries, what could have been drafted in pencil or paint (as in many of the artist's other works) instead is expressed through elements of domesticity—ironing and stitching—added to the artistic process: "I collect white fabric from around the world, and spend many happy hours ironing and folding and looking at these things."[9]

Embroidered ciphers identified the linens of queens; personal ciphers, of carefully chosen poetry and portraits of her mother, mark the embroideries of Maira Kalman.

Donna Ghelerter is an independent textile and costume historian in New York.

Notes

1 Gertrude Stein, *Ida* (1941. Reprint, New York: Vintage Books, 1968), 27.

2 See Carol Humphrey, *Samplers* (Cambridge, UK: Cambridge University Press, 1997), fig. 38, for an example.

3 See ibid., figs. 47 and 48, for examples.

4 The Metropolitan Museum of Art, accession number 57.122.375.

5 Donald King, *Samplers* (London: Her Majesty's Stationery Office, 1960), fig. 31.

6 Cora Ginsburg LLC catalogue, 1995.

7 The Metropolitan Museum of Art, accession number 57.122.792.

8 For an example, see Adolph S. Cavallo, *Needlework* (New York: Cooper-Hewitt Museum, Smithsonian Institution, 1979), pl. 10.

9 Maira Kalman, *The Principles of Uncertainty* (New York: Penguin Press, 2007), 112.

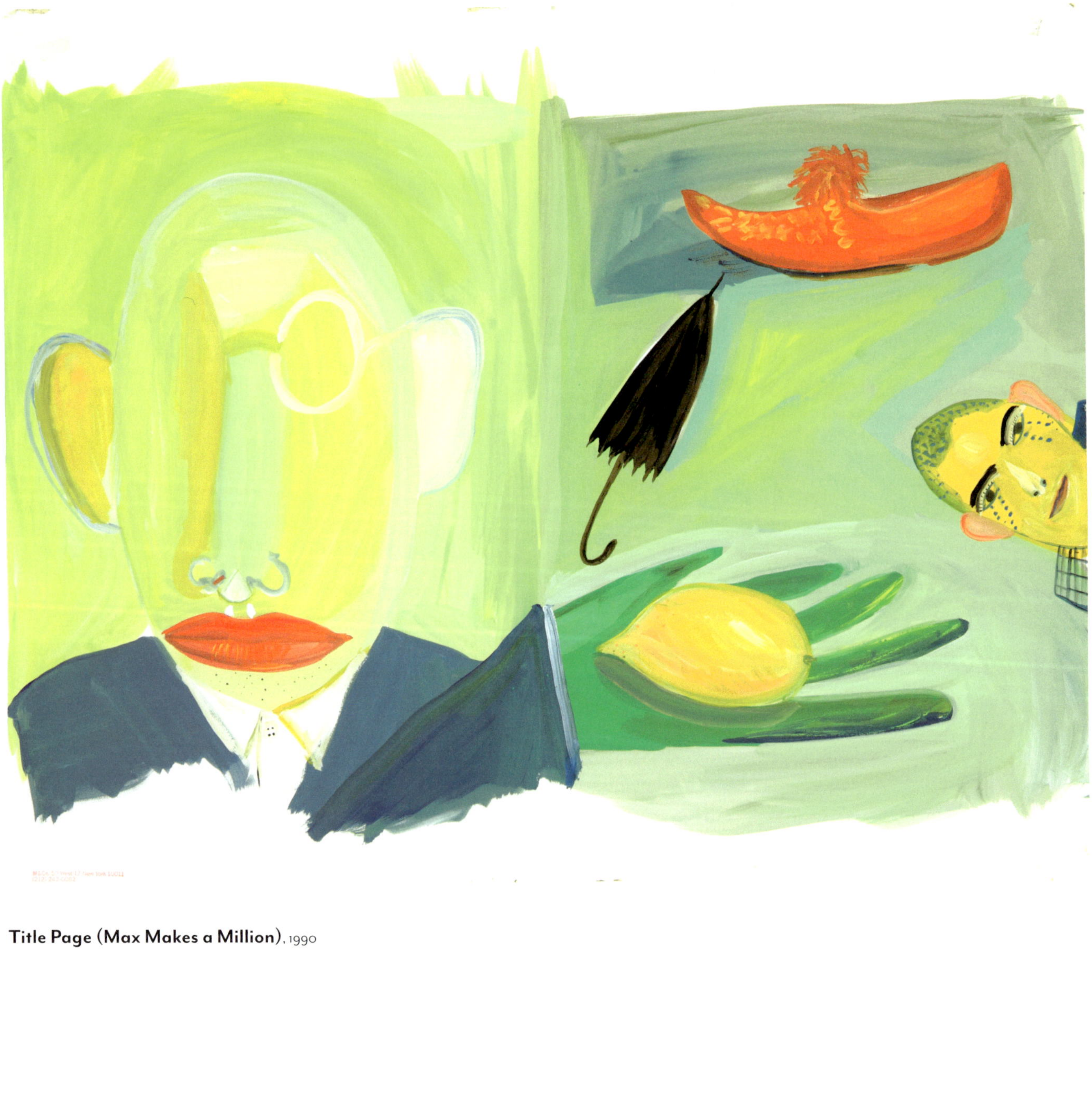

Title Page (Max Makes a Million), 1990

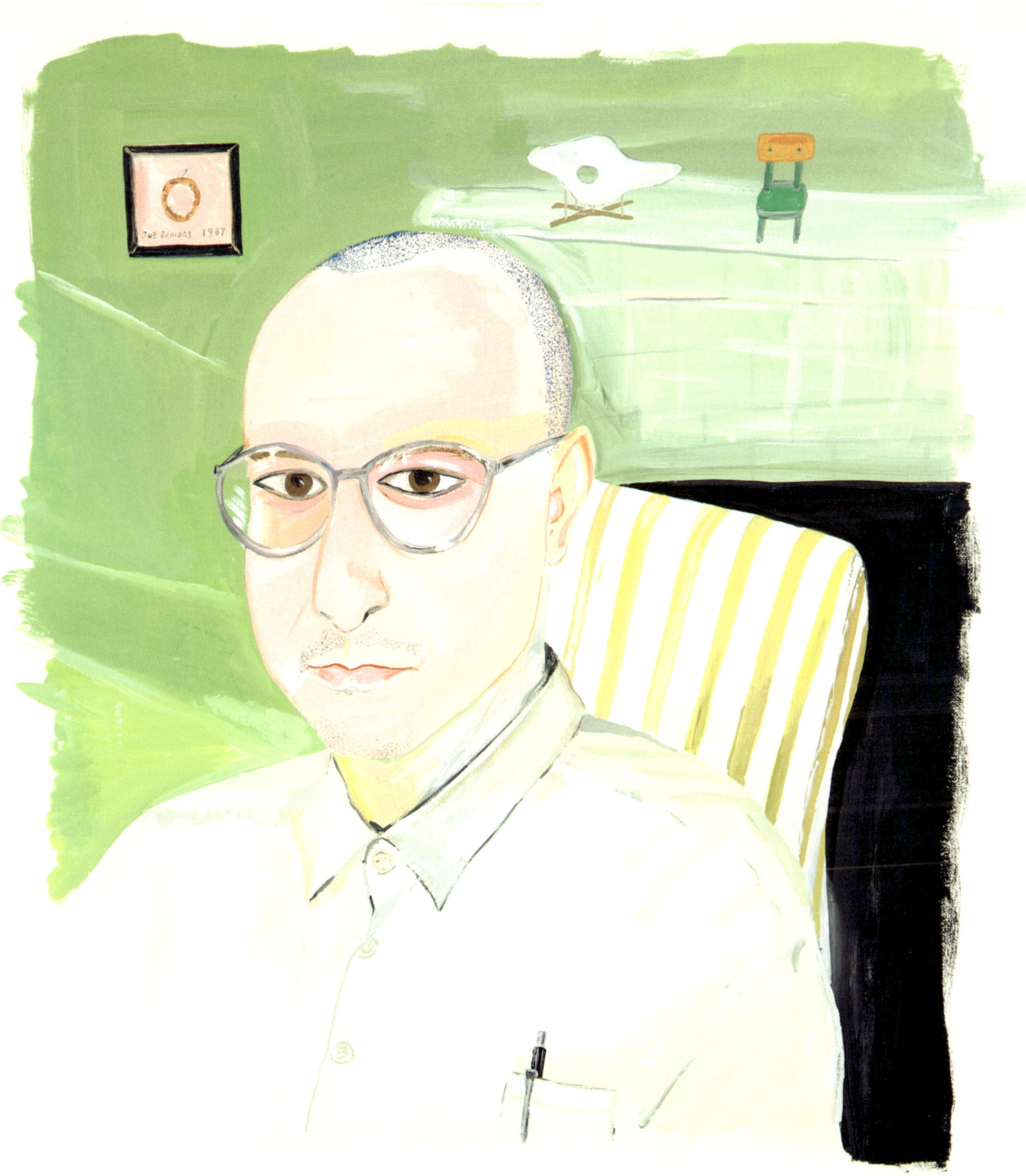

Tibor Kalman, 1998

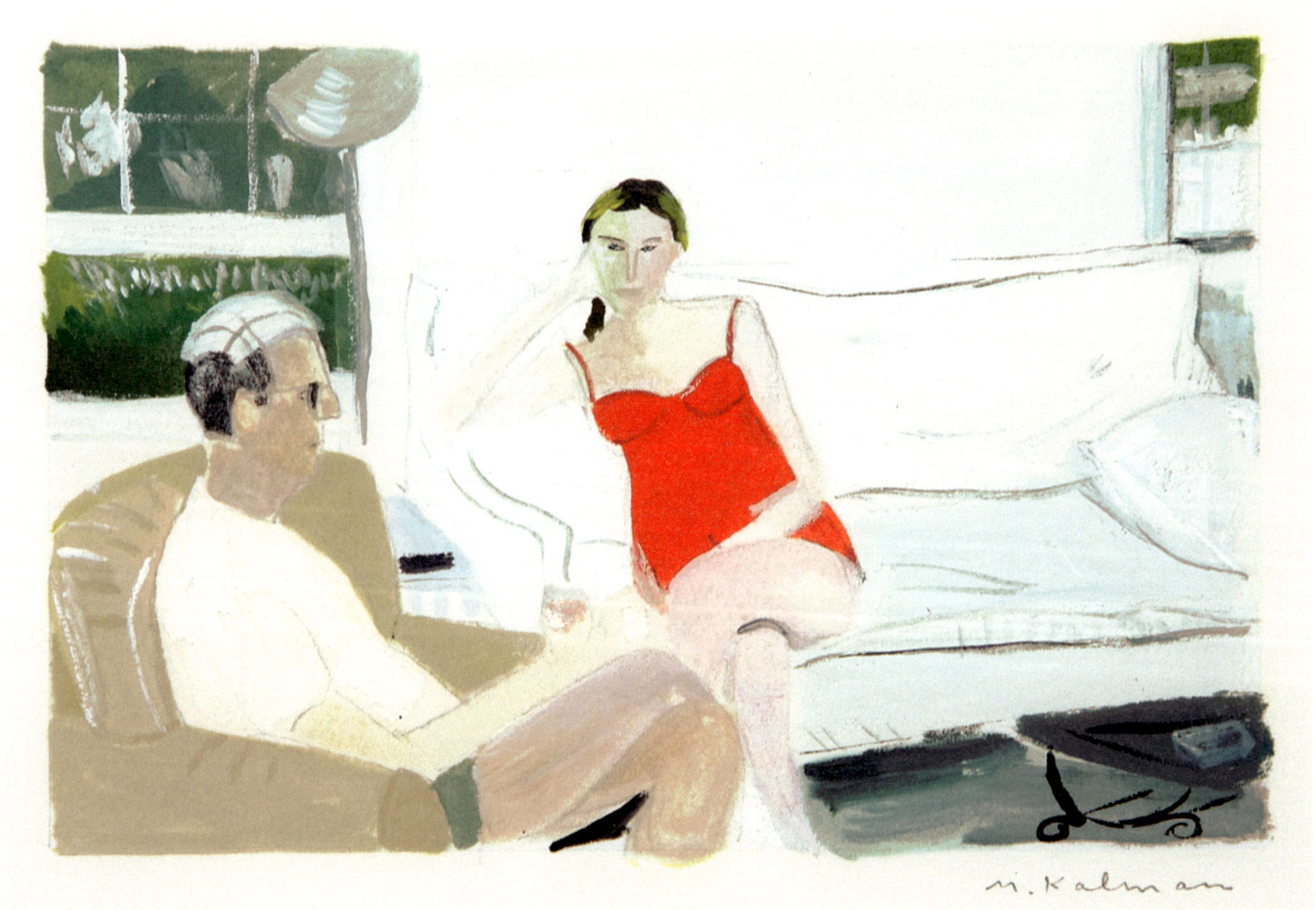

Tibor and Elissa, 1996

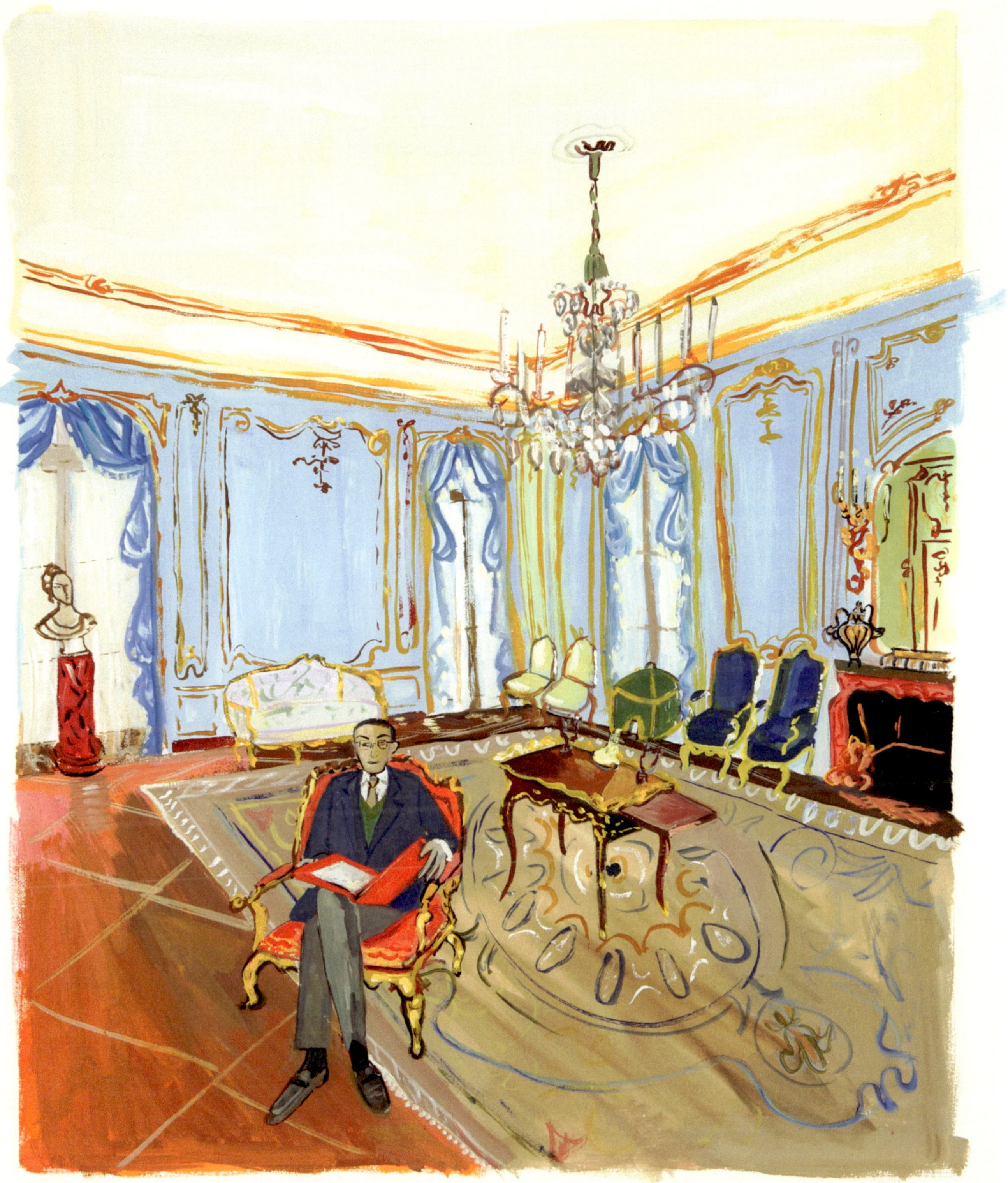

Philippe, 2008

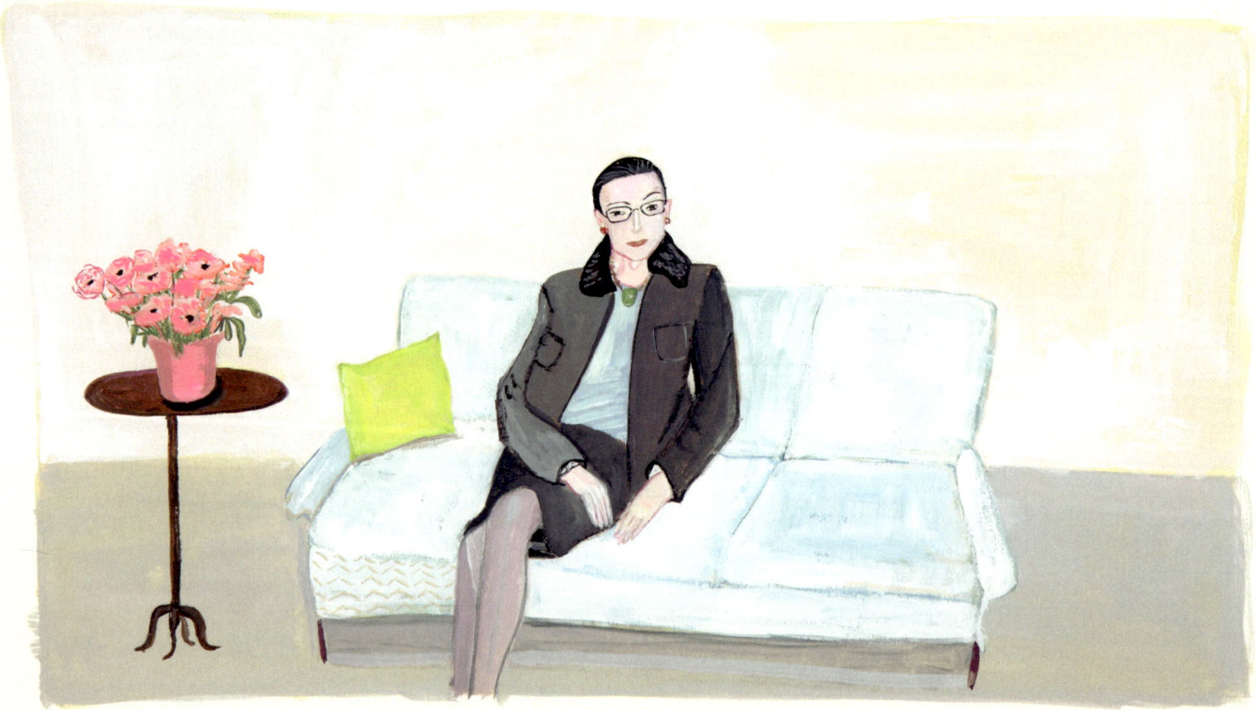

Ruth Bader Ginsburg, 2009

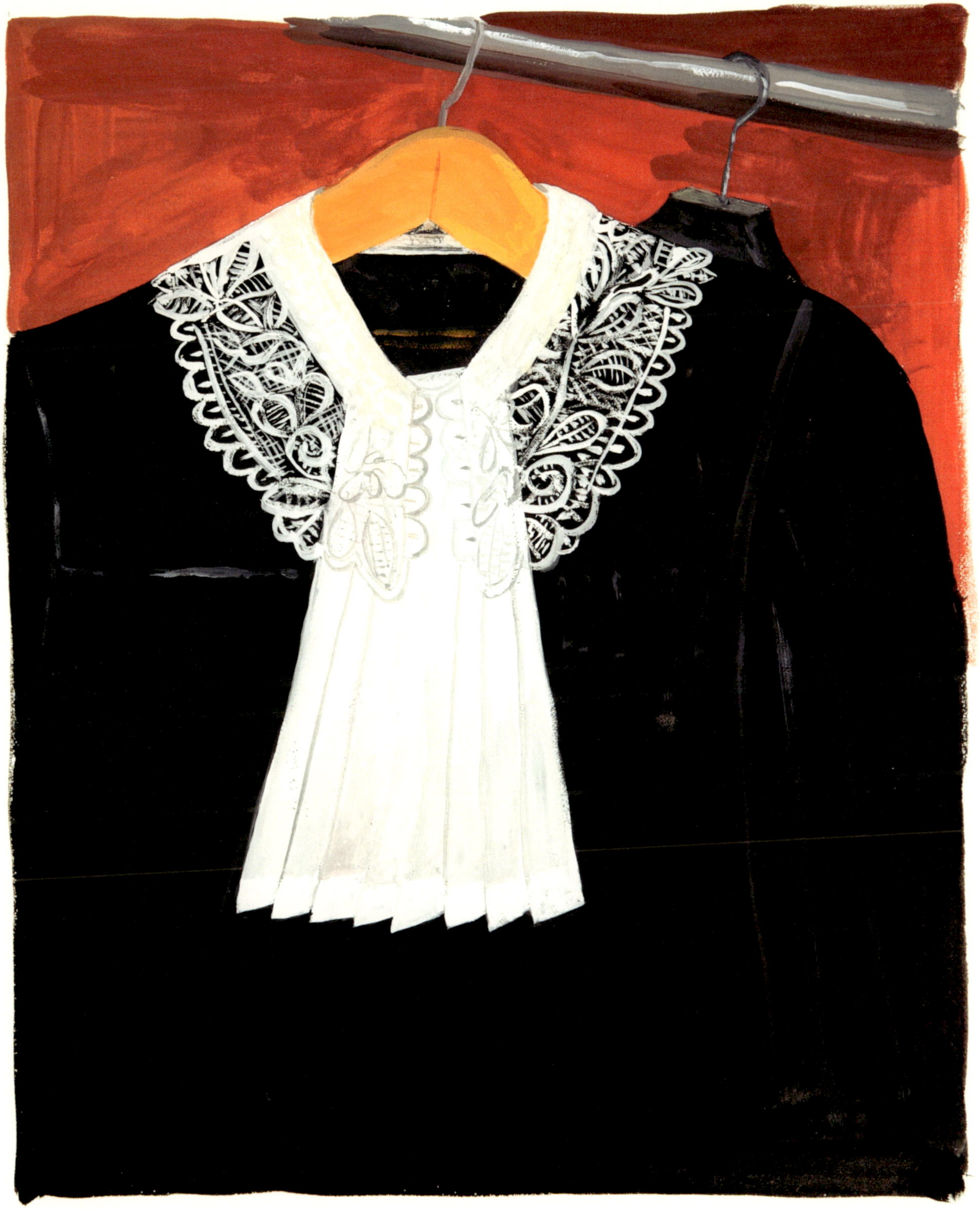

Ruth Bader Ginsburg/Robe, 2009

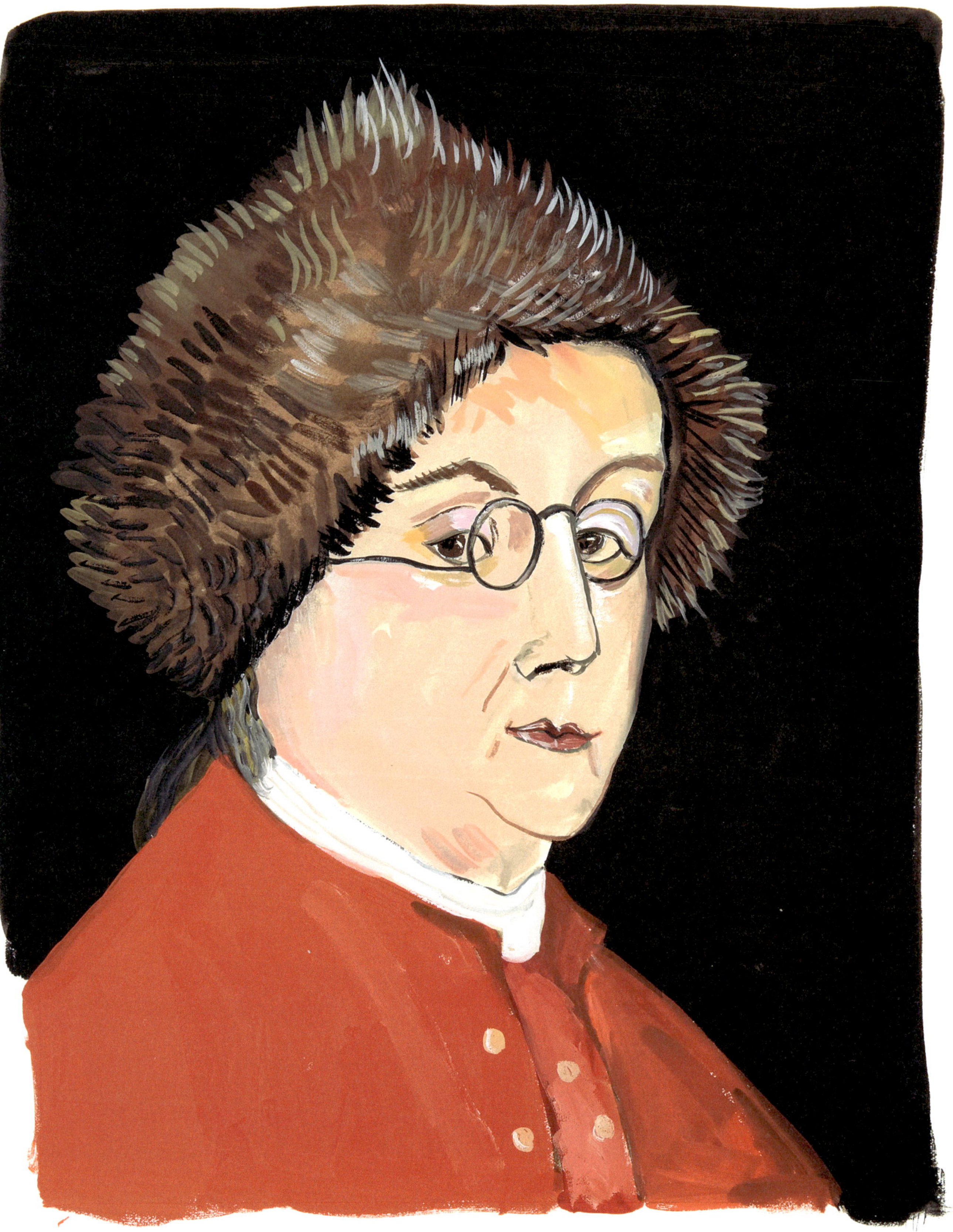

Benjamin Franklin in Fur Hat, 2009

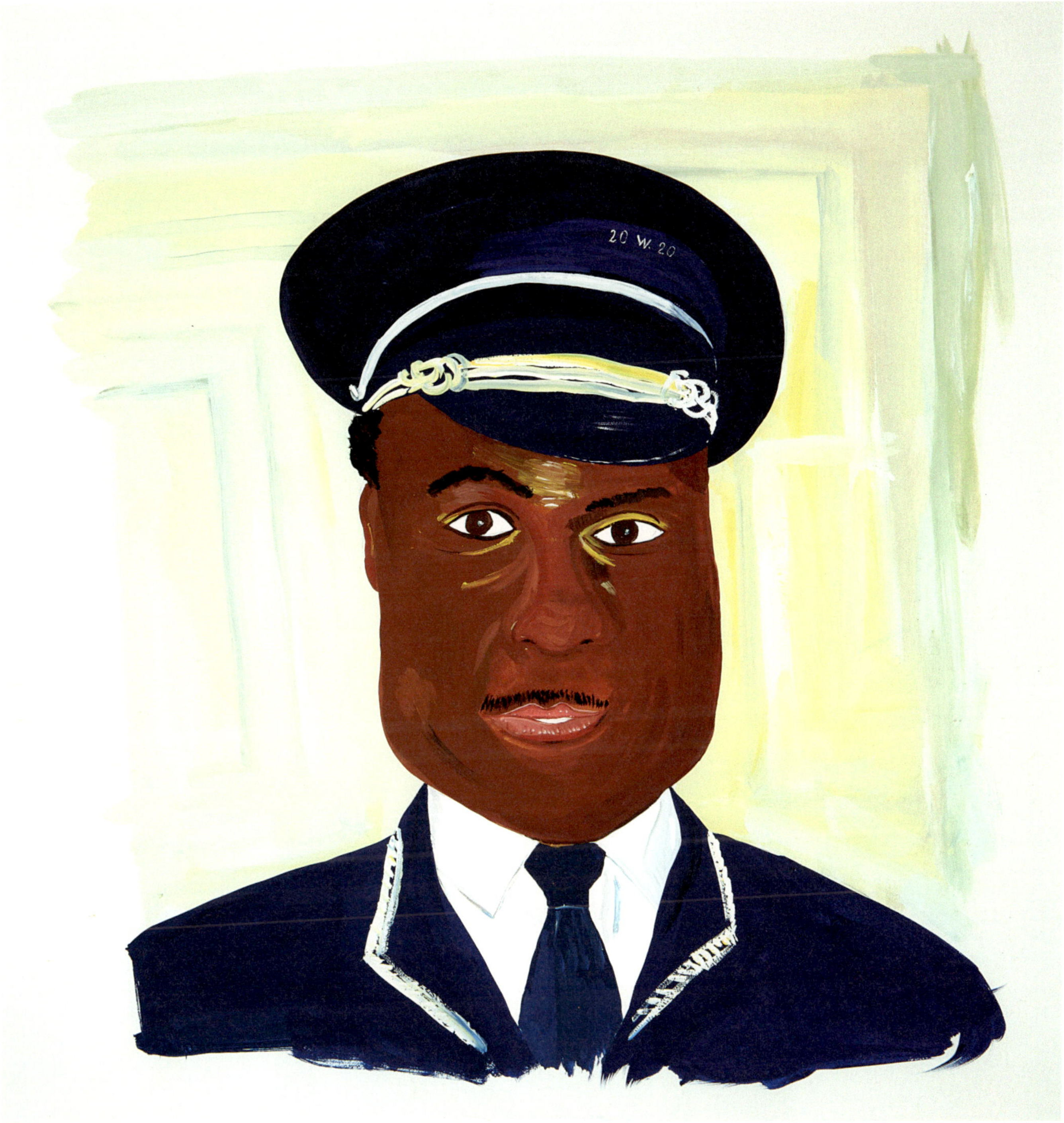

James Bell, 1993

The Contradictoriness of Ideas: Maira Kalman's Blogging

Stamatina Gregory

IN 1967, ROLAND BARTHES, FRENCH THEORIST AND lover of the sentimental and absurd, declared the idea of the "author" dead.[1] But then, Barthes himself didn't make it to the twenty-first century. These days, every academic reiteration of the author's supposed disappearance is answered by the springing up of a new crop of personal websites, listservs, blogs, tweets, and status updates.[2] Social media's power to quickly, nearly effortlessly, elevate the personal and private to the public is alternately hailed as democratizing and empowering and denounced as ushering in a new tyranny of banality. We are all photographers, writers, critics, commenters, theorists, *auteurs*. In 2006 alone, an average of more than seventy-five thousand new blogs emerged each day.[3]

Enter Maira Kalman and her first blog, "The Principles of Uncertainty," hosted by *The New York Times*. In its first entry in May of 2006 she asks, "How can I tell you everything that is in my heart?" and as if realizing both the enormity and futility of the task, she presents us with an illustration of a hapless dodo. In her second entry, she writes, "My brain is exploding. Trying to make sense out of nonsense, trying to tell you everything (*everything*?) And all the while time is fleeing, and the air around me vibrates with so many images." Succinctly and poetically, she encapsulates either (or both) the generalized anxiety of the creative process and the experience of navigating a relatively new and potentially seditious social medium.

Throughout the run of "The Principles of Uncertainty," Kalman constructed her entries with a supreme awareness of their context—not an echo chamber of news, not a pure exploration of the personal, but a poetic thread of interactions between her psyche and the world. Her

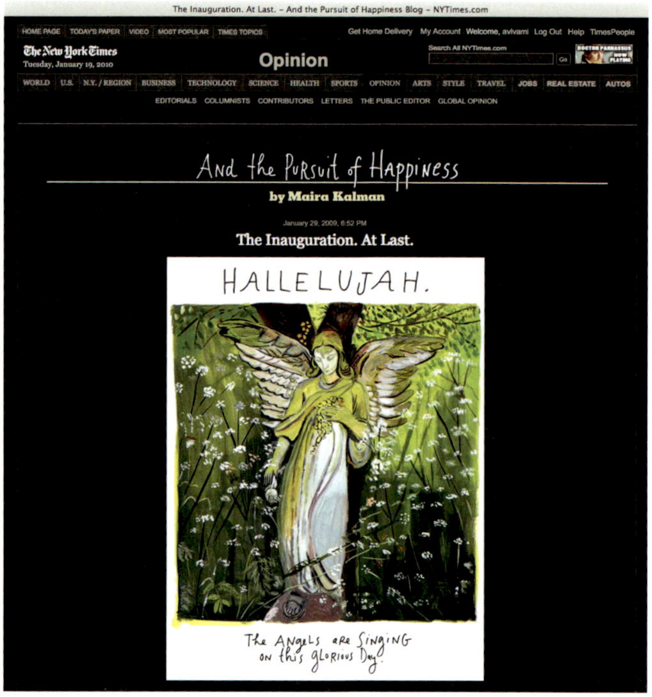

And the Pursuit of Happiness (blog), screen grab from *The New York Times* (online), posted January 29, 2009

blogging underscores the conditions of critically engaging with a public, participatory medium that straddles permanence and ephemerality; fleeting glances and leisurely consumption; reportage and punditry; the tenuous filaments of narrative within a tide of media culture. "Stalin was a paranoid man," writes Kalman. "Even more than my father."[4] In words and the images that perform them, Kalman reiterates the indisputable cultural condition that history and politics are inextricable from our most intimate processes of identification. In writing about the Bolsheviks, the flux of Russian history is made tangible through the experiences of her family, as she shifts from ruminating on the almost certain alienation Vladimir Nabakov felt when uprooted from his home to her mother's flight to the United States. On a trip to Israel during the 2006 war with Lebanon, she reflects on the pettiness of neighbors at a time of local war and global crisis; she visits a cemetery, imploring her buried relatives to "do something," thinking they "must talk to someone who knows someone – pull some strings" for peace.[5]

In her later blog, "And the Pursuit of Happiness," begun in 2008 and also hosted by *The New York Times*, she takes on the United States itself: the mind-bogglingly byzantine legislative process, the curious idiosyncrasies of particular Founding Fathers, the alien innards of civic waste management.[6] Here, Kalman swaps her strolls through her neighborhood, her family memories, and her piles of ephemera for explorations of more highly controlled spaces: military training bases, the Pentagon, the Supreme Court, the Senate. The structure of her entries is inevitably one of discovery: a series of visual and linguistic sequiturs that both instruct the basics of American civics and grapple with their inherent contradictions. After a visit to the Department of Homeland Security, reflecting on immigration reform, undocumented workers, the lyrics of Belorussian immigrant Irving Berlin, and the urban multiculturalism that allows her to enjoy (and subsequently render in creamy pastels) a mango lassi in a Jackson Heights diner, she states, "Is it naïve of me to think, while acknowledging the myriad problems, that the system is basically just?" Recalling a day at the army base at Fort Campbell, Kentucky, where she learned about MRAP vehicles, fatal funnels, *Hooah!* power candy bars, and the stark tenacity of military wives, she asks, "And the horrors of war? And the terror?. . . Who can handle the contradictions?"[7]

Kalman finds the answers (or rather, defers them) through colors, forms, and words: a red slice of cherry pie, the sight of her sister under a pink bougainvillea, a plea to smartly dressed officials or hunched old ladies. In a conversation appropriated for discussions on hypertext, and apt to an understanding of Kalman's blog work, Jean Baudrillard has stated, "As for ideas, everyone has them. What counts is the poetic singularity of the analysis. . . . There will never be any resolving the contradictoriness of ideas, except in the energy and felicity of language."[8]

Predictably – and, I argue, purposefully – Kalman's deliberate conceptual lapses, rhetorical spaces, escapist anecdotes, and occasional resigned haplessness in the face of the convolutions of domestic and geopolitical affairs incite reams of responses from readers. Aside from popular repetitive adulations, Kalman's readers energetically respond with essays of their own. Some are measured, some reactionary, and some informed deconstructions of the positions – across the political spectrum – they identify in her words and pictures. To the extent that they incite and accommodate dissent and eschew, even on the smallest of levels, monologue for dialogue, blogs are media on a communal or social scale. To engage with public and private efforts to maintain that dialogue – the word as privilege and as pleasure – is Kalman's project.

Stamatina Gregory is an independent curator and critic based in New York.

Notes

1 Roland Barthes, "The Death of the Author," *Aspen* 5–6 (1967).

2 Nicholas Rombe frames this phenomenon not as a contradiction but as the ultimate realization of Barthes' claim in "The Rebirth of the Author," in *Critical Digital Studies: A Reader*, ed. Marilouise Kroker (Toronto: University of Toronto Press), 437.

3 "State of the Blogosphere, April 2006 Part 1: On Blogosphere Growth," http://blog.technorati.com (accessed October 30, 2009).

4 Maira Kalman, *The Principles of Uncertainty* (New York: Penguin Books, 2007), 6.

5 Ibid., 79.

6 Maira Kalman, "And the Pursuit of Happiness," http://kalman.blogs.nytimes.com.

7 Maira Kalman, "At Ease," posted May 28, 2009, http://kalman.blogs.nytimes.com/2009/05/28/at-ease (accessed November 1, 2009).

8 Jean Baudrillard, *The Perfect Crime* (New York: Verso, 1996), 103.

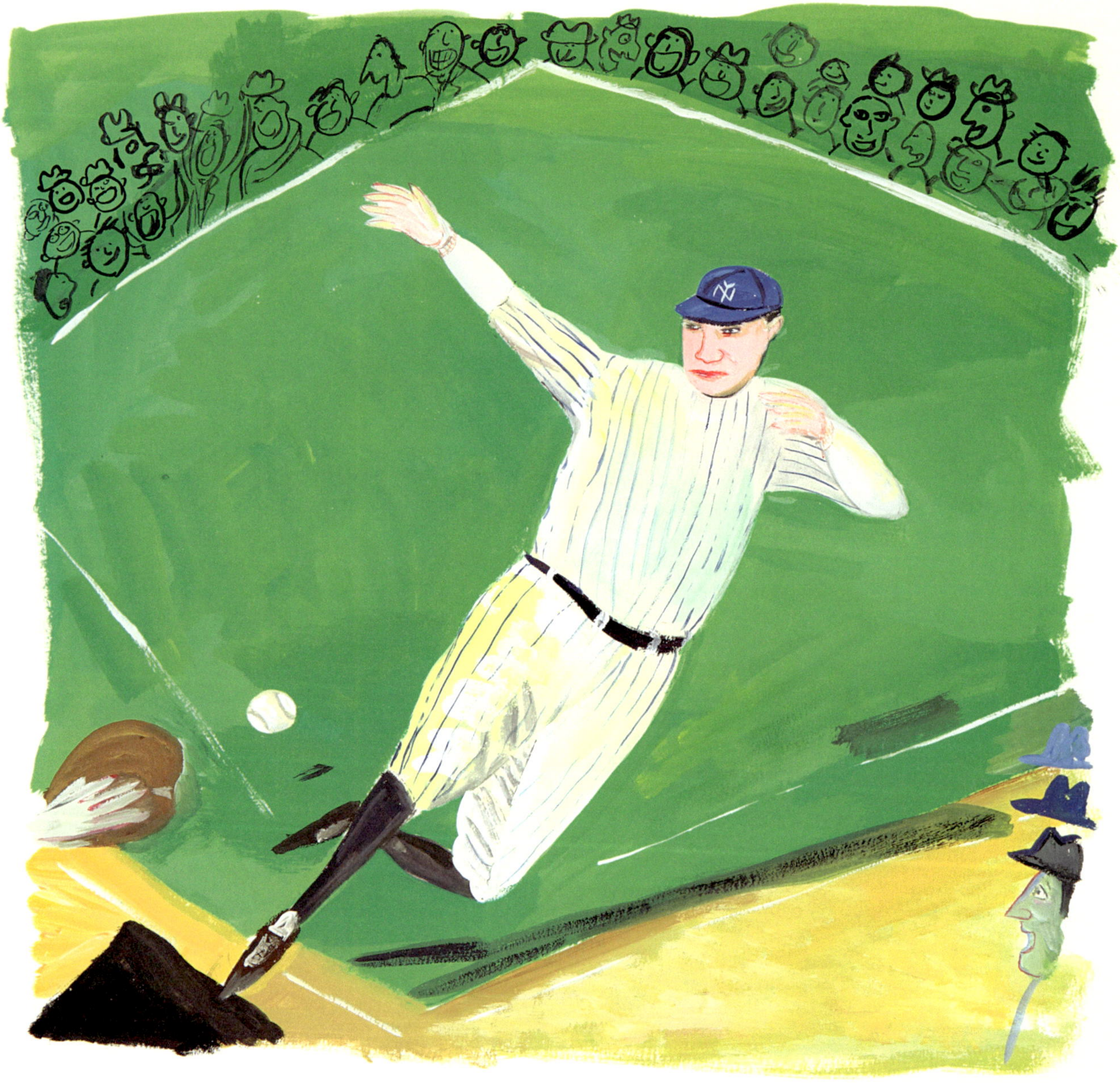

Babe Ruth, 2002

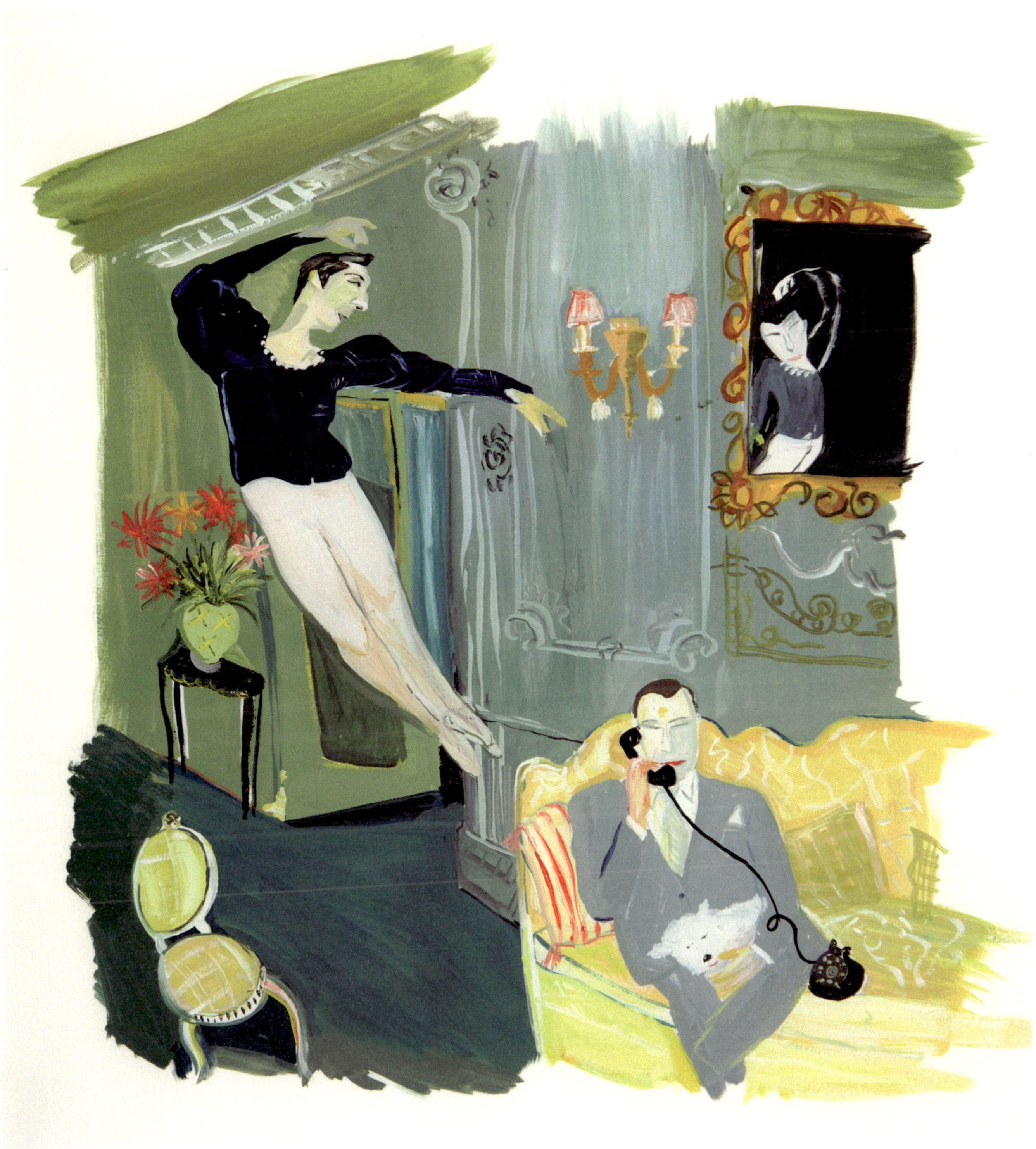

Man Leaping While Man Talks on Phone, 1991

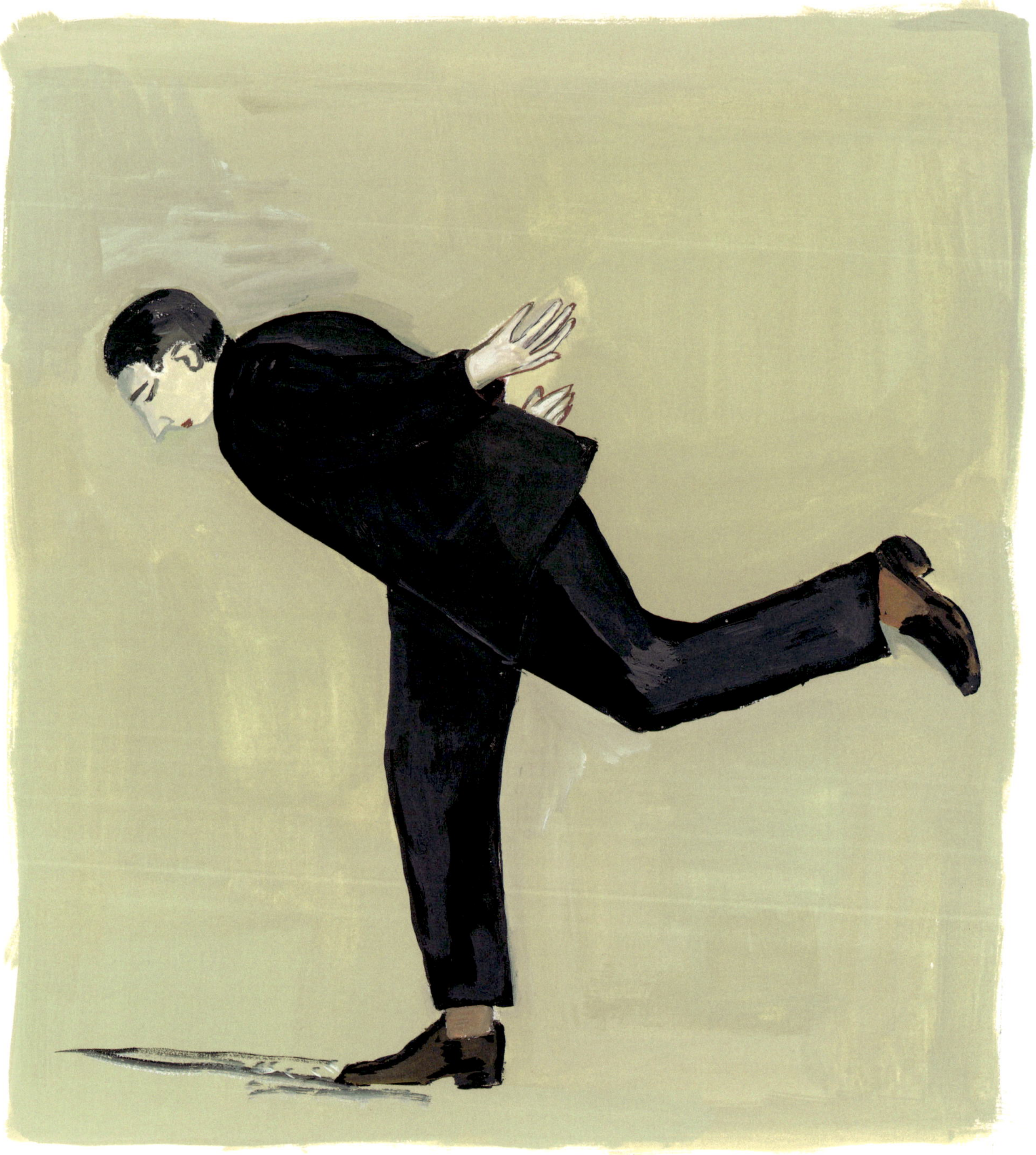

Man Dances on Salt, 2007

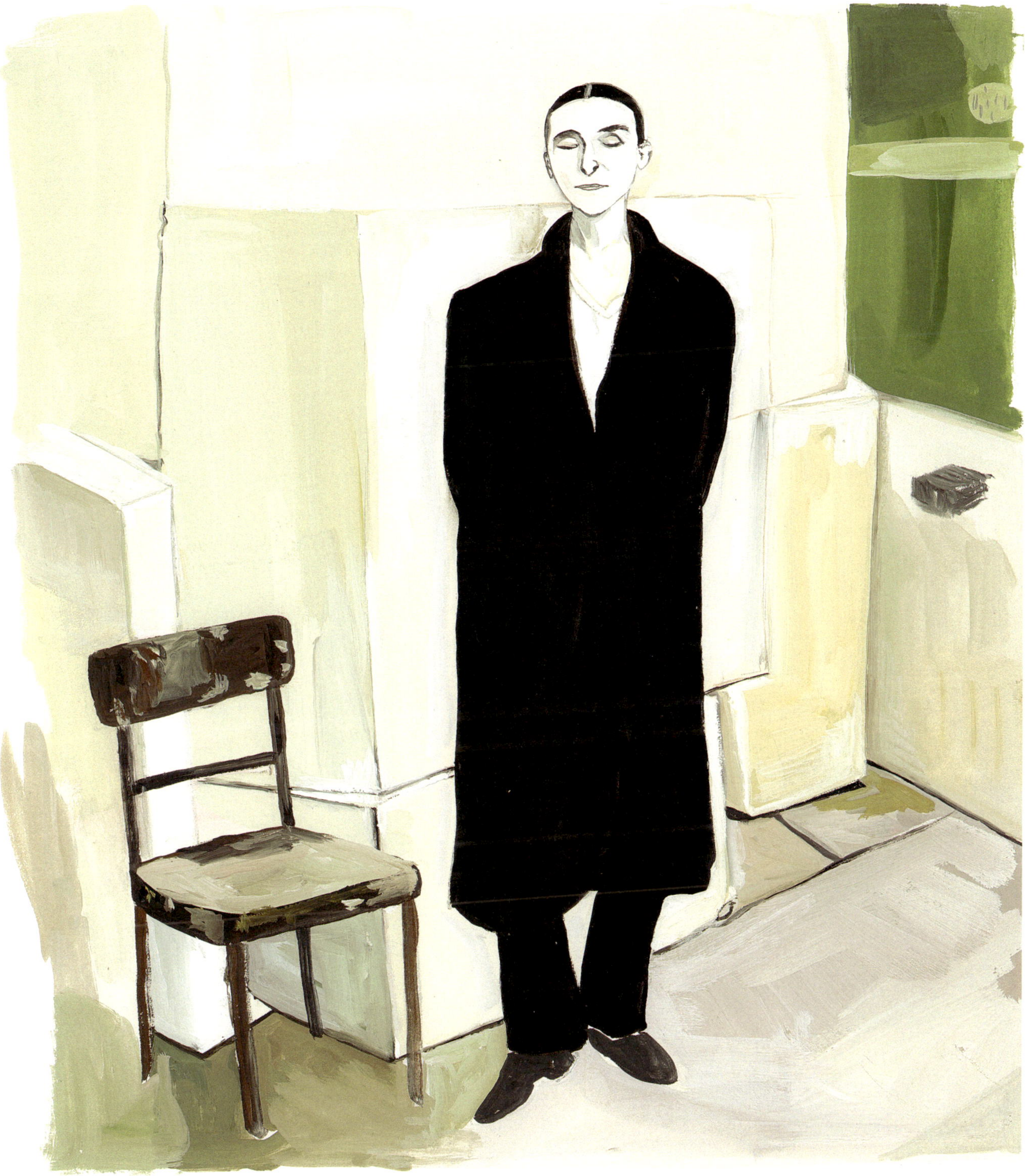

Pina Bausch, 2004–5

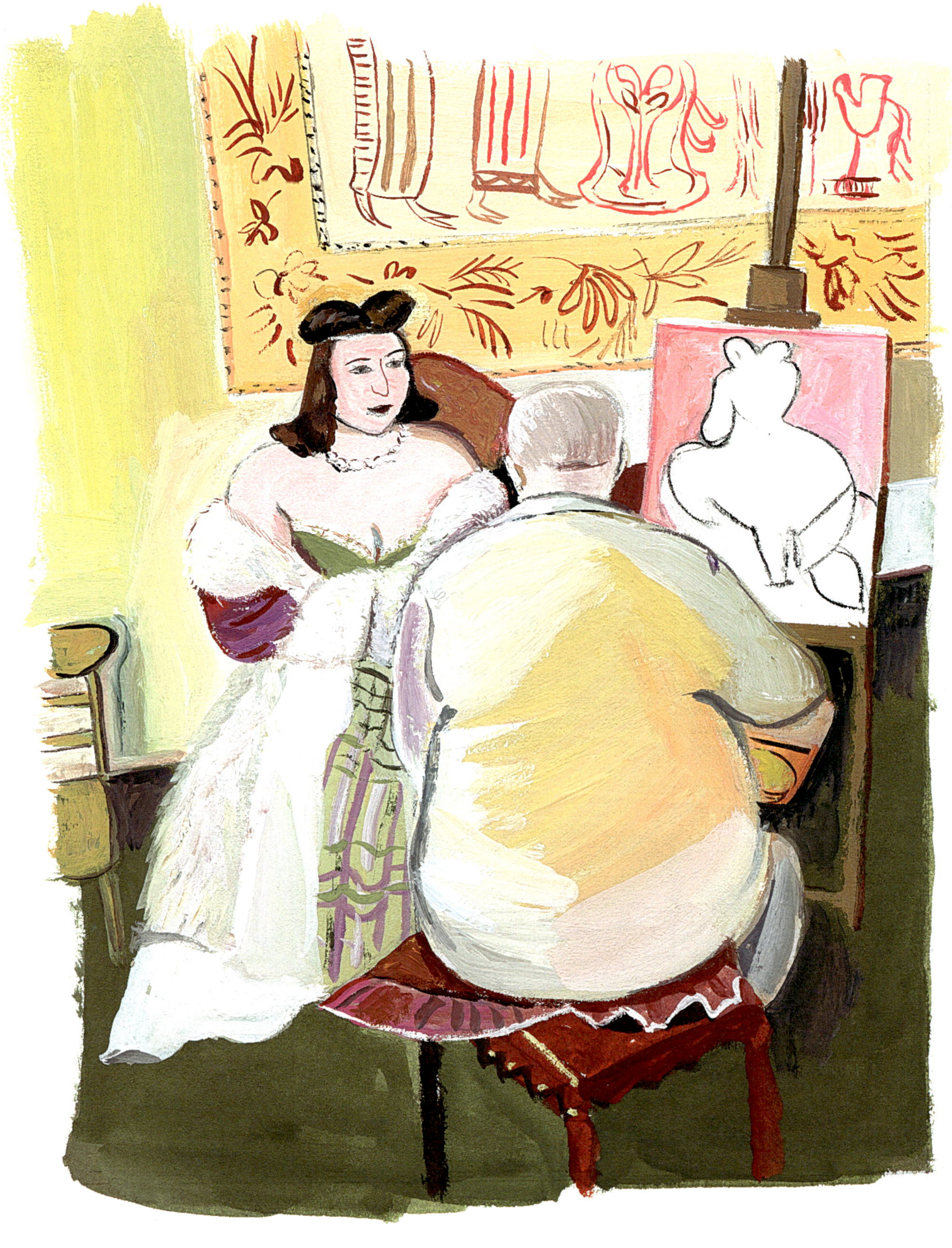

Matisse in Nice, 2004–5

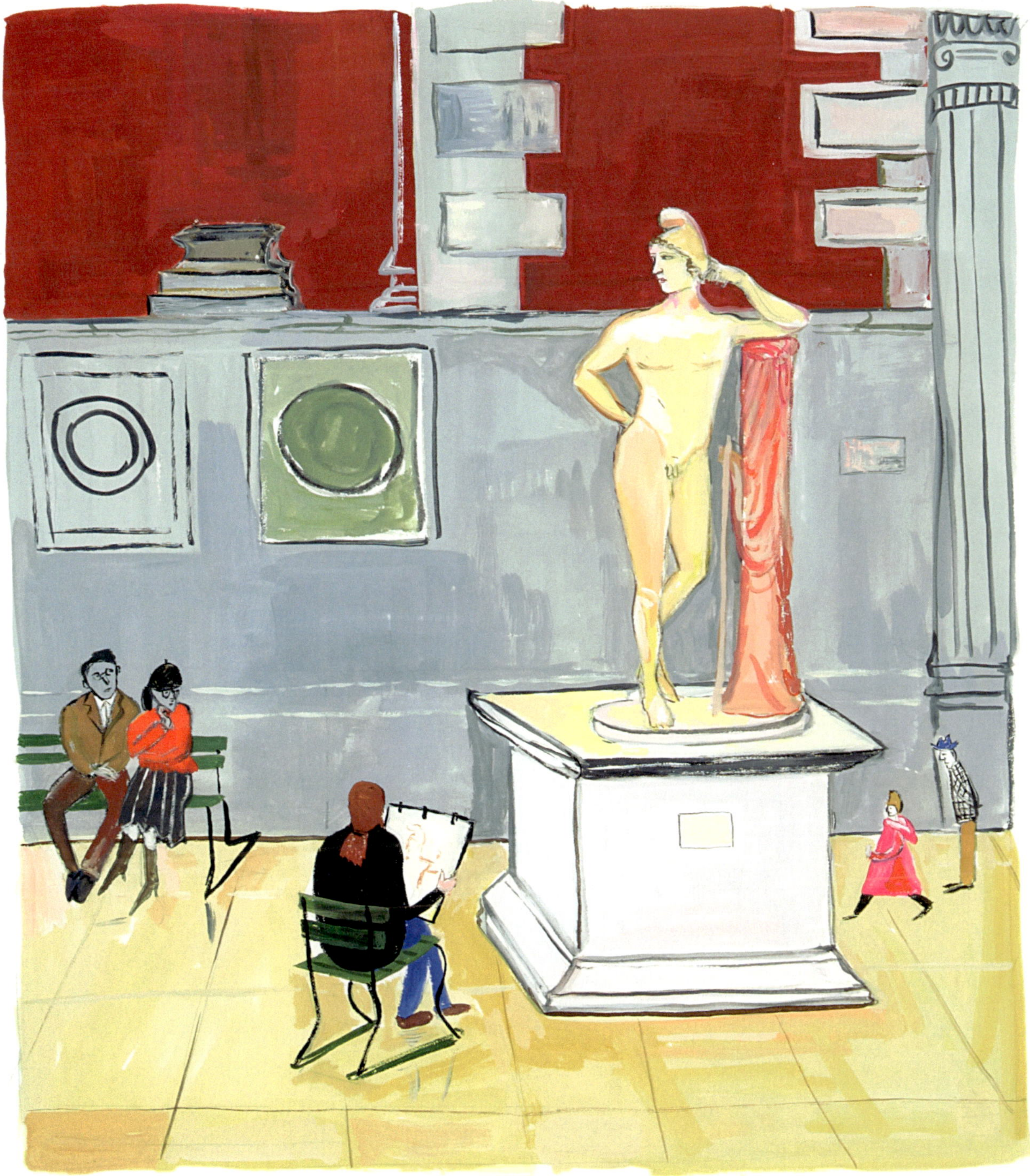

Metropolitan Museum, 2008

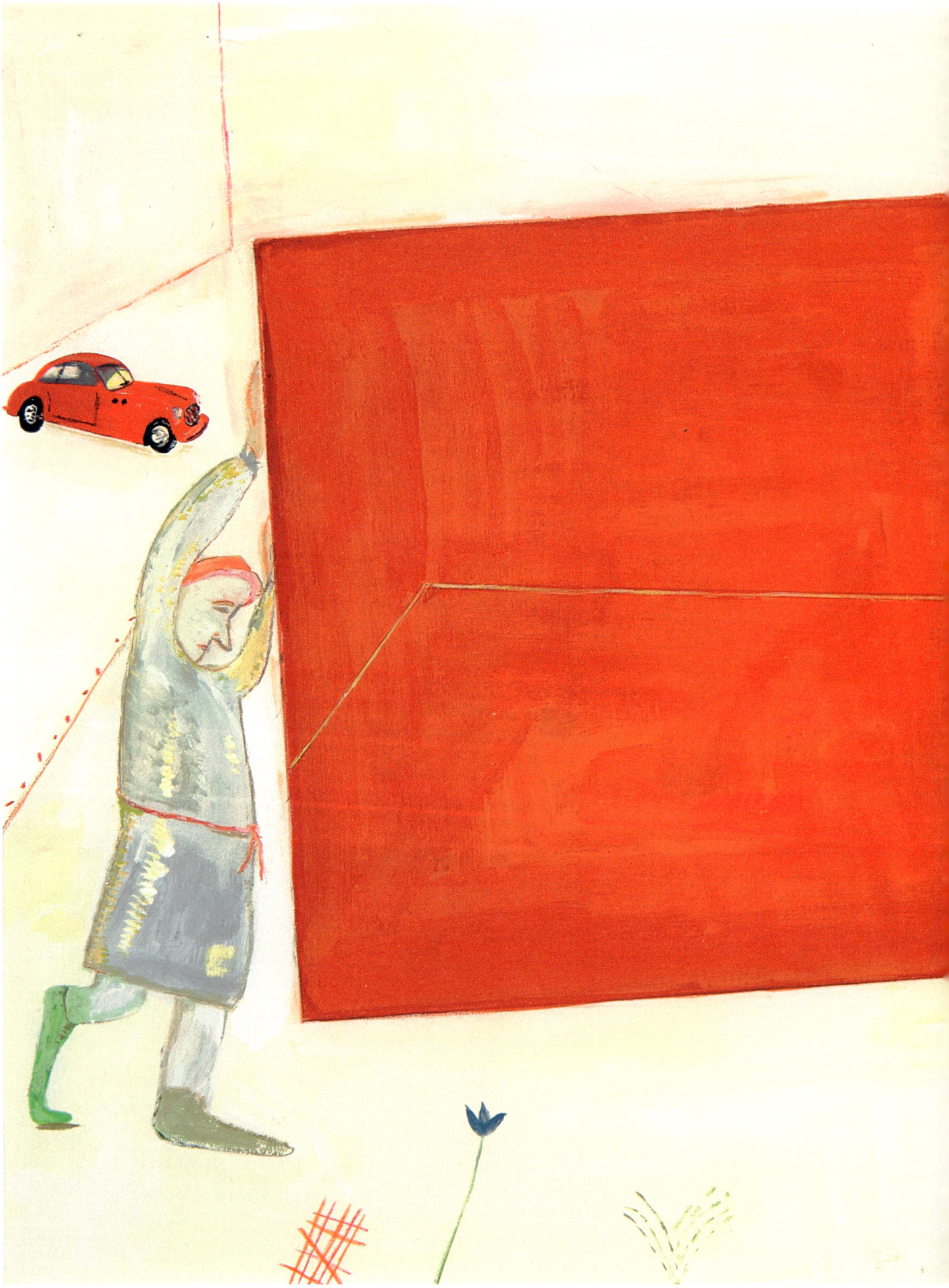

MoMA Moves to Queens, 2002

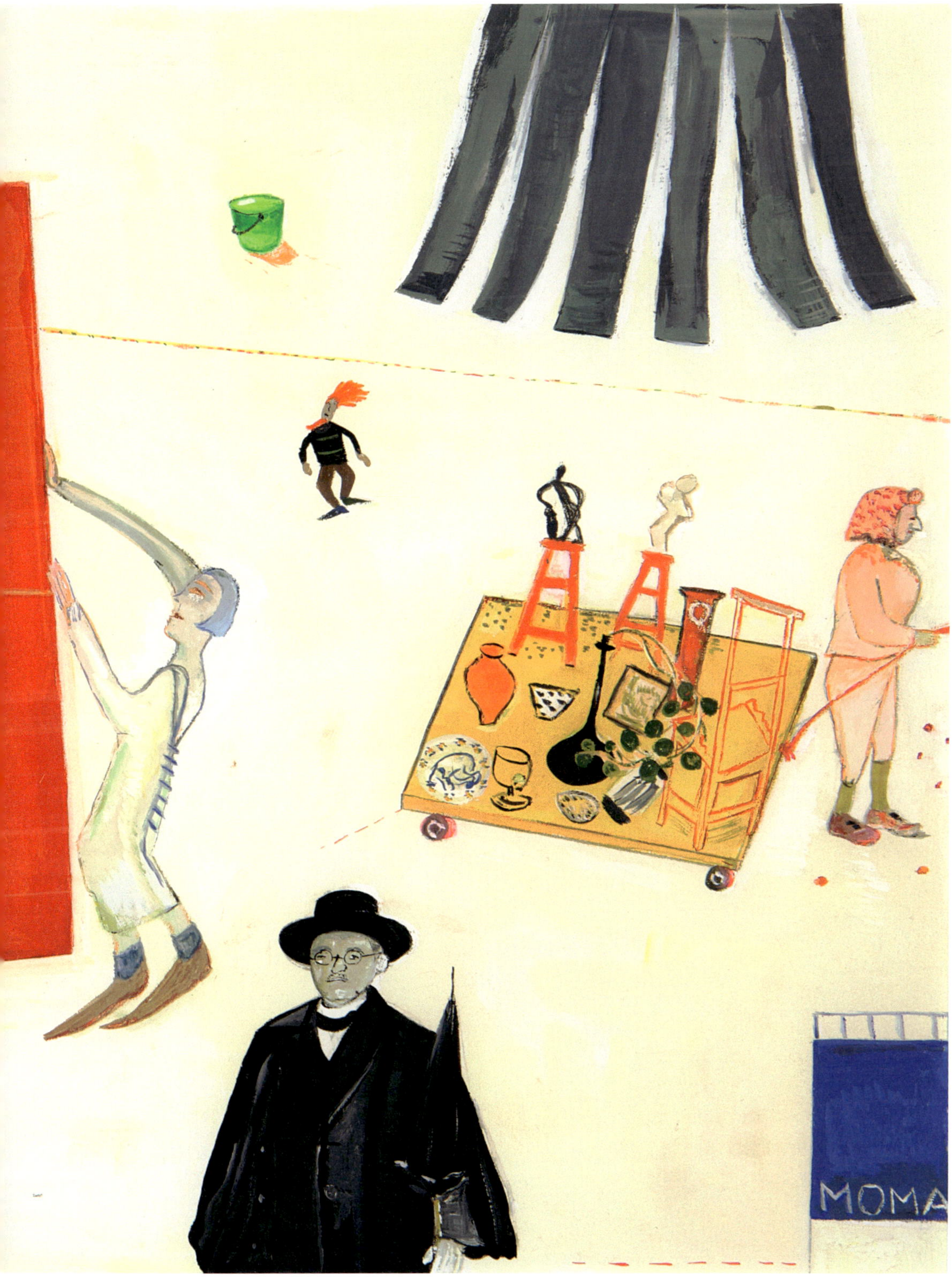
MOMA

One Thing Leads to Another: Maira Kalman's Murals

Kenneth E. Silver

A QUINTESSENTIALLY PUBLIC FORM OF ART, THE mural might seem ill suited to Maira Kalman's highly personal and idiosyncratic aesthetic. But Kalman is a master at making the insignificant important and turning the fleetingly observed into the durably meaningful. Powerful circumstance determined one of her first forays into the mural genre. When the students of Public School 234 in New York's Tribeca neighborhood, near the World Trade Center, were forced to evacuate their building on September 11, 2001, Kalman decided to create a mural for their temporary quarters on West 13th Street. At that grim moment, when so many New Yorkers felt bereft, Kalman was determined to give "a bit of laughter" to the suddenly displaced children, something they could "take with them and not be grim."[1] As if in somatic translation of the young students' spatial and psychic disorientation, Kalman's painted wall made light of a world turned upside down. **What's What?**, as the mural was titled, featured a shower of mislabeled beings and things (although skewed identities were systematically paired – an umbrella was labeled "cake," the cake labeled "umbrella"; a shoe was labeled "fish," and vice versa). Belgian Surrealist René Magritte, of course, got a good deal of deconstructive mileage by telling us what wasn't a pipe, and thereby alerting us to the arbitrary nature of language. We might refer to the style of **What's What?** as "Grade School Classicism": simple forms, bright colors, awkward perspective. It's a variation on Kalman's usual faux-naïf mode and includes a few mischievous, typical Kalman touches, like the black-and-white talking dog at the lower right, a kind of all-knowing, order-restoring narrator, who says: "Hi. I was just walking by. I know I am a dog."

Maira Kalman's children's world is only, anyway, a mislabeled adult's world (since her adults seem as guileless as children, her children as self-conscious as adults). The murals she made for New York's Grand Central Station as it was undergoing renovation in 1999 recapitulated the utterly grown-up, infantile hubbub of midtown Manhattan at rush hour, an organized daily chaos of purposeful movement, exhibitionism, distraction,

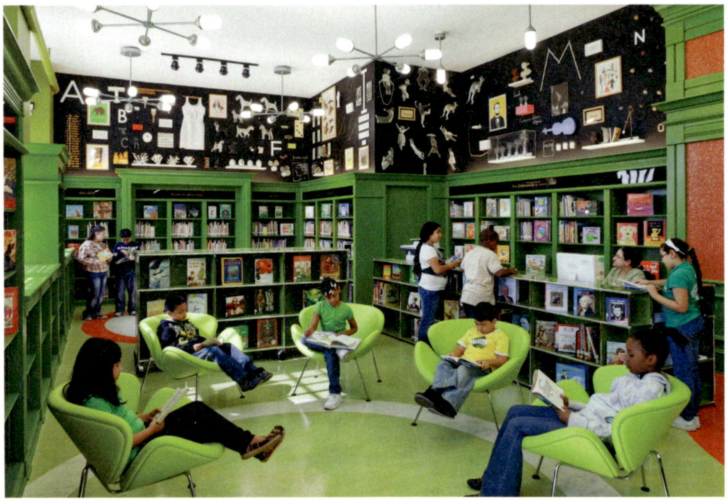

Maira Kalman's natural history alphabet at P.S. 47, 2009

Maira Kalman's natural history alphabet at P.S. 47, 2009

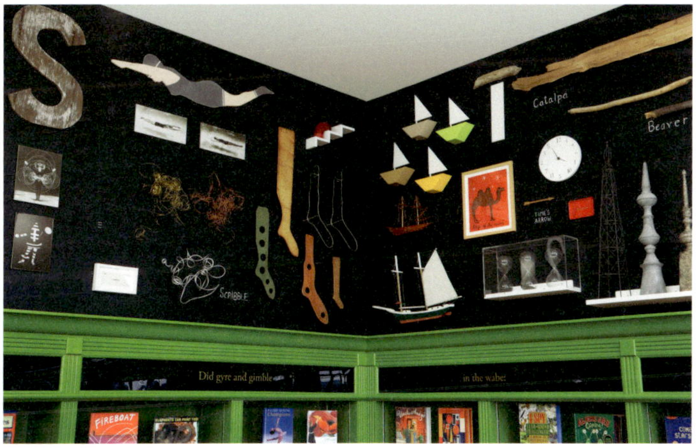

salesmanship, and lolling about. As densely packed as the city itself, the Grand Central murals (the basis for her children's book of 2001, **Next Stop Grand Central**) made a wallpaperlike overall pattern of rushing commuters, haranguing vendors, and lunching ladies and their escorts. These multitudes were rendered in the tertiary magentas, ceruleans, and ochers that convey the coloristic sophistication of Kalman's adults as surely as red, yellow, blue, and green mean "childhood" in Kalmanville.

For her most recent and ambitious mural, Kalman has returned to a New York City public school, specifically to the library of P.S. 47, in the Soundview neighborhood of the Bronx. Completed in the winter of 2009 with support from the Robin Hood Foundation, the superb new facility, designed by architect Richard H. Lewis, is the first dedicated library the school has had in years (due to overcrowding, most spaces at P.S. 47 were long ago repurposed). Kalman created a three-dimensional mural based on the alphabet for the space above the bookshelves, *A* through *Z* meandering their way around three walls of the large room. With its black ground color, the mural looks like a gigantic blackboard, or a night sky filled with the constellations of Maria Kalman's personal cerebral hemispheres. Letters, words, objects, and images form a running commentary on language and its properties. Sometimes signifier and signified are matched in uncomplicated pairings, like the brushes floating up from the letter *B*, the abacus at *A*, the window at *W*, all real "found" objects that in their utter ordinariness betray their debt to ironic Duchampian understatement. Other letters beget onomatopoeic or near abstract surrogates: a group of four *O*s are composed of round faces, perfect circles from which issue a series of sighs: "Oh, Oh, Oh, Oh"; at the letter *S* written language seems to dissolve entirely, into colorful three-dimensional scribbles. Sometimes, though, the obvious semiotic pairing of word and thing is not quite as simple as we might think. The antique sheet-metal hat at *H*, for instance, turns out to offer a quick phonics lesson: the words "HAT" and "His HAT" are so stacked that the coincidence of the letters *H* is readily apparent and can be sounded out. Then, only a few feet away, two portraits of Abraham Lincoln materialize, hard by the letter *L*–is it *his* hat, in fact, that we just encountered at *H*? One thing leads to another! Doesn't this mean that language–like this alphabet that wraps itself around a second-floor room in the Bronx–is propulsive, that it unfolds in time, that we must learn to recollect what we see and hear, note similarity and difference, and make associations? Alongside Noah Webster, Sigmund Freud presides over Maira Kalman's *Kunstkammer* of a language lesson.

But words should not be given more than their due. Nearby, also at the letter *L*, when "looking" is invoked, we recognize that Kalman's connection to language is first and foremost *visual*. Here we encounter two busts of Victorian-looking looking women (they look to their right in the direction of *J*, "Jumped," with photos of Fred Astaire, kangaroos, and a girl jumping rope), and a group of three (*L*) lightbulbs–big-bigger-biggest!–just below two more lightbulbs mounted on a pink pedestal, labeled "luminous dream object." Luminous dream object? Why not "luxuriously nonsensical things I love?" As if by magic, Maira Kalman has turned the utilitarian into the aesthetic–creating a Surrealist object worthy of her High Modernist artistic predecessors–suggesting to the attentive grade-schooler at P.S. 47 that libraries and the books that live in them are filled not only with facts but also with the stuff of dreams.

Kenneth E. Silver is a professor of art history at New York University in New York. He is also a contributing editor at *Art in America* and Adjunct Curator of Art at the Bruce Museum in Greenwich, Connecticut.

Notes

1 Maira Kalman, quoted in Chee Pearlman, "First Look: Unleashing Her Inner Child," *The New York Times*, November 1, 2001.

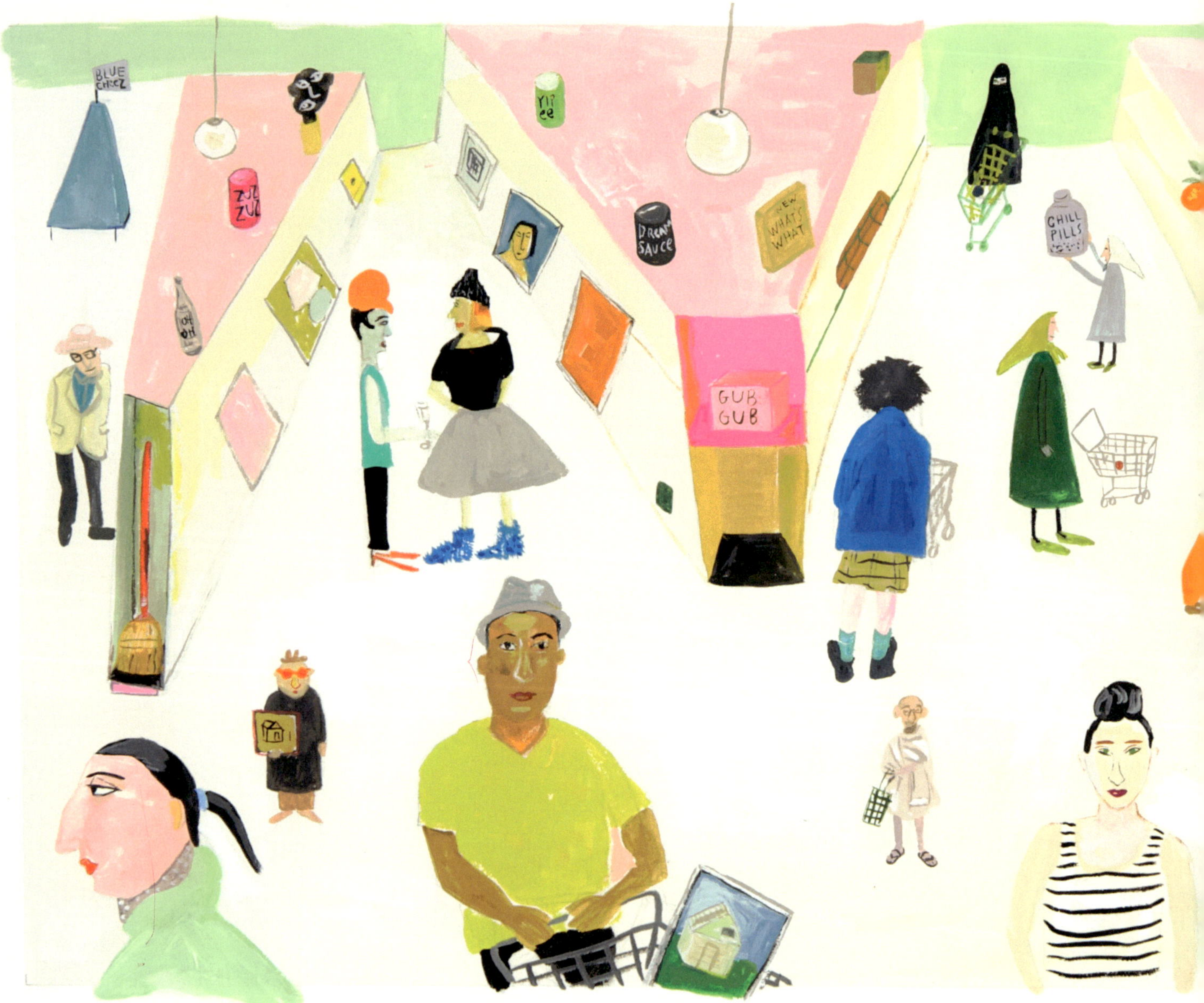

Pop Shop, 1999

Works in the Exhibition

Unless otherwise noted, all works are courtesy of Maira Kalman. Publication information cites first appearance in print. Major publications of Kalman's work include: *Elements (The Elements of Style*, 2005); "Principles" ("The Principles of Uncertainty," 2006–7); and "Pursuit" ("And the Pursuit of Happiness," 2009). References to *Elements* are annotated with the relevant caption. References to the latter two sources include date of publication in *The New York Times* (online). Extended bibliographic information can be found in the Chronology.

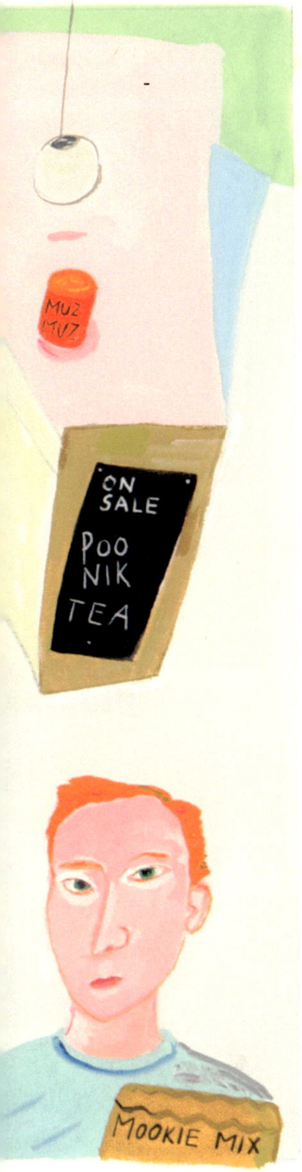

In the Apartment, 1972
ink on paper
12⅝ x 10⅝ inches
[page 21]

R. Esterbrook Pens, 1977
ink, pencil, and colored pencil on paper
13⅞ x 11 inches
[page 20]

The Guzelofkowitzes Visit Daughter Veronica Guzé (Know Your Roots), 1978
pencil, colored pencil, and ink on paper
11½ x 8⅝ inches
Published: "New York File 1: Maira Berman," *Illustration* (Japan), February 1983
[page 9]

Presidents, 1978
graphite, ink, correction fluid, and paper collage on vellum, taped to board
12⅝ x 11⅝ inches
Published: "Centerfold," *The Village Voice*, August 21, 1978
[page 84]

Cindy Sherman, 1982
pastel on paper
6 x 8 inches
Collection of Beth Rudin DeWoody
[page 88]

Laurie Anderson, 1982
ink, pencil, correction fluid, and vellum on paper
10⅞ x 13⅛ inches
Published: Debra Rae Cohen, "Laurie Anderson Lost in Translation," *The Village Voice*, June 8, 1982
[page 87]

Suitcase, ca. 1982
colored pencil and pencil on paper
8½ x 8½ inches
Published: "New York File 1: Maira Berman," *Illustration* (Japan), February 1983
[page 74]

Little Baby Goes Wooo/ All Night Long, 1985
gouache and pencil on paper
13⅝ x 12 inches
Published: *Stay Up Late*, 1987
[page 10]

Blow the Saxophone, 1988
gouache on paper
17 x 14 inches
Published: *Max Makes a Million*, 1990
"He meant to blow the saxophone/ but man, he blew his nose instead/ and his glasses flew off his head onto the bed."
[page 23]

My Cousin Ervin, 1988
gouache on paper
14½ x 12¾ inches
Published: *Hey Willy, See the Pyramids*, 1988
[page 94]

Tower of Babel, 1989
gouache on paper
14 x 17 inches
Published: Garry Wills, "The Private Ministry of Colonel Thieme," *Wig Wag*, October 1989
[page 27]

Title Page (Max Makes a Million), 1990
gouache on paper
14 x 17⅛ inches
Published: *Max Makes a Million*, 1990
[page 98]

Man Leaping While Man Talks on Phone, 1991
gouache on paper
14 x 13 inches
Private collection
Published: *Ooh-la-la (Max in Love)*, 1991
[page 109]

Max, 1991
gouache on paper
17 x 14 inches
Published: *Ooh-la-la (Max in Love)*, 1991
[page 12]

The Poet Wrote on the Sidewalk, 1991
gouache on paper
16¼ x 20 inches
Published: *Ooh-la-la (Max in Love)*, 1991
[page 35]

Séance, 1991
gouache on paper
16⅞ x 14 inches
Published: *Ooh-la-la (Max in Love)*, 1991
[page 92]

Self-Portrait (Favorite Jacket), 1991
pencil and colored pencil on paper; ink on paper
12⅝ x 9¾ inches
Published: Frank De Caro, "Mizrahi Loves Company," *Mademoiselle*, January 1991
[page 2]

Red Room, 1992
gouache on paper
17 x 14 inches
Published: *Max in Hollywood, Baby*, 1992
[page 75]

James Bell, 1993
gouache on paper
17 x 14 inches
Published: *Chicken Soup, Boots*, 1993
[page 105]

Crosstown Boogie Woogie, 1995
gouache on paper
15⅜ x 11½ inches
Published: *The New Yorker*, December 4, 1995, cover
[page 38]

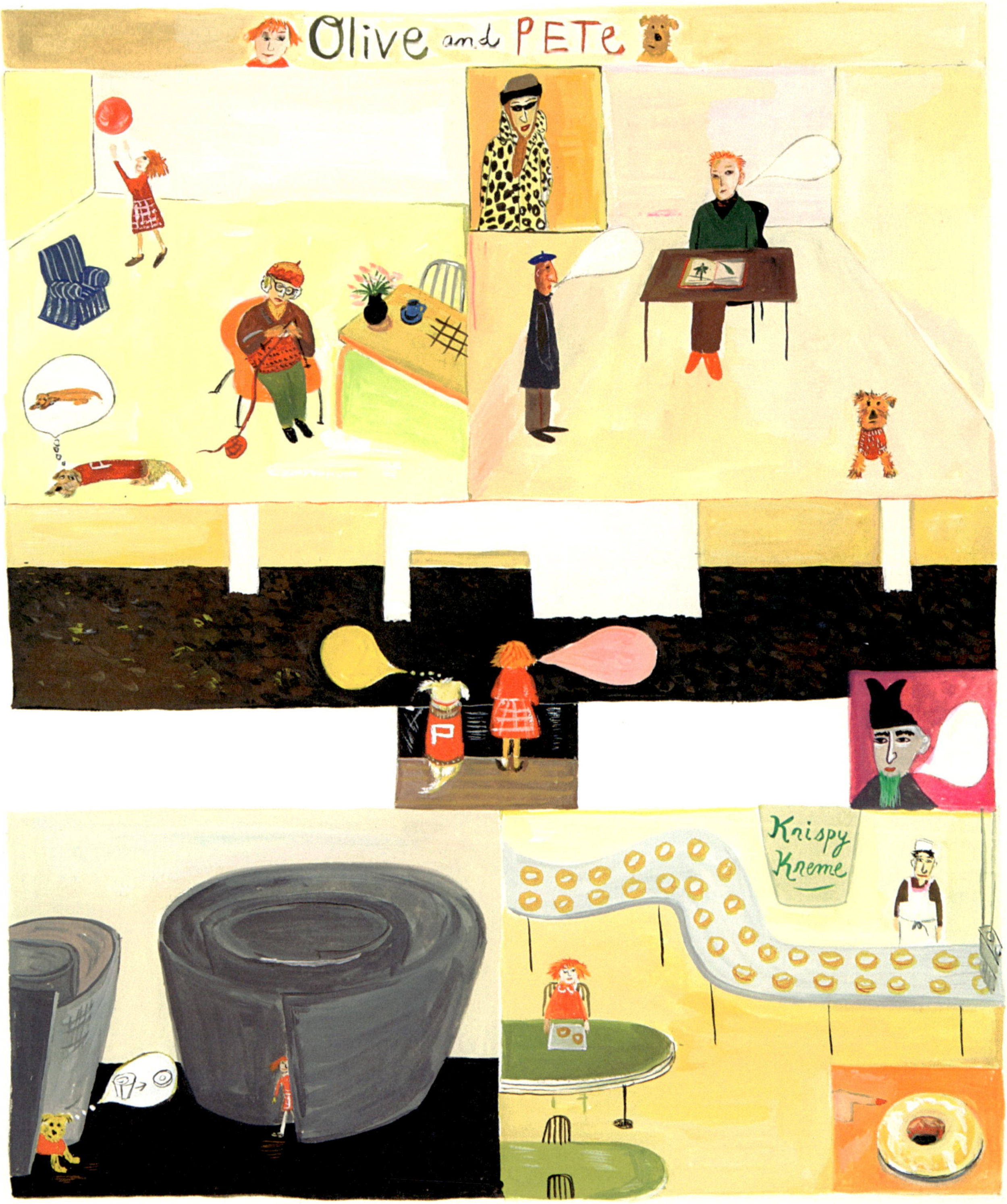

Olive and Pete in New York, 1998

Glass, 1996
gouache on paper
15 7/8 x 11 7/8 inches
Published: *Domus*, February 1996
[page 41]

I Saw Her, 1996
pencil and colored pencil on paper
6 x 4 inches
[page 1]

Tibor and Elissa, 1996
gouache on paper
5 x 8 inches
Collection of Elissa Santisi and Jim Keller
[page 100]

My Mother in Palestine, 1998
ink, tape, and correction fluid on paper; ink on vellum
11 x 8 1/2 inches
Published: "Op-Ed: In Case you Forgot to Buy a Card," *The New York Times*, May 10, 1998
[page 7]

Olive and Pete in New York, 1998
gouache on paper
15 3/4 x 11 7/8 inches
Published: "The Travels of Olive and Pete, This Time: New York," *Travel & Leisure Family*, Spring/Summer 1998
[page 120]

Tibor Kalman, 1998
gouache on paper
15 1/4 x 11 3/4 inches
Published: *Tibor Kalman: Perverse Optimist*, 1998
[page 99]

White House. Black Dots., 1998
gouache on paper; pencil on vellum
15 x 11 1/8 inches
Published: *Tibor Kalman: Perverse Optimist*, 1998
[page 60]

Dog Reads Book, 1999
gouache on paper
17 1/4 x 13 1/2 inches
Published: *The New Yorker*, February 1, 1999, cover
[page 125]

New York, Grand Central Station, 1999
gouache and ink on paper
15 3/8 x 22 1/4 inches
Published: *Next Stop Grand Central*, 1999
[pages 36–37]

Pop Shop, 1999
gouache on paper
14 3/8 x 18 inches
Published: Glenn D. Lowry, "The State of the Art Museum, Ever Changing," *The New York Times*, January 10, 1999
[pages 118–19]

Labs on Cheetah Print (Dolce and Gabbana's Yellow Labradors, Lola and Dalí), 2000
gouache on paper
12 1/2 x 10 inches
Collection of Madalyn and Stephen Tobias
Published: "Fashion Pet Portraits," *Interview*, June 2000
[page 16]

Lady Birley, 2000
gouache on paper
11 1/2 x 7 3/4 inches
Collection of Mark Sena and Linda Saul Sena
Published: "Principles," June 7, 2006
[page 65]

Viktor & Rolf, 2000
gouache on paper
18 x 15 inches
Published: "Couture Voyeur," *The New York Times Magazine*, November 5, 2000
[page 78]

Woman with Face Net, 2000
gouache on paper
17 x 14 3/4 inches
Published: "Couture Voyeur," *The New York Times Magazine*, November 5, 2000
[page 86]

Annual Misery Day Parade, 2001
gouache and pencil on paper
14 3/4 x 13 1/8 inches
Published: *The New Yorker*, February 5, 2001, cover
[page 39]

Dream in Venice, 2001
gouache on paper
18 1/4 x 15 inches
Published: *What Pete Ate from A to Z*, 2001
[page 76]

Endpaper (What Pete Ate), 2001
gouache on paper
14 7/8 x 22 1/4 inches
Published: *What Pete Ate from A to Z*, 2001
[pages 18–19]

Maira Kalman and Rick Meyerowitz
New Yorkistan, 2001
gouache and pencil on paper
20 x 14 3/4 inches
Collection of Erica and Eric Schwartz
Sketch for *The New Yorker*, December 10, 2001, cover
[page 26]

Babe Ruth, 2002
gouache on paper
12 x 12 inches
Published: *Fireboat: The Heroic Adventures of the John J. Harvey*, 2002
[page 108]

MoMA Moves to Queens, 2002
gouache on paper
9 1/2 x 14 1/2 inches
Collection of Hope and Michael Proper
Published: "Sketchbook," *The New Yorker*, April 22 and 29, 2002
[pages 114–15]

The Planes Attacked, 2002
gouache on paper
12 x 22 inches
Published: *Fireboat: The Heroic Adventures of the John J. Harvey*, 2002
[pages 28–29]

Snickers, 2002
gouache on paper
11 1/8 x 12 inches
Published: *Fireboat: The Heroic Adventures of the John J. Harvey*, 2002
[page 70]

Fred, 2003
gouache and ink on paper
15 x 13 inches
Published: "Look," *Print*, September/October 2003; *Elements*, "A basic structural design underlies every kind of writing."; "Pursuit," February 26, 2009
[page 49]

My Mother in Organza, 2003
gouache and pencil on paper
14 x 11 1/4 inches
Published: *Boston Globe–Horn Book Award Magazine*, 2003, cover
[page 6]

Her Story Is Strange, 2004
gouache on paper
17 x 14 7/8 inches
Published: Lawrence Osborne, "Inward Bound," *The New York Times Magazine*, July 18, 2004; *Elements*, "Her story is strange."
[page 62]

Sunny Day at Park, 2004
gouache on paper
8 1/4 x 8 3/4 inches
Collection of Julie Saul
Published: "Principles," April 4, 2007; "Mind's Eye," *Aperture*, Winter 2007
[page 64]

Abraham Lincoln, 2004–5
gouache on paper
15 x 11 inches
Published: *Elements*, "Lincoln, Abraham"; "Principles," October 4, 2006
[page 85]

Cardboard Box, 2004–5
gouache on paper
12 1/2 x 11 1/2 inches
Published: *Elements*, "Illusion. See allusion."
[page 46]

Chocolate and Champagne Party, 2004–5
gouache on paper
10 1/4 x 13 3/4 inches
Published: *Elements*, "Be obscure clearly! Be wild of tongue in a way we can understand."
[pages 68–69]

The Glass House, 2004–5
gouache on paper
9 x 11 inches
Published: *Elements*, "People who live in glass houses shouldn't throw stones."
[page 79]

Matisse in Nice, 2004–5
gouache on paper
12 x 10 3/8 inches
Published: *Elements*, "She was part in, part out."
[page 112]

Pina Bausch, 2004–5
gouache on paper
12 1/2 x 11 1/2 inches
Published: *Elements*, "Do you mind my asking a question?"
[page 111]

Young Nabakov, 2006

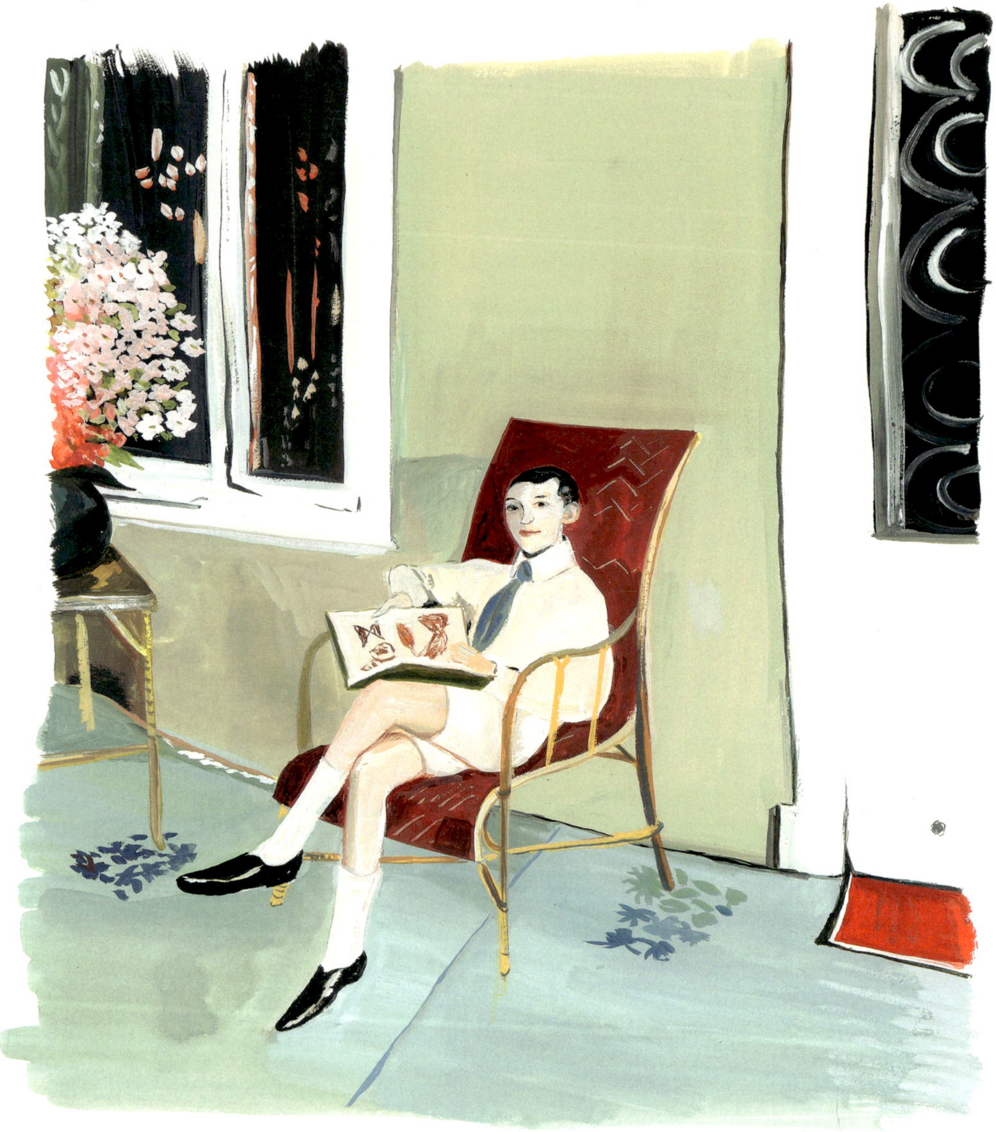

Pink Package, 2004–5
gouache on paper
14¼ x 11½ inches
Published: *Elements*, "Contents"; "Principles," October 4, 2006
[page 48]

Rajastani Room, 2004–5
gouache on paper
13¾ x 11¾ inches
Published: *Elements*, "'Spontaneous me,' sang Whitman."
[page 83]

Self-Portrait (with Pete), 2004–5
gouache on paper
16 x 15 inches
Published: *Elements*, "Hot day. Book found. Aha!/ Words cannot express./ If only I could./ Without a doubt./ Goodness./ Good. Good. Good."
[page 5]

Sentence Fragment, 2004–5
gouache on paper
12¾ x 10¾ inches
Published: *Elements*, "sentence fragment"
[page 58]

Susan, 2004–5
gouache on paper
11⅝ x 9 inches
Published: *Elements*, "Well, Susan, this is a fine mess you are in."
[page 14]

The Temple of Isis, 2004–5
gouache on paper
12 x 10¾ inches
Published: *Elements*, "The temple of Isis"
[page 34]

Zermatt, 2004–5
gouache on paper
15¾ x 11½ inches
Published: *Elements*, "The best way to see a country, unless you are pressed for time, is to travel on foot."
[page 59]

Don't Cry Over Spilt Milk, 2005
silk and cotton thread on linen and cotton
26½ x 27¼ inches
Collection of Elizabeth Hilpman
[page 40]

Goethe: An Embroidery in Four Parts, 2005
I Feel a Sense of Dread
My Rigid Heart
What I Possess
What Had Disappeared
silk and cotton thread on linen and cotton
49½ x 19½ inches
Published: "Principles," October 4, 2006
[pages 30–31]

Pink Dress, 2005
silk and cotton thread on silk
30 x 56 inches
Courtesy of the artist and Julie Saul Gallery, New York
[page 77]

To the Stars, 2005
silk and cotton thread on burlap
42 x 18¾ inches
Collection of Edwina von Gal
[page 22]

Celeste Hotel, 2006
gouache on paper
6¾ x 10¼ inches
Collection of Andrea Popowich Meislin and Robert Meislin
[page 63]

Celeste Hotel, Petit Salon, 2006
gouache on paper
7 x 8¾ inches
Collection of Susan Grant Lewin
Published: "Principles," October 4, 2006
[page 82]

Edith Sitwell, 2006
gouache on paper
12 x 10 inches
Published: "Principles," September 6, 2006
Private collection
[page 95]

Exaltations/Observations, 2006
ink and correction fluid on paper with collage
11 x 11⅞ inches
Sketch for "Principles," December 6, 2006
[page 24]

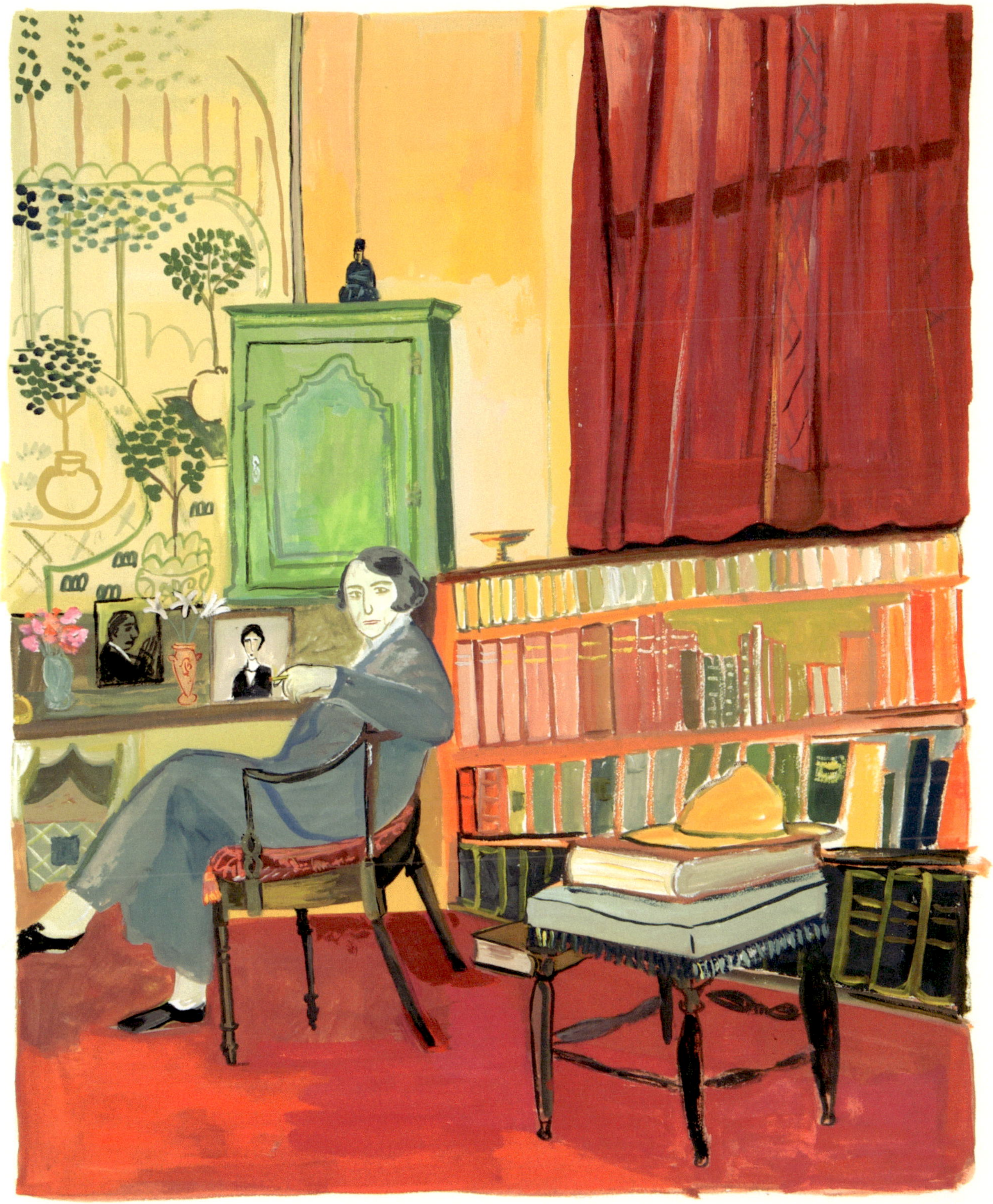

Vita Sackville-West, 2007

Herring and Philosophy Club, 2006
gouache on paper
9¾ x 14½ inches
Collection of Ellen and Robert Grimes
Published: "Sunny-Side Up: On the Love of Breakfast," *Gourmet* (supplement), August 2006
[page 73]

Le Corbusier Sink, 2006
gouache on paper
7¾ x 7½ inches
Collection of Jane and Patrick Curley
Published: "Principles," November 1, 2006
[page 56]

Mosses of Long Island, 2006
gouache on paper
7 x 8¾ inches
Collection of Edwina von Gal
Published: "Principles," October 4, 2006
[page 47]

My Beautiful Mother's Map, 2006
gouache on paper
11⅝ x 15⅛ inches
Courtesy of the artist and Julie Saul Gallery, New York
Published: "Principles," May 3, 2006
[page 25]

Outside the Proust Room, 2006
gouache on paper
7 x 7½ inches
Collection of Christopher and Deborah Buck
Published: "Principles," November 1, 2006
[page 55]

Sofa, 2006
gouache on paper
8 x 11½ inches
Courtesy of the artist and Julie Saul Gallery, New York
Published: "Principles," December 6, 2006
[pages 52–53]

Woman with Bow, 2006
gouache on paper
7 x 6¾ inches
Collection of Victoria E. Schonfeld
Published: "Principles," November 1, 2006
[page 93]

Wooden Box, 2006
gouache on paper
10¾ x 11 inches
Courtesy of the artist and Julie Saul Gallery, New York
Published: "Principles," October 4, 2006
[page 45]

Young Nabakov, 2006
gouache on paper
9¾ x 8½ inches
Private collection, Brooklyn
Published: "Principles," May 3, 2006
[page 122]

Dead Man, 2007
gouache on paper
6¼ x 7 inches
Published: "Principles," February 7, 2007
[page 61]

Keep Calm, 2007
gouache on paper
11¾ x 8¾ inches
Collection of Barbara Becker and Chad Gallant
Published: "Principles," April 4, 2007
[page 33]

London Blitz, 2007
gouache on paper
10½ x 15¾ inches
Collection of Catherine Hong and David Ferris
Published: "Principles," March 7, 2007
[pages 80–81]

Man Dances on Salt, 2007
gouache on paper
9 x 7¾ inches
Collection of Tom and Claire O'Connor
Published: "Principles," February 7, 2007, and *Principles* (book cover)
[page 110]

Museum Guard with Bow, 2007
gouache on paper
11 x 8¾ inches
Collection of Pam Remick
Published: "Principles," January 3, 2007
[page 91]

Schlafzimmer with Folded Quilts, 2007
gouache on paper
8½ x 8½ inches
Published: "Principles," January 3, 2007
[page 54]

Steinberg Camera, 2007
gouache on paper
9½ x 11¾ inches
Private collection, New York
Published: "Principles," March 7, 2007
[page 44]

Vita Sackville-West, 2007
gouache on paper
18 x 15 inches
Courtesy of the artist and Julie Saul Gallery, New York
Published: "The Splendid Garden(er)," *Culture + Travel*, Winter 2007
[page 123]

Walter Benjamin, 2007
gouache on paper
10½ x 8¼ inches
Published: "Principles," March 7, 2007
[page 66]

Aalto Vase with Poppies, 2008
gouache on paper
21 x 15 inches
Courtesy of the artist and Julie Saul Gallery, New York
Published: "Stem Sell: Alvar Aalto's Design Still Holds Water," *The New York Times Style Magazine*, May 4, 2008
[page 67]

After Ingres, 2008
gouache on paper
19 x 19⅜ inches
Courtesy of the artist and Julie Saul Gallery, New York
Published: "Mad about the Met," *Departures*, May/June 2008
[page 90]

Broken Chair in Tel Aviv, 2008
gouache on paper
15⅛ x 11¾ inches
Courtesy of the artist and Julie Saul Gallery, New York
Published: "My Tel Aviv," *Tablet* (online magazine), September 5, 2008
[page 51]

Damien Hirst/Manolo Blahnik, 2008
gouache on paper
13⅝ x 10⅞ inches
Courtesy of the artist and Julie Saul Gallery, New York
Published: "Mad about the Met," *Departures*, May/June 2008
[page 50]

Emily Dickinson, 2008
gouache on paper
15 x 14 inches
Courtesy of the artist and Julie Saul Gallery, New York
Published: Judith Thurman, "Her Own Society," *The New Yorker*, August 4, 2008
[page 15]

Metropolitan Museum, 2008
gouache on paper
19 x 19⅜ inches
Courtesy of the artist and Julie Saul Gallery, New York
Published: "Mad about the Met," *Departures*, May/June 2008
[page 113]

Philippe, 2008
gouache on paper
19½ x 16 inches
Published: "Mad about the Met," *Departures*, May/June 2008
[page 101]

Tel Aviv Bauhaus Building, 2008
gouache on paper
10⅜ x 14⅞ inches
Courtesy of the artist and Julie Saul Gallery, New York
Published: "My Tel Aviv," *Tablet* (online magazine), September 5, 2008
[page 57]

Benjamin Franklin in Fur Hat, 2009
gouache on paper
15⅛ x 10⅞ inches
Courtesy of the artist and Julie Saul Gallery, New York
Published: "Pursuit," July 30, 2009
[page 104]

Butter and Eggs, 2009
gouache on paper
11⅛ x 15 inches
Courtesy of the artist and Julie Saul Gallery, New York
Published: "Pursuit," January 29, 2009
[page 72]

Hole Punch, 2009
gouache on paper
11¼ x 15⅛ inches
Courtesy of the artist and
Julie Saul Gallery, New York
Published: "Pursuit,"
May 28, 2009
[page 42]

Panache, 2009
gouache on paper
11 x 18 inches
Published: *13 Words*, 2010
[page 11]

Red Jacket, 2009
gouache on paper
15⅛ x 11 inches
Published: "Pursuit,"
September 24, 2009
[page 17]

Rubber Band, 2009
gouache on paper
9 x 12 inches
Published: "Pursuit,"
July 30, 2009
[page 43]

Ruth Bader Ginsburg, 2009
gouache on paper
10⅞ x 16 inches
Published: "Pursuit,"
April 23, 2009
[page 102]

Ruth Bader Ginsburg/Robe, 2009
gouache on paper
13⅝ x 9⅝ inches
Courtesy of the artist and
Julie Saul Gallery, New York
Published: "Pursuit,"
April 23, 2009
[page 103]

Soldier, 2009
gouache on paper
15⅛ x 11⅛ inches
Published: "Pursuit,"
May 28, 2009
[page 89]

2 Million People, 2009
gouache on paper
10¾ x 15 inches
Courtesy of the artist and
Julie Saul Gallery, New York
Published: "Pursuit,"
January 29, 2009
[page 32]

Pickle Tag, 2010
gouache on paper
14¾ x 11 inches
[page 71]

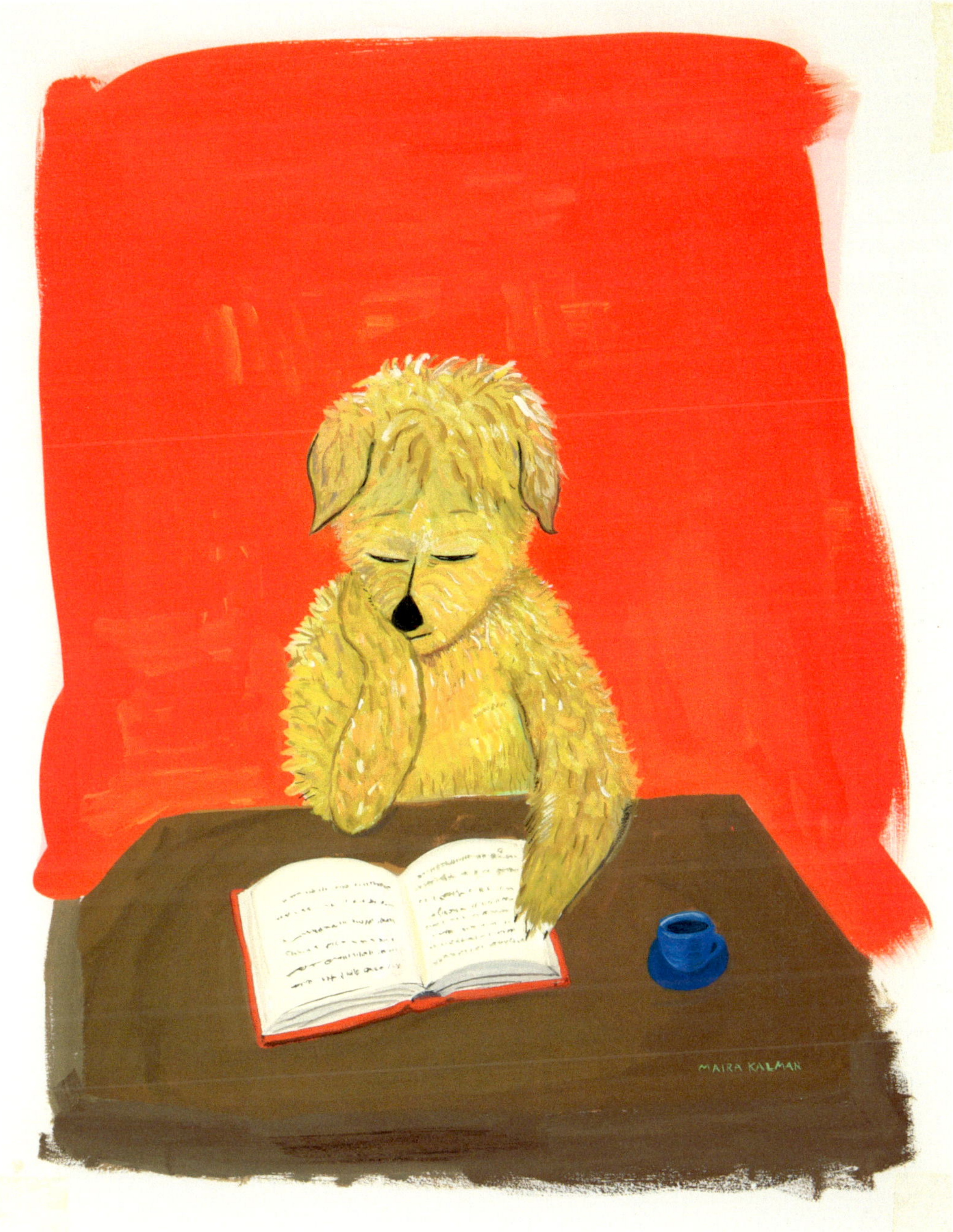

Dog Reads Book, 1999

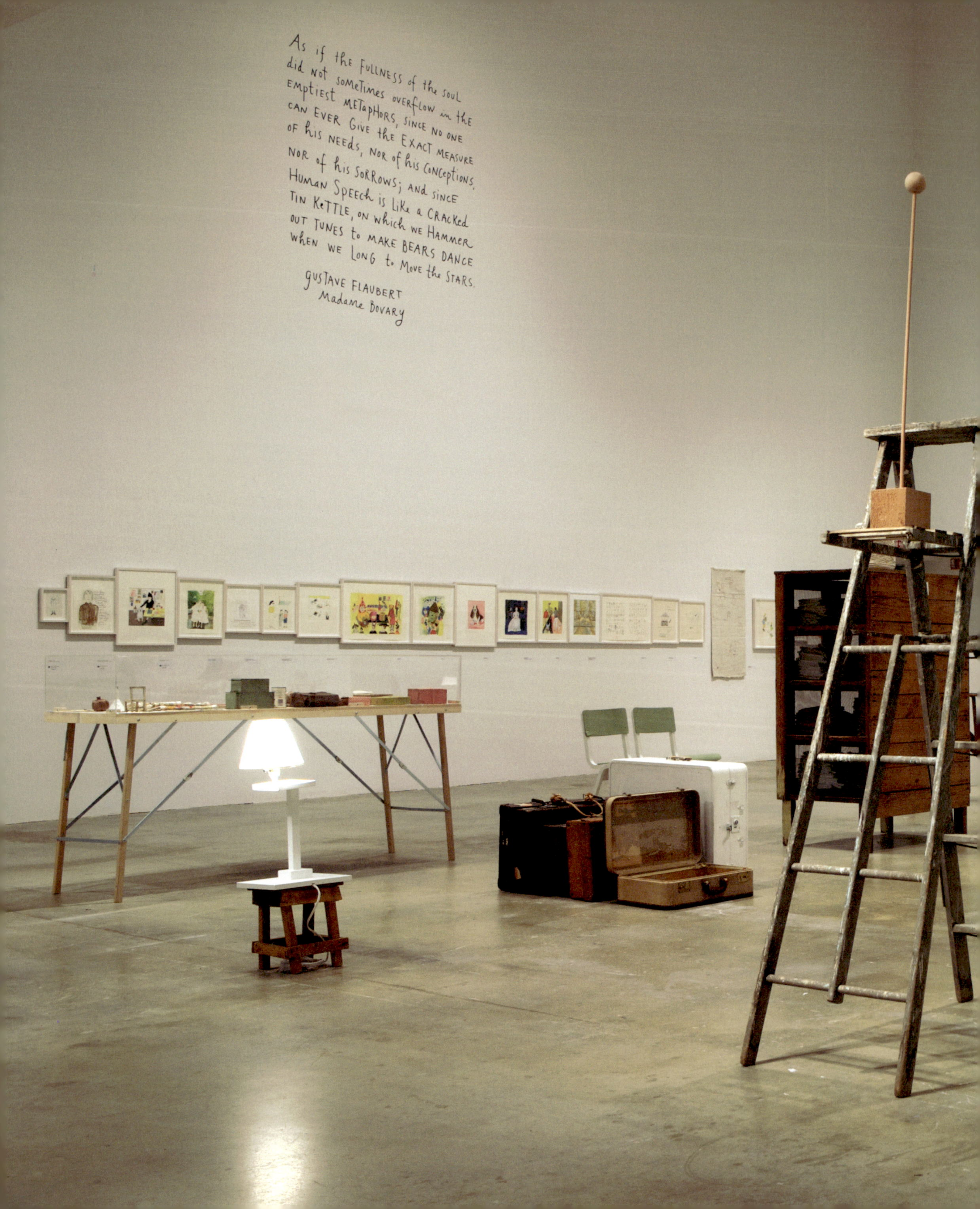
As if the Fullness of the soul
did not sometimes overflow in the
emptiest metaphors, since no one
can ever give the exact measure
of his needs, nor of his conceptions,
nor of his sorrows; and since
Human Speech is like a cracked
tin kettle, on which we hammer
out tunes to make bears dance
when we long to move the stars.
Gustave Flaubert
Madame Bovary

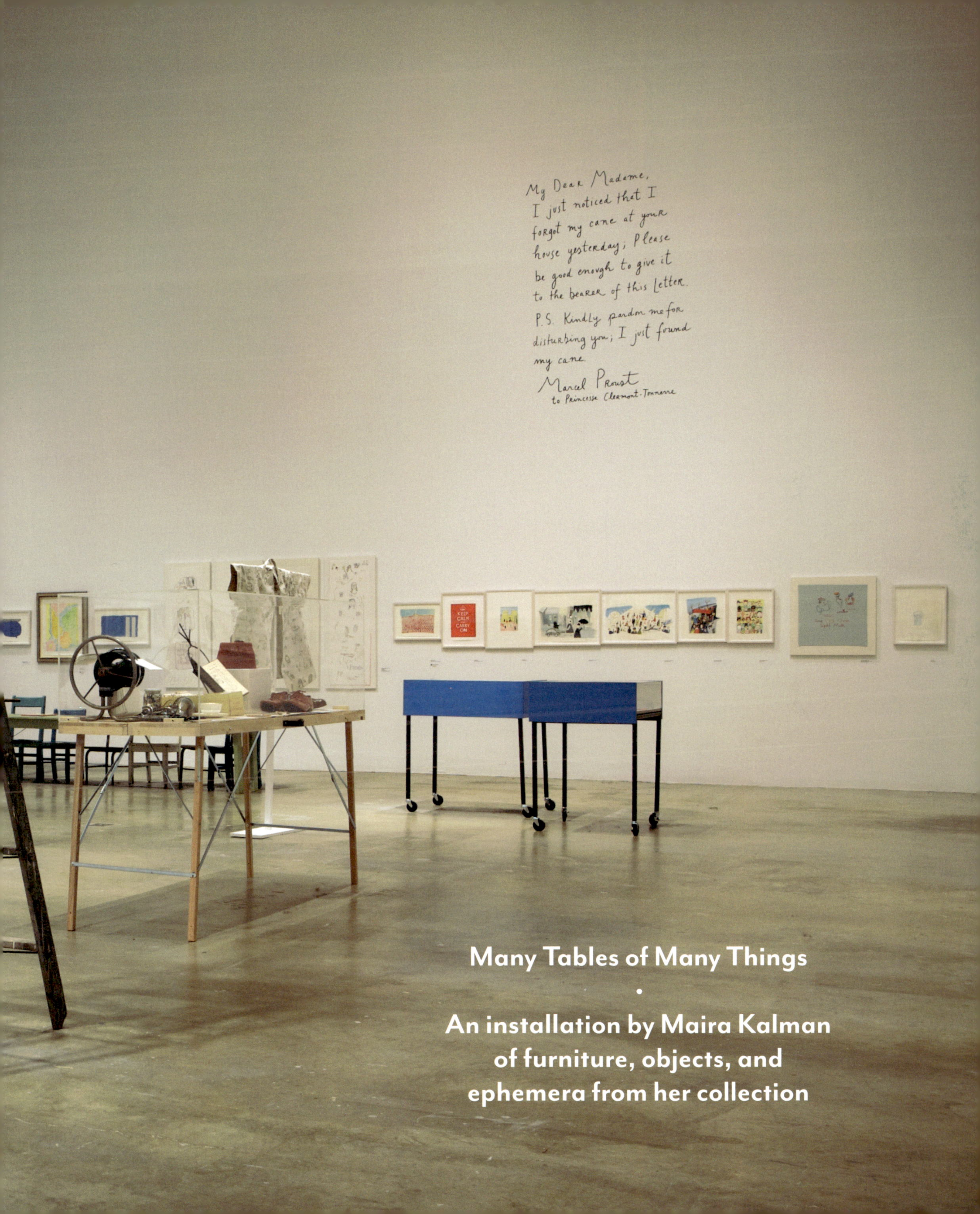

Many Tables of Many Things

•

An installation by Maira Kalman of furniture, objects, and ephemera from her collection

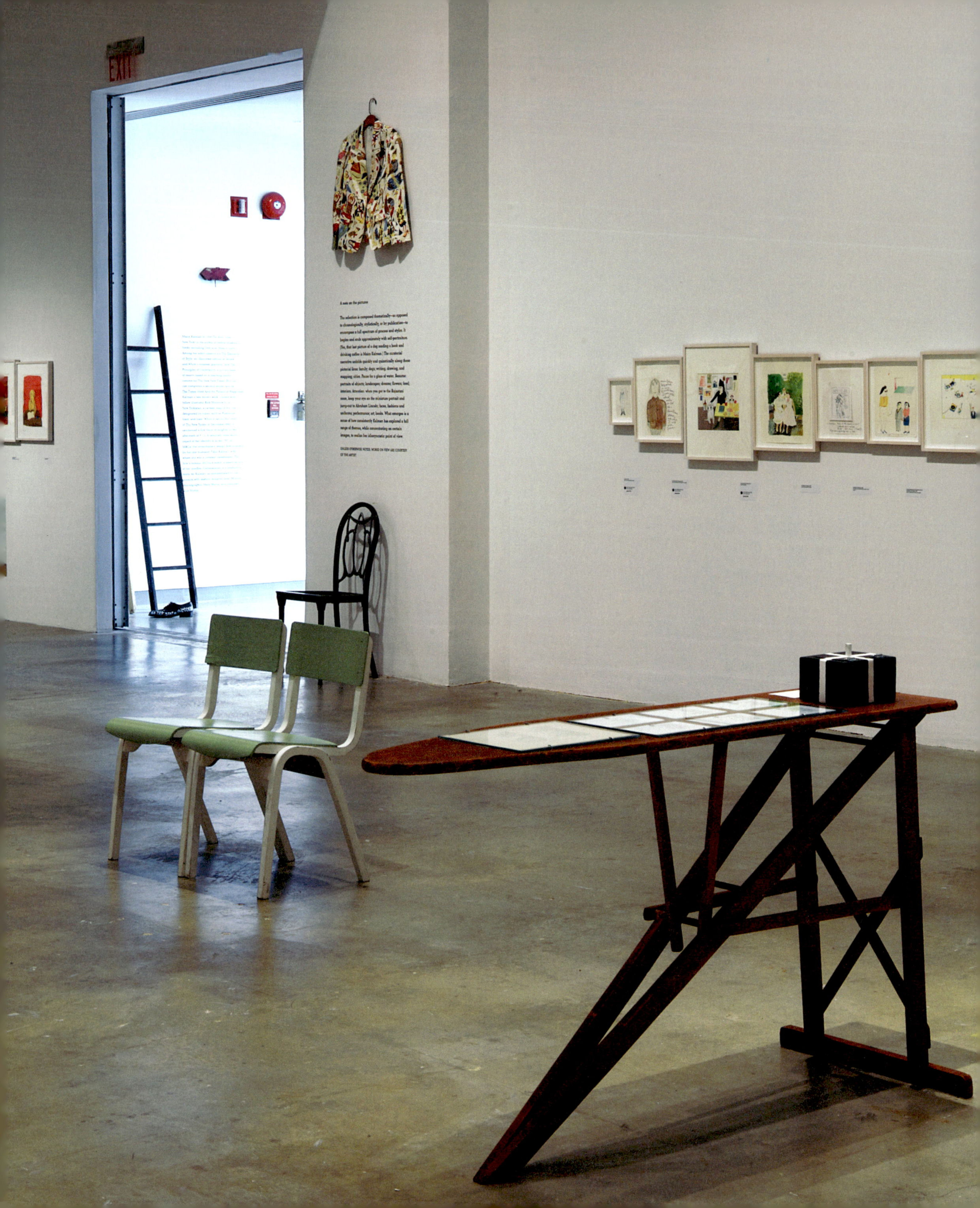
EXIT

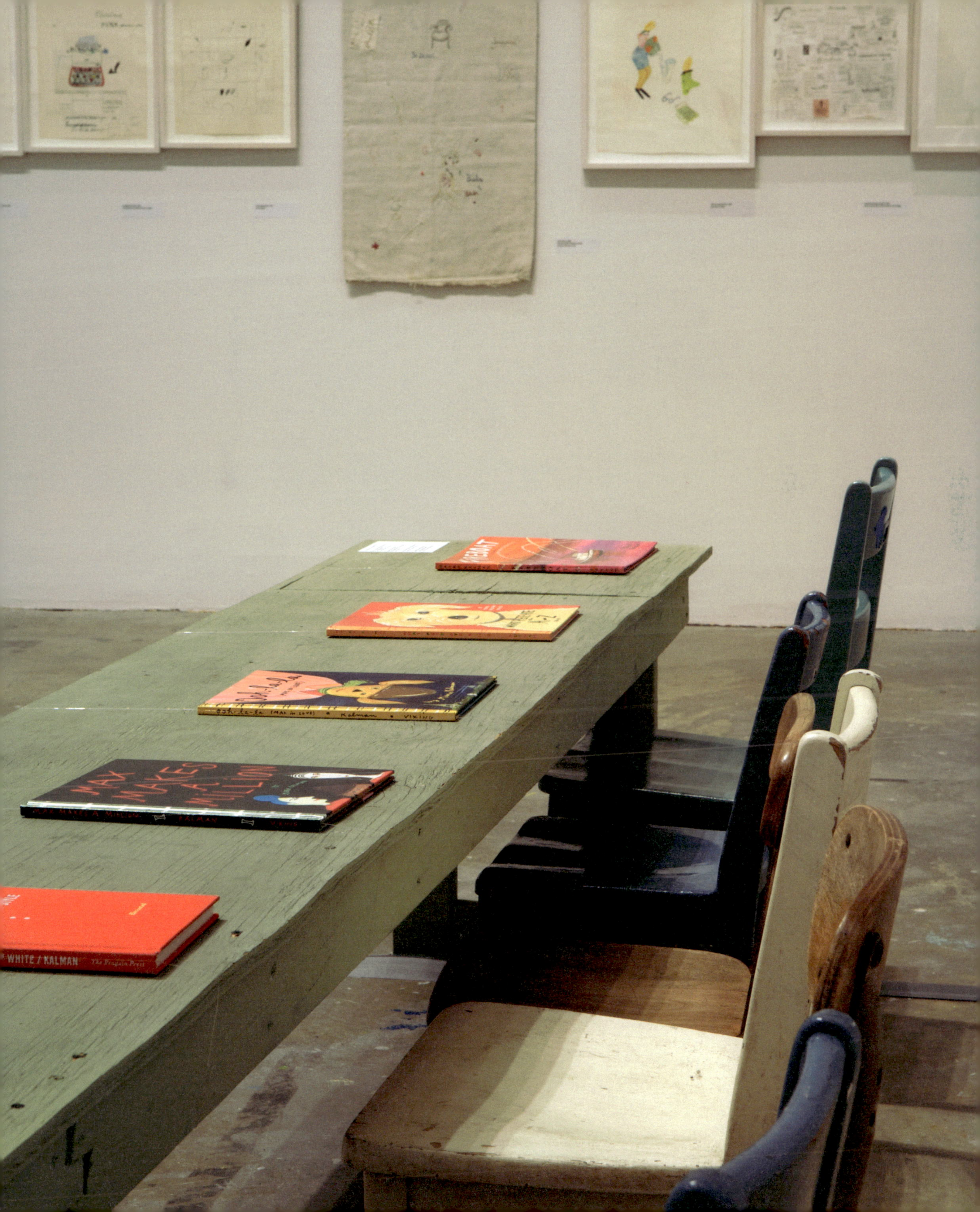
MAX MAKES A MILLION
WHITE / KALMAN

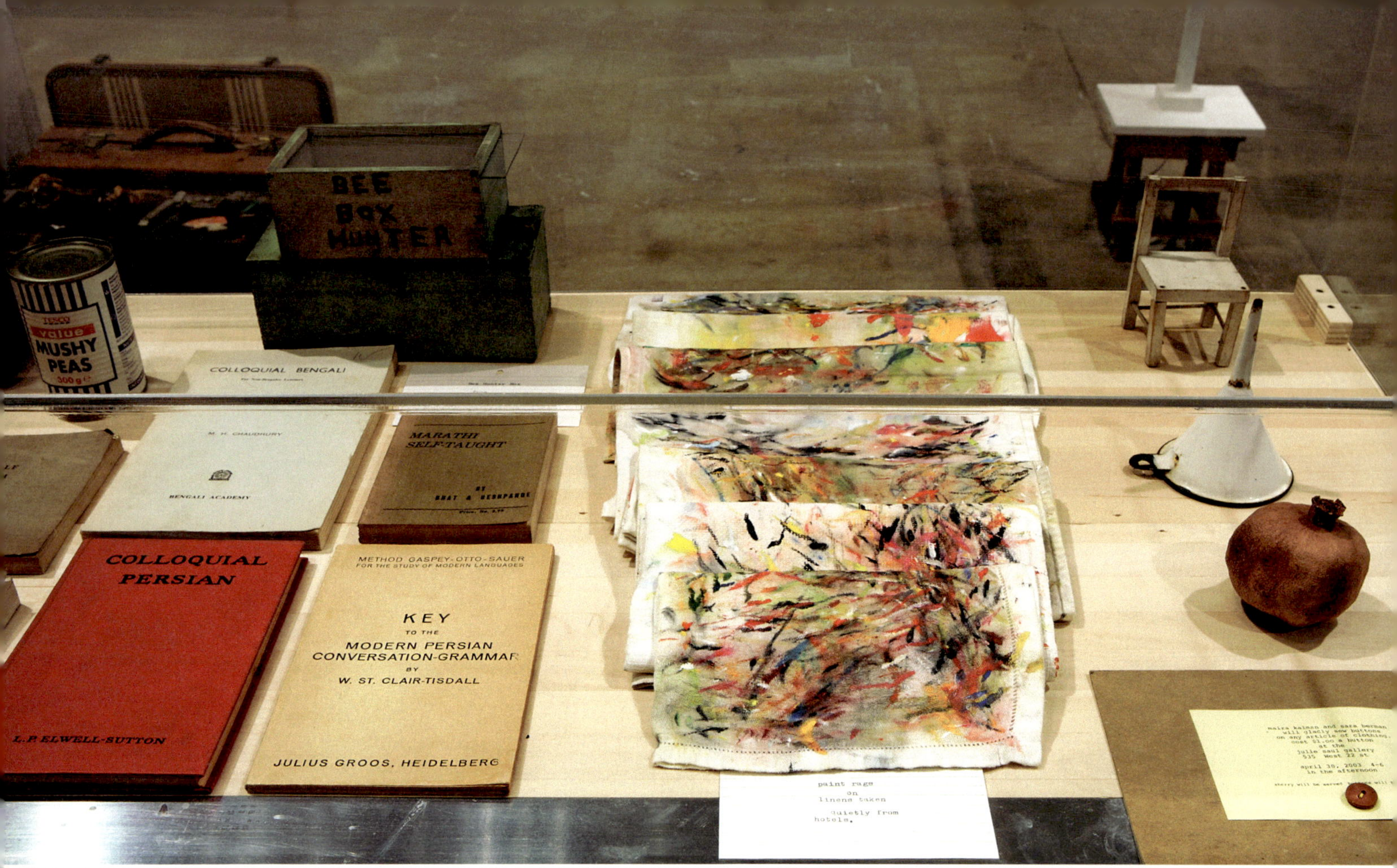
BEE
BOX
HUNTER
value
MUSHY PEAS
COLLOQUIAL BENGALI
BENGALI ACADEMY
MARATHI SELF-TAUGHT
COLLOQUIAL PERSIAN
L.P. ELWELL-SUTTON
METHOD GASPEY-OTTO-SAUER
FOR THE STUDY OF MODERN LANGUAGES
KEY
TO THE
MODERN PERSIAN
CONVERSATION-GRAMMAR
BY
W. ST. CLAIR-TISDALL
JULIUS GROOS, HEIDELBERG
paint rags
on
linens taken
quietly from
hotels.
maira kalman and sara berman
will gladly sew buttons
on any article of clothing.
cost $1.00 a button
at the
julie saul gallery
535 West 22 st
april 30, 2003 4-6
in the afternoon

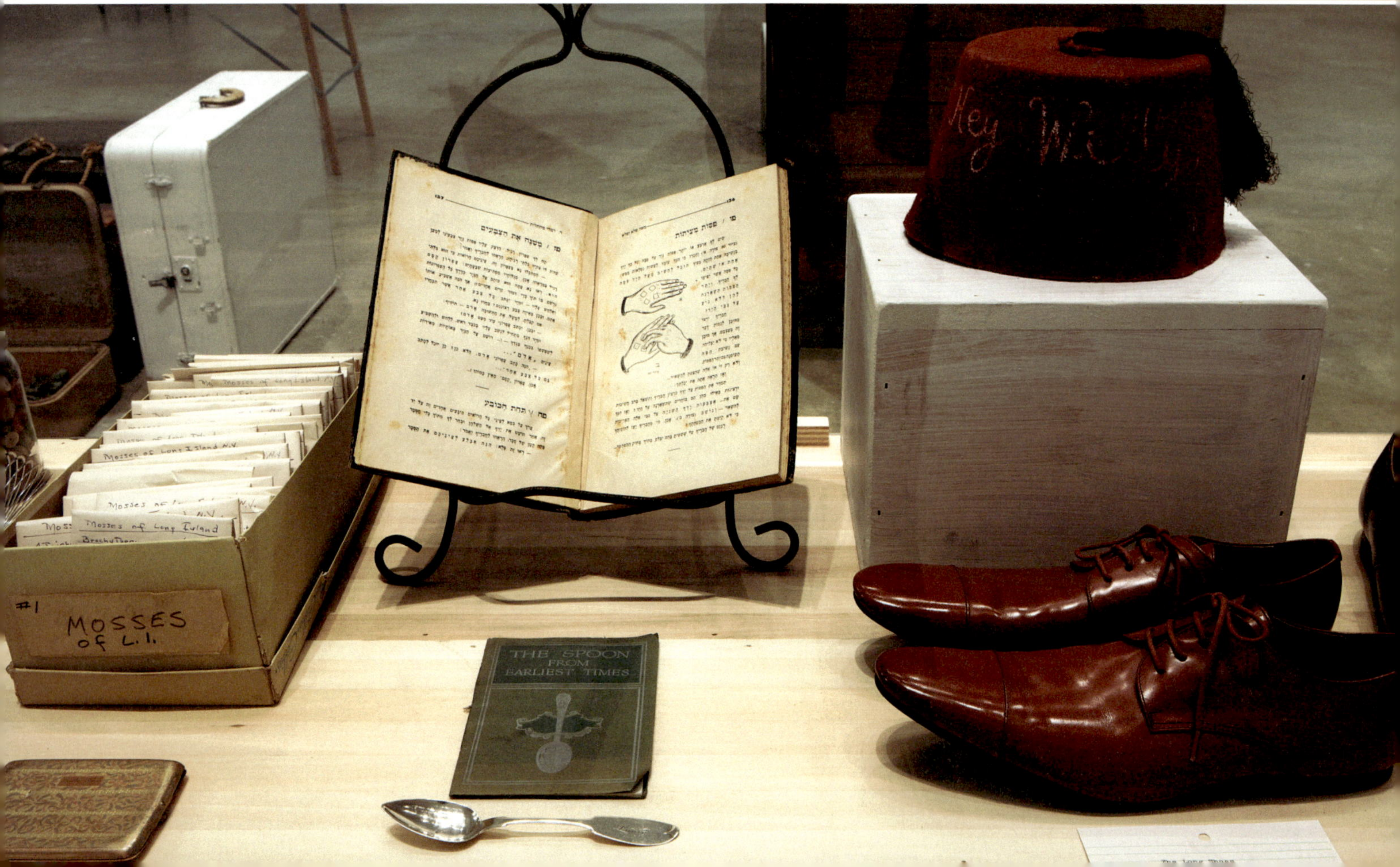
#1
MOSSES
of L.I.
Mosses of Long Island
THE SPOON
FROM
EARLIEST TIMES

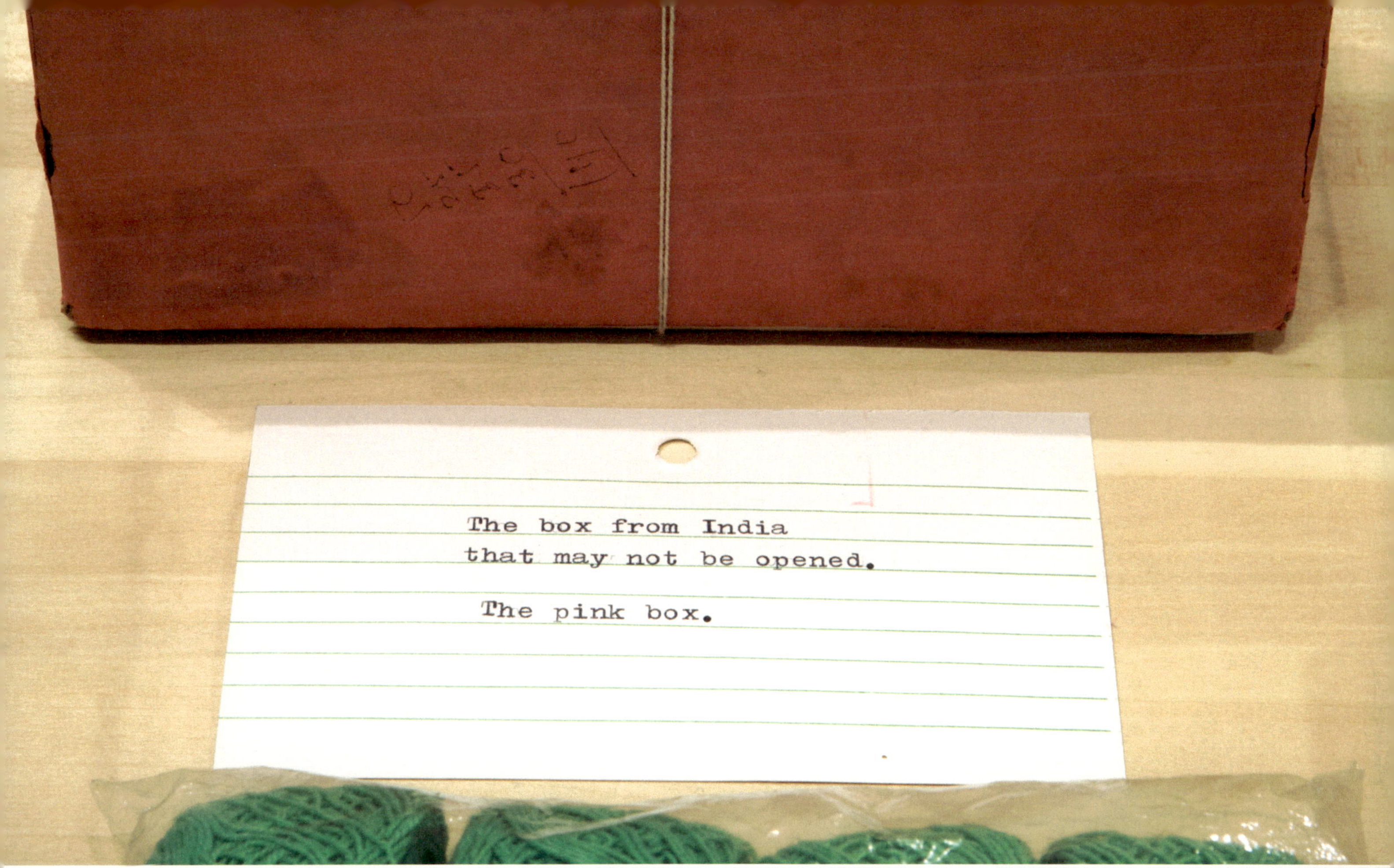
The box from India
that may not be opened.
The pink box.

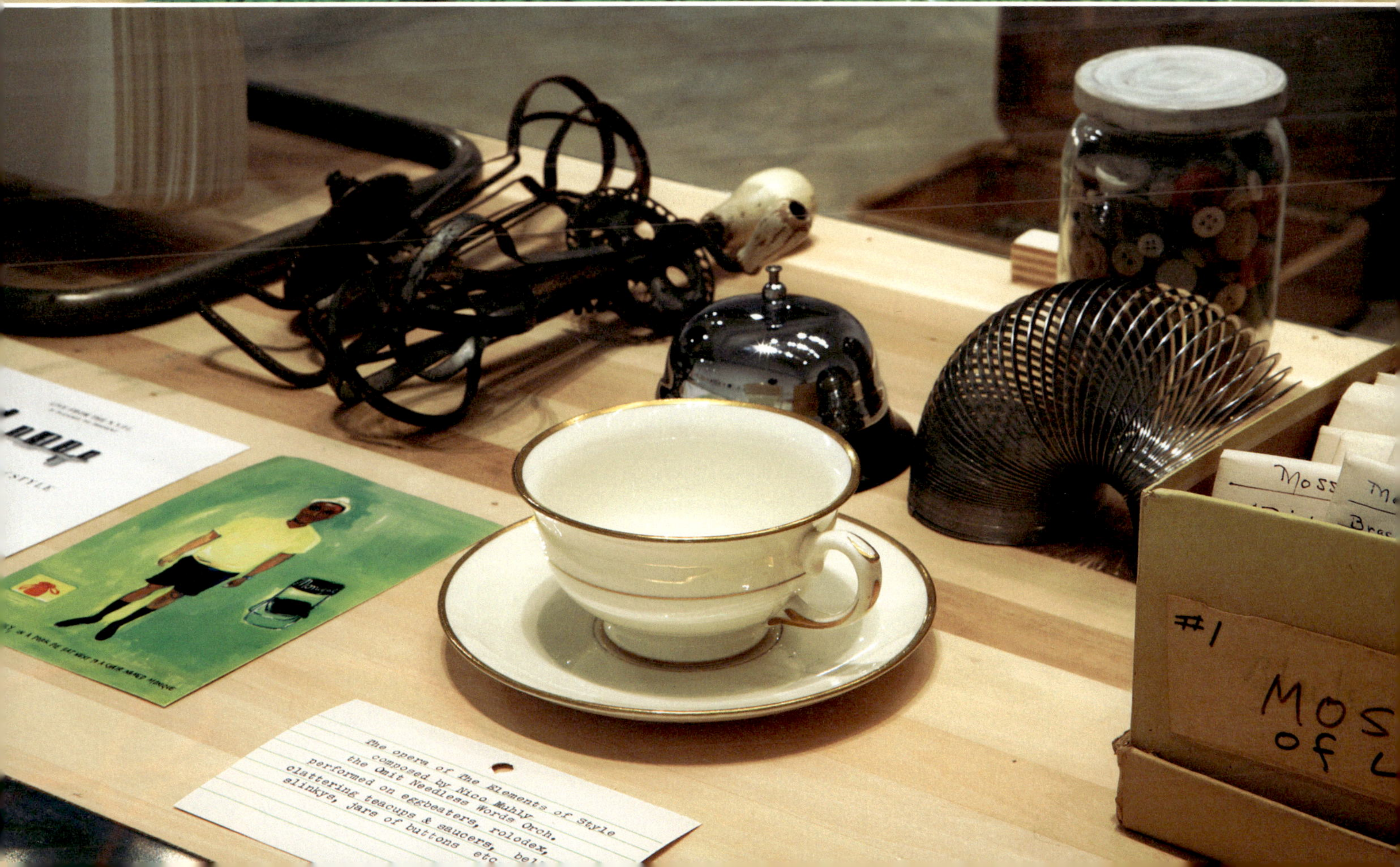
The opera of The Elements of Style
composed by Nico Muhly
the Omit Needless Words Orch.
performed on eggbeaters, rolodex,
clattering teacups & saucers,
slinkys, jars of buttons etc
#1

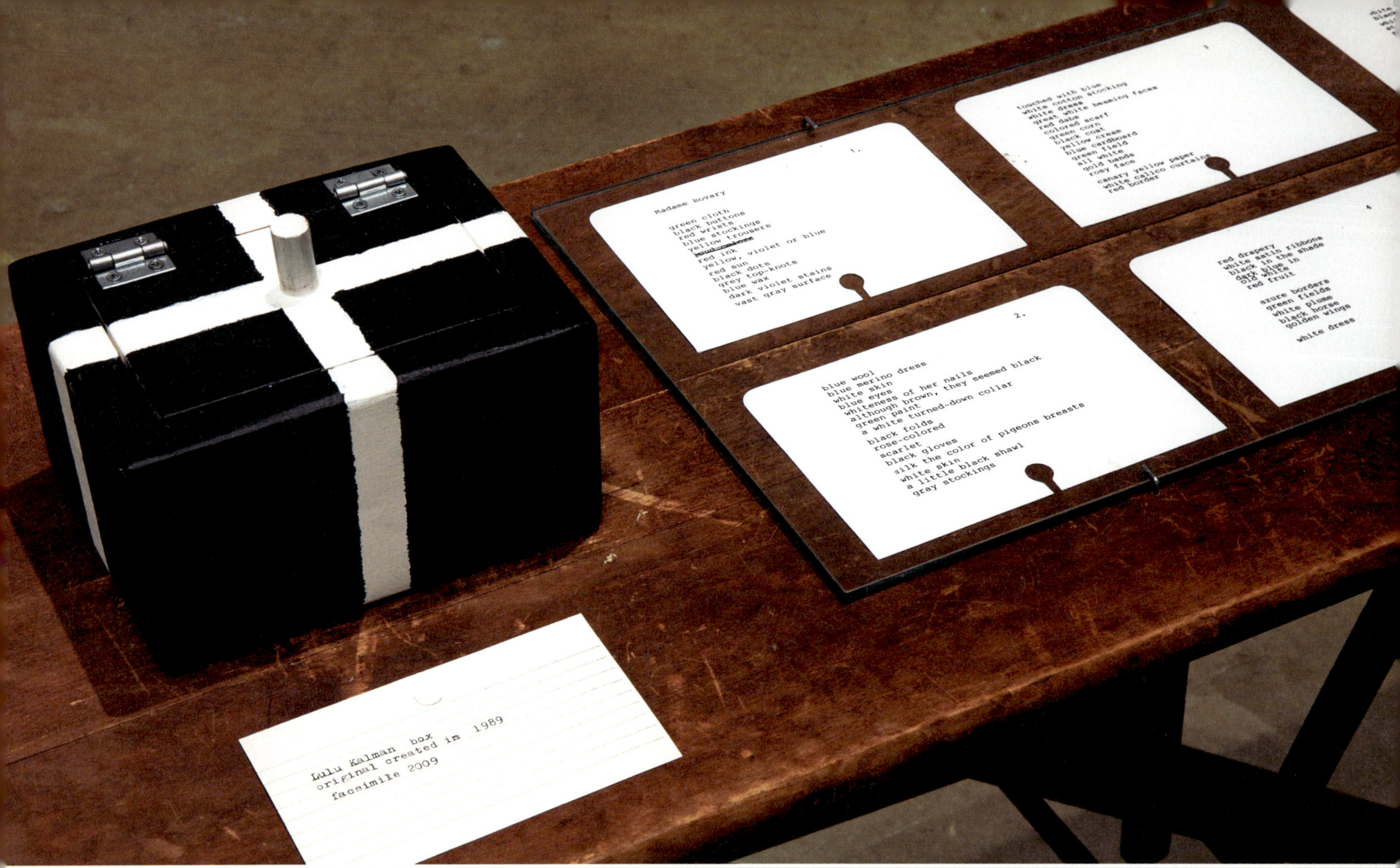

1.
Madame Bovary
green cloth
black buttons
red wrists
blue stockings
yellow trousers
red ink
yellow, violet or blue
red sun
black dots
grey top-knots
blue wax
dark violet stains
vast gray surface
touched with blue
white cotton stocking
white dress
great white beaming faces
red dabs
colored scarf
green coat
black coat
yellow cream
blue cardboard
green field
all white
gold bands
rosy face
canary yellow paper
white calico curtains
red border
2.
blue wool
blue merino dress
white skin
blue eyes
whiteness of her nails
although brown, they seemed black
green paint
a white turned-down collar
black folds
rose-colored
scarlet
black gloves
silk the color of pigeons breasts
white skin
a little black shawl
gray stockings
red drapery
white satin ribbons
black in the shade
dark blue in
old white
red fruit
azure borders
green fields
white plume
black horse
golden wings
white dress
Lulu Kalman box
original created im 1989
facsimile 2009

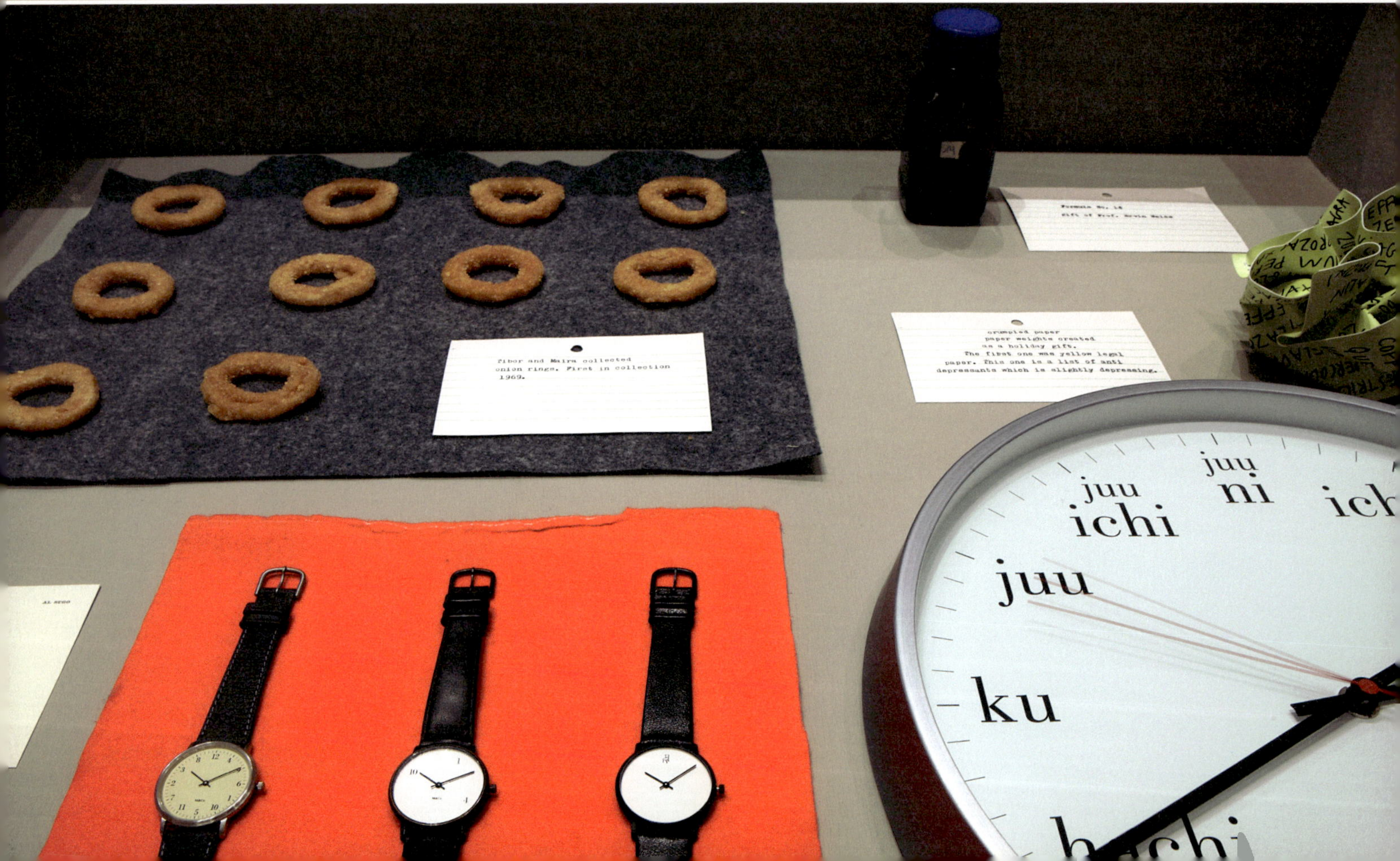

Tibor and Maira collected onion rings. First in collection 1969.
crumpled paper
paper weights created
as a holiday gift.
The fisst one was yellow legal
paper. This one is a list of anti
depressants which is slightly depressing.
juu ichi
juu ni
ichi
juu
ku

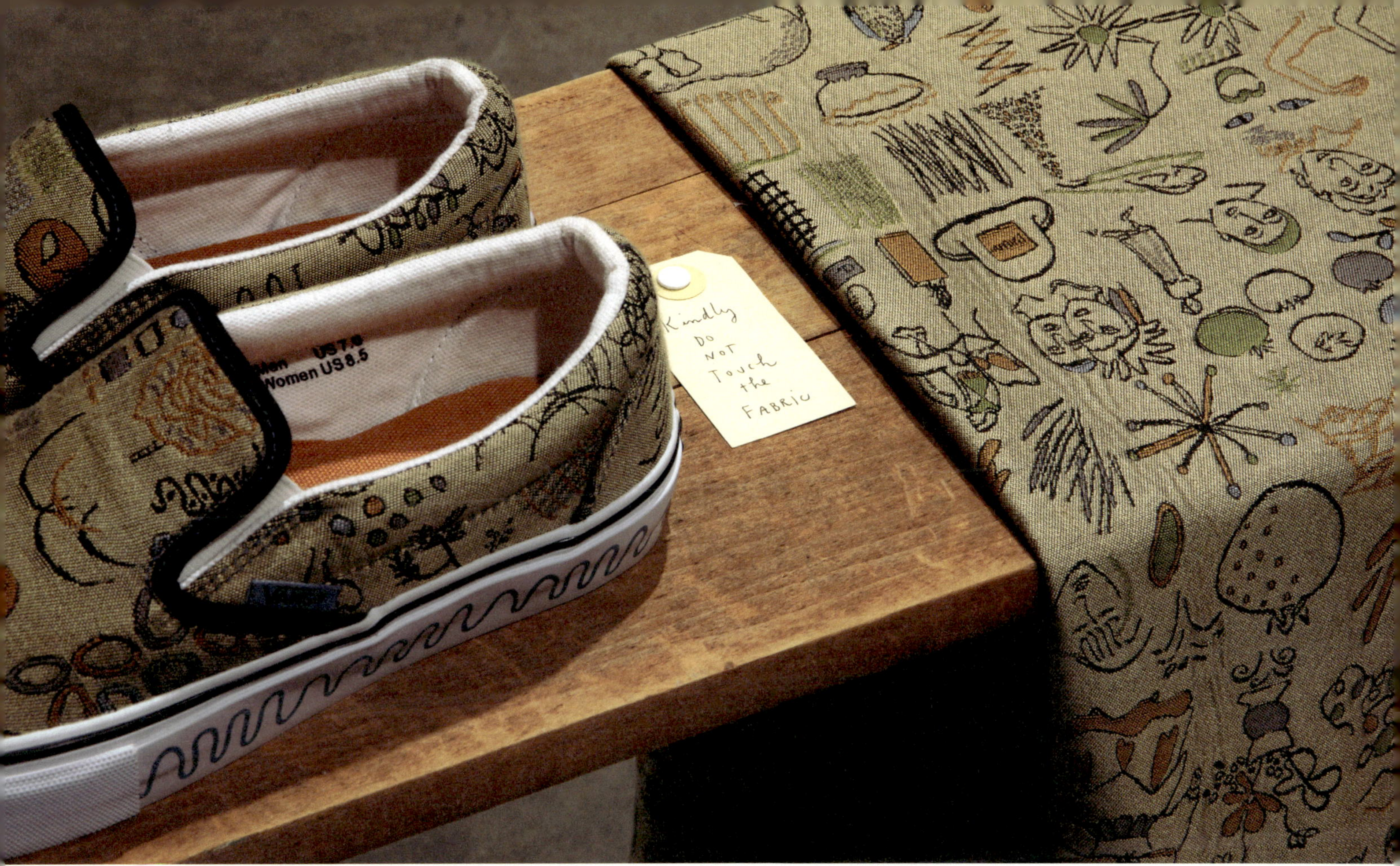
Women US 8.5
Kindly
DO
NOT
Touch
the
FABRIC

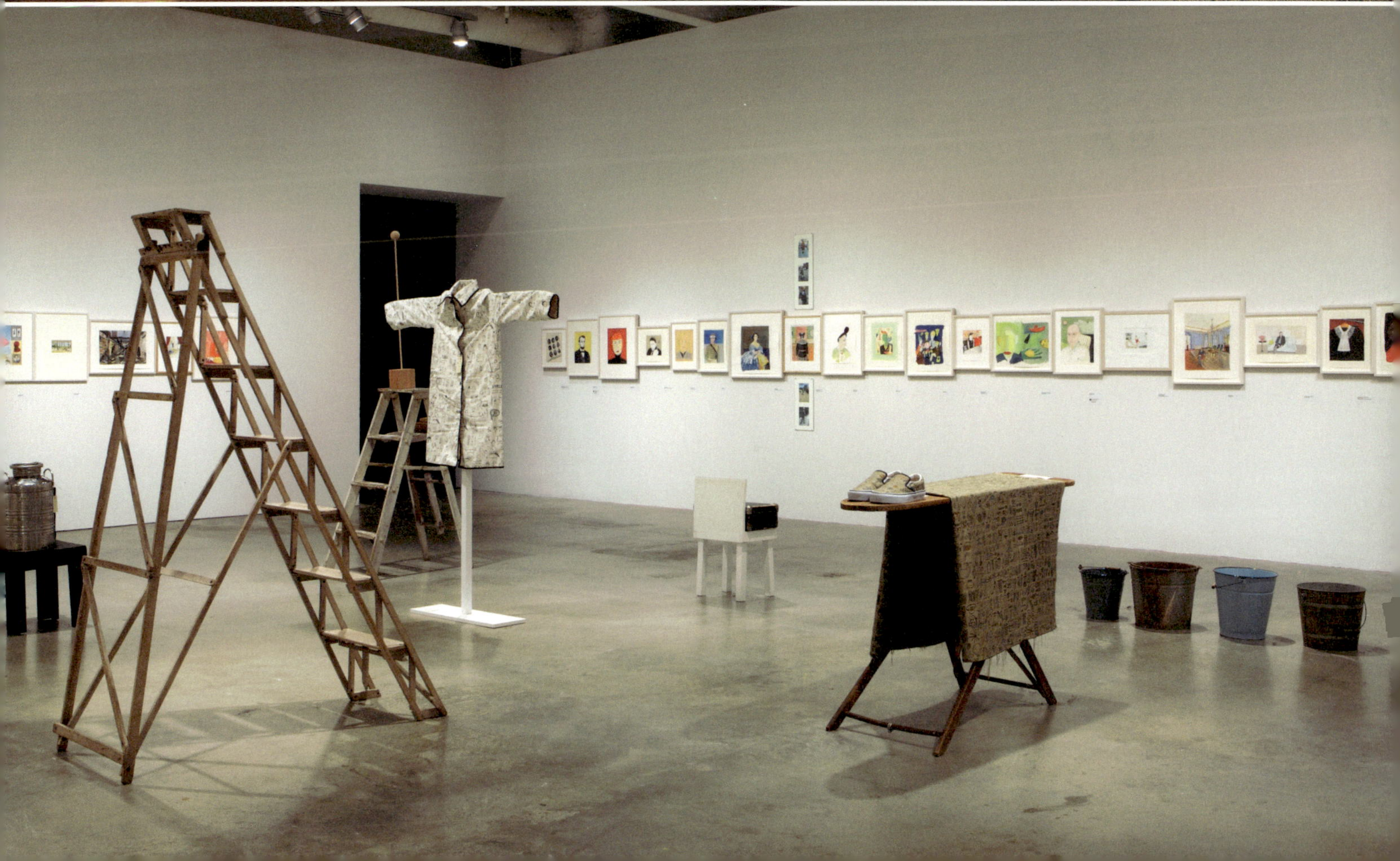

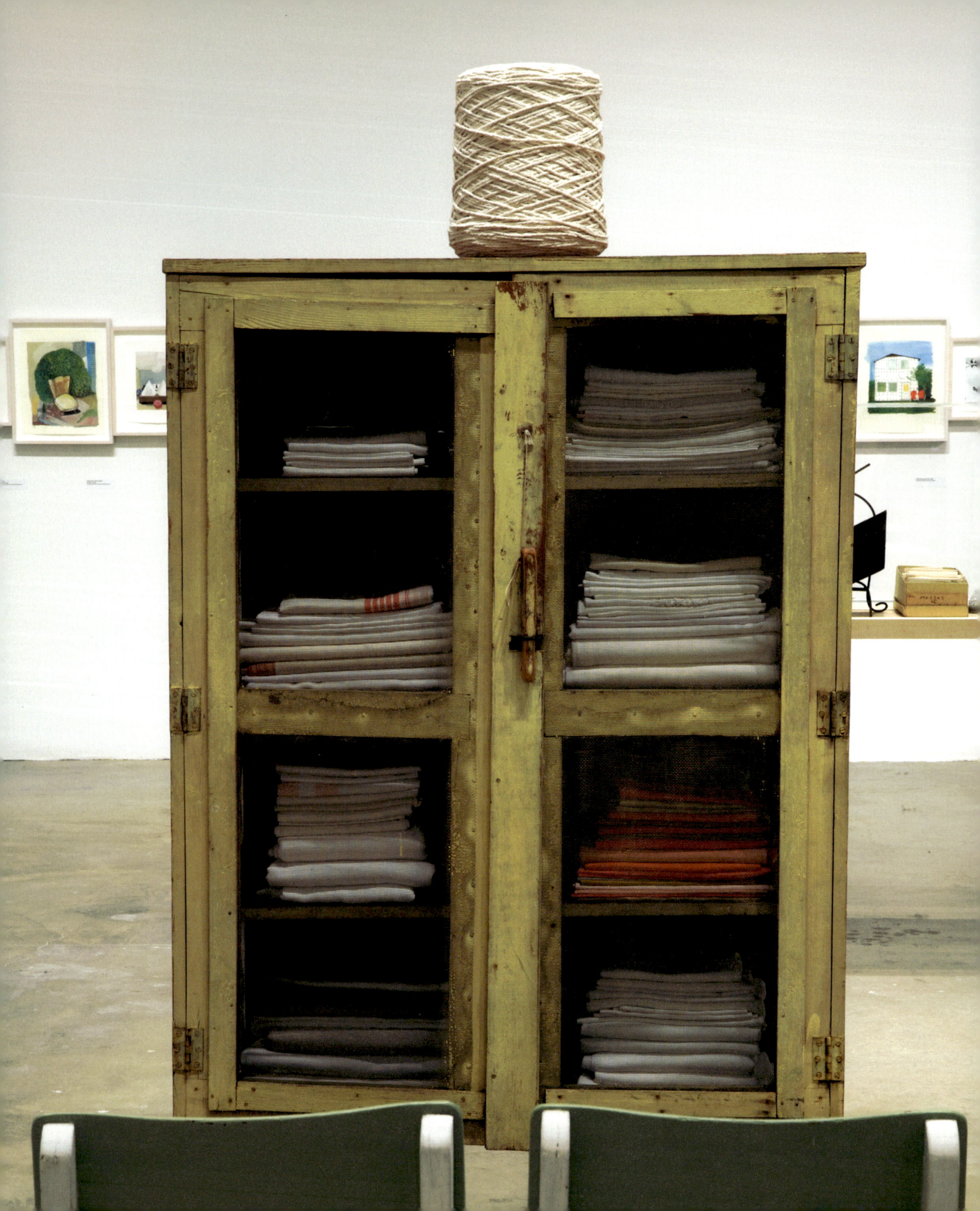

The following inventory is based on Kalman's notes:

Two wallpaper tables
Table one: 2 wooden wheels, green twine, paper tags, pink box tied with string, 8 balls of string, 1 blue linen binding, 2 spools *Kismet*-brand thread, the story of "Pesach Berman" printed on rubber, blue block, 5 boxes, bag with brown clasp, golden egg, "M" lock and key, George's money clip, ACME *Thunderer* whistle, key, 5 notebooks tied with string, can of *Mushy Peas,* wooden BEE BOX HUNTER, 6 language books, 7 linen paint rags, chair, funnel, pomegranate, button-sewing event announcement card.

Table two: Announcement card, program and objects from *The Elements of Style* opera (performed on eggbeaters, Rolodex, teacups and saucers, bell, slinky, pinking shears, jar of buttons), collection in a shoebox of mosses of Long Island, engraved *Milton Fine* cigarette case, book of magic tricks on stand, book of spoons, engraved Laura spoon, *Hey Willy* fez, Junya Watanabe shoes (not to wear), brown shoes (to slow down time).

Ironing board with *The Story of My Life* fabric by Maharam, and shoes.

Little stool (from Fez) with MOLLY LAMP
3 ladders
5 metal buckets
1 little white chair with funnel from Jaipur
Black cardboard suitcase on LUBA CHAIR
Milk can on RAIN CHAIR
Kate Spade raincoat
2 pastel boxes
2 wooden hat stands by Kika Schoenfeld

Pie chest: big spool of string, 100 linens, all ironed.

2 chairs (for viewing linens)
1 French iron chair
5 suitcases (with linens, lavender and eucalyptus)
2 Isaac Mizrahi jackets
Ironing board with LULU BOX, list of names from Dostoevksy's *The Idiot*, list of color phrases from Flaubert's *Madame Bovary*

Long green table with books: *The Principles of Uncertainty*, *The Elements of Style*, *Max Makes a Million*, *What Pete Ate from A to Z*, *Fireboat*.

2 blue vitrines, made by Alex Kalman, with objects related to Tibor Kalman and M&Co: 10 onion rings on felt, *Prozac* paperweight, bottle of no. 14 potion, 3 M&Co watches, Japanese M&Co clock, Askew M&Co clock, *Anyu* handkerchief, Karl Marx potato chips, new location announcement printed on rubber ball.

2 LULU LADDERS
1 *Falcon* fire detector
1 red wooden arrow

Short films by Alex Kalman/Red Bucket Films: *The Elements of Style* opera performed at Dia:Beacon (with composer Nico Muhly), Mark Morris dance lesson, Pete and Maira, Robin Hood Library.

Quotations on the walls from the writings of Flaubert, Proust, and Freud.

Chronology

Selected publications, projects, exhibitions, and events

Compiled by Kate Kraczon and annotated
by Maira Kalman

1949

Born Maira Berman in Tel Aviv, Israel

SUNNY. SANDY.
The FLuttering AWNINGS of
SEASide Cafés.

1954

Moves with family to Riverdale, New York

BLUE and GRAY.
ONIONS FRYING
in
COFFEE SHOPS.
PIANO LESSONS.
BALLet LESSONS.

1964–1968

Attends the High School of Music and Art, New York

MICHAEL GOLDENTHAL.
BROKEN Heart.
BOB DYLAN.

1968–1971

Attends New York University, New York

Studies English literature

Meets Tibor Kalman

LEATHER JACKET. GLASSES.
"DO YOU WANT to have
COFFEE?"
(HE SAID)

1973

Collaboration: *Our Town! An Insider's Guide to New York Brought to You by the People of Barnes & Noble Bookstores*, contributes text to a promotional guide to New York designed by Tibor Kalman

CORNELIA STREET.
FIFTH FLOOR WALKUP.
TUB in Kitchen.
ONION RING ON WALL.

1978

First published illustration: "Centerfold." *The Village Voice*, August 21.

1979

Tibor Kalman founds M&Co with
Carol Bokuniewicz and Liz Trovato

Works for *National Lampoon* as a pasteup artist
from 1979 to 1981

MAIRA IS
EVER PRESENT
BUT UNOFFICIAL.

1981

Marries Tibor Kalman

Collaboration (with M&Co): *The Fully Unauthorized 1981 Semi-Official Guide to Fort Lauderdale/Daytona Beach*. New York: National Lampoon, Inc.

Illustration for album cover designed by M&Co: *Three Big Songs* by David Byrne. Sire Records.

1982

Daughter Lulu Bodoni Kalman born

MOVE TO 12th STREET
JOE JUNIOR'S Coffee Shop
ON CORNER

1984

Designs M&Co 10-One-4 watch

1985

Son Alex Onomatopoeia Kalman born

1987

Book: *Stay Up Late*. Text by David Byrne.
New York: Viking Penguin.

DRAWN in the BEDROOM

1988

Book: *Hey Willy, See the Pyramids*.
New York: Viking Penguin.

FAMILY STORIES.
BELOVED SARA.
SISTER KIKA
COMES UP with
TITLE.

1989

Book: *Sayonara, Mrs. Kackleman*. New York: Viking Kestrel.

Designs tapestry fabric for Isaac Mizrahi, the first of many collaborations with the fashion designer

Exhibition: *An Evening with Maira Kalman in Nervous*, solo show, The Ginza Art Space, Japan, October 7–October 27

TRAVELS TO KYOTO.
SEES MOSS GARDEN.
GOES TO HOT SPRING
in PINE FOREST.
ALEX Thought he WENT.

1990

Book: *Max Makes a Million*.
New York: Viking Penguin.

SISTER KIKA COMES UP
with TITLE.
MEETS CHARLOTTE Sheedy.
AGENT

1991

Book: *Roarr: Calder's Circus*.
New York: Whitney Museum of American Art.

Book: *Ooh-la-la (Max in Love)*.
New York: Viking Penguin.
The New York Times "Best Illustrated Book"

Review: Linda Wertheimer. "An American Dog in Paris."
The New York Times Book Review, November 10.

1992

Book: *Max in Hollywood, Baby*. New York: Viking Penguin.

Exhibition: *The Child's World*, group show, The Illustration Gallery, New York

Profile: Trish Hall. "For Young Readers, Picasso, Not Bunnies." *The New York Times*, January 9.

1993

MAIRA TIBOR LULU ALEX MOVE to ROME FOR TWO YEARS. Apt. on VIA di PANICO. DOLCE FAR NIENTE

Book: *Chicken Soup, Boots*. New York: Viking Penguin.

Review and illustration: "A Review in Pictures." For *1-800-Am-I-Nuts? And Other True Tales of the Nineties* by Margo Kaufman. *Los Angeles Times*, April 18.

1994

Designs TANGO collection of mannequins for Ralph Pucci International

Text and illustration: "Piccolo Mondo: Spring Children's Wear takes a Roman Holiday." *The New York Times Magazine*, March 6.

Exhibition: *Maira Kalman's Max (a Dog)*, solo show, Children's Museum of Manhattan, October 1994–October 1995

1995

Book: *Swami on Rye*. New York: Viking Penguin.

RETURN to NEW YORK. Kiss the GROUND.

Designs Sony Building window display in New York with Ralph Pucci TANGO mannequins

Profile: Debra Hotaling. "It's a Dog's World: The Exploits of that Famous Canine Poet, Max Stravinsky, Are Delighting All Ages." *Los Angeles Times*, June 15.

Cover illustration: *The New Yorker*, December 4 (*Crosstown Boogie Woogie*).

1996

Designs KIDS line of mannequins for Ralph Pucci International

Profile: Akiko Busch. "Mondrian and Maira." *Metropolis*, January/February.

Illustration: *Domus*, February, cover (*Glass*).

Illustration: *The New Yorker*, April 8, cover (*Easter Parade*).

Text and illustration: "Small Wonders, The Pig on a Leash and Other Childhood Tales," *Travel & Leisure*, September.

Illustration: *The New Yorker*, September 9, cover (*Readin, Ritin & Ritalin*).

1997

Text: "I Don't Like Little Angels." *Little Angels*. Los Angeles and New York: Picture This Publications.

Illustration: "Opining on Icons" by Chee Pearlman. *Icons: Magnets of Meaning*. San Francisco: San Francisco Museum of Modern Art and Chronicle Books.

Text and illustration: "The New Year on Other Planets." *The New York Times*, January 1.

Illustration: *The New Yorker*, April 7, cover (*Einstein, Zweistein, Dreistein*).

1998

Designs murals for Grand Central Station, New York

Text and illustration: "Some Things You Don't Know About Tibor." *Tibor Kalman: Perverse Optimist*. Edited by Peter Hall and Michael Bierut. New York: Princeton Architectural Press.

SUPERMARKET PARTY THEREMIN in AISLE 5

Illustration: *Domus*, February, cover.

Text and illustration: "The Travels of Olive and Pete, This Time: New York." *Travel & Leisure*, Spring/Summer.

Text and illustration: "The Travels of Olive and Pete, This Time: Anguilla." *Travel & Leisure*, Fall/Winter.

Text and illustration: "Letters to Harold" (a photo essay with Pucci mannequins). *The Book* (Neiman Marcus), November.

Profile: James Kaplan. "(T&)M&Co." *New York Magazine*, November 23.

Profile: Barbara Aria. "All Aboard." *Time Out New York*, December 31, 1998–January 7, 1999.

1999

Tibor Kalman dies on May 2

The OCEAN.
The END.
The ROCK.

Book: *Next Stop Grand Central*. New York: Penguin Putnam.

Review: Kyle Crichton. "Crossroads of Half a Million Lives." *The New York Times Book Review*, April 11.

Illustration: *The New Yorker*, February 1, cover (*Dog Reads Book*).

Text and illustration: "The Travels of Olive and Pete, This Time: Cairo to Cairo." *Travel & Leisure*, Spring/Summer.

2000

Book (with Tibor Kalman): *(un)FASHION*. New York: Abrams, 2000.

Book (editor): *T.BOR: A Book (to Keep) + 30 Postcards (to Send)*. New York: The Little Bookroom.

Text and illustration: "Tibor Swimming in the Ocean." *The New York Times Magazine*, January 2.

Illustration: "Instant Solutions." *The New Yorker*, April 10.

Illustration: "A Cut Above and Beyond." *Interview*, May.

Copresents *TIBOR IN ORBIT*, a public art project honoring Tibor Kalman, in conjunction with the New Museum and Creative Time, New York, May/June

Illustration: "Fashion Pet Portraits." *Interview*, June.

Designs stage drops for *Four Saints in Three Acts* by the Mark Morris Dance Group/English National Opera. The Coliseum, London, June 2000; Brooklyn Academy of Music, March 2006

Illustration: *The New Yorker*, August 7, cover (*A Place in the Sun*).

Text and illustration: "Couture Voyeur." *The New York Times Magazine*, November 5.

Coorganizes *Tiborocity: Design and Undesign by Tibor Kalman 1979–1999*, San Francisco Museum of Modern Art and the New Museum, New York

Designs "DNA Deli Cup" for Creative Time, New York

2001

Book: *What Pete Ate from A to Z*. New York: Putnam.

Cofounds (with Alex Melamid) the Rubber Band Society, New York

BASEd ON the LOVE of
RUBBeR BANdS

Article: "The Talk of the Town: How-to-Dept: Art, a Crash Course." *The New Yorker*, January 15.

Illustration: *The New Yorker*, February 5, cover (*Annual Misery Day Parade*).

Profile: Steven Heller. "Maira Kalman, the surviving spirit of M&Co." *Eye*, Spring.

Text and illustration: "Airports Inevitable." *The New York Times Magazine*, May 13.

Profile: Chee Pearlman. "Unleashing Her Inner Child." *The New York Times*, November 1.

Illustration (with Rick Meyerowitz): *The New Yorker*, December 10, cover (*New Yorkistan*).

Review: Sarah Boxer. "A Funny New Yorker Map Is Again the Best Defense." *The New York Times*, December 8.

RICK and I WERE ON
OUR WAY TO A PARTY.

Designs mural (*What's What?*) at Public School 234's temporary location following September 11

Text and illustration: "The Family Way." *The Book* (Neiman Marcus), December.

2002

Book: *Fireboat: The Heroic Adventures of the John J. Harvey*.
New York: Puffin Books.
Boston Globe–Horn Book Nonfiction Award
Child Magazine "Best Book of the Year"

Book (editor). *Colors: Tibor Kalman, Issues 1–13*
(an anthology of the magazine under Tibor Kalman).
New York: Thames & Hudson.

Finalist for National Design Award for Communication Design

Joins the board of AIGA
(American Institute of Graphic Arts),
New York, 2002–4

Joins the Fine Arts Department, MFA faculty, at the
School of Visual Arts, New York

Text and illustration: "Martin Fell Down."
The Ganzfeld (no. 2).

Illustration: "Art Moves Art." *The New Yorker*,
April 22 and 29.

Illustration: *The New Yorker*, September 2, cover
(*School Daze*).

Illustration (with Rick Meyerowitz):
"New York Transit Strike Contingency Plan" (op-ed piece).
The New York Times, December 12.

Text and illustration: "The Party: A Fashion Fantasy."
The New York Times Magazine, December 12.

2003

Book: *Smartypants (Pete in School)*. New York: Putnam.

Designs fabric and rainwear for Kate Spade

Illustration (with Rick Meyerowitz): "Things to Do on Valentine's
Day" (op-ed piece). *Los Angeles Times*, February 14.

Profile: Steven Heller. "Interview: Maira Kalman." *Eye*, Spring.

Profile: Elaine Louie. "Bellows and Barks to Soothe the Soul."
The New York Times, April 20.

Exhibition: *Just Looking*, solo show, Julie Saul Gallery,
New York, April 25–June 14. Maira and her mother
sew buttons on clothing at gallery on April 30 ($1 a button).
"Sherry will be provided. Buttons will be provided."

JULIE SAUL CALLS.
HELLO.
HELLO.

Illustration (with Rick Meyerowitz): "Ask Your Doctor."
The New Yorker, September 8.

Text and illustration: "Look." *Print*,
September/October, cover.

IN Search of JANE AUSTEN.

Text and illustration: "On Desiring Stuff."
Newsweek, October 27.

The shoes were
Long and Pointy and
NEVER WORN.

2004

Profile: "Bedtime Story." *O! At Home*, Spring.

Profile: Kim Hastreiter. "What They Do." *Paper*, May.

Featured: "Through a Glass, Brightly; Amid the Frenzy,
a Nice Odd Place." *The New York Times*, June 13.

Illustration: *The New Yorker*, June 14 and 21,
cover (*Twice Removed*).

Exhibition: *The Voting Booth Project*, group show
curated by Chee Pearlman, Parsons, The New School,
New York, October 8–December 5 (catalogue)

Text and illustration (with Rick Meyerowitz): "The New York City
Sub Culinary Map." *The New Yorker*,
September 6, 2004; published as a poster.

2005

Illustration for book: *The Elements of Style*. Text by William Strunk Jr. and E. B. White. New York: Penguin.

Review: Jeremy Eichler. "'Style' Gets New Elements." *The New York Times*, October 19.

Review: Lynn Neary. "'Elements of Style' Goes Beyond Words." National Public Radio, November 2.

Found at a Church jumble SALE.
Read on a Green Couch.

Designs "The Story of My Life," upholstery-weight fabric for Maharam

Michael. Sabine.
Sabine. Michael.

Featured: Jennifer New. *Drawing from Life: The Journal as Art*. New York: Princeton Architectural Press.

Illustration: *The New Yorker*, March 14, cover (*Duck Hat*).

Text and illustration: "Little London." *The New York Times Travel Magazine*, March 20.

Profile: Jane Margolies. "Kalman's Sampler." *I.D. Magazine*, May.

Exhibition: *The Art of The New Yorker: Eighty Years in the Vanguard*, group show, The Norman Rockwell Museum, Stockbridge, Massachusetts, June 11–October 31

Text and illustration: "Vis-à-vis the Venice Biennale." *The New Yorker*, August 22.

Lulu Got Sick
on Little Bed.
Then Better.
Then WALK.

Profile: Catherine Hong. "Mad about Maira." *W Magazine*, October.

Performance: "Style: Maira Kalman," *The Elements of Style* set to music by Nico Muhly, New York Public Library, October 19

Composer Nico Muhly.
Blue Rubber Shoes.
Performance in
Main Reading Room
of the Library.

Exhibition: *Maira Kalman: Elements of Style*, solo show curated by Sid Sachs, The Rosenwald-Wolf Gallery of The University of the Arts, Philadelphia, October 19–December 5

Exhibition: *I Can't Stand All the Excitement*, solo show of embroideries, Julie Saul Gallery, New York, October 28–December 10

On Linens taken
From
Restaurants and Hotels.

2006

Blog: "The Principles of Uncertainty." *The New York Times* online (nytimes.com/opinion), May 2006–April 2007.

Mary Duenwald.
David Shipley.

Illustration: *Poetry Magazine*, July/August, front and back covers, endpapers.

Has Title Changed to
PEOTRY
for Humor issue.

Text and illustration: "Sunny-Side Up: On the Love of Breakfast." *Gourmet* (supplement), August.

Profile: Conversation with Junot Diaz, Maira Kalman, Ruth Reichl, and Jane Smiley on *The Charlie Rose Show*, August 18.

2007

Book: *The Principles of Uncertainty*. New York: Penguin Press.

Review: Alison Stewart. "Maira Kalman Sure of 'Uncertainty.'" National Public Radio, October 19, 2007.

Review: Barbara Yablon Maida. "Maira Kalman's New York: Goethe Rides the F Train." *The New York Observer*, October 22.

Review: Heller McAlpin. "A Year in the Life." *Los Angeles Times Book Review*, October 28.

MUCH WANDERING
AROUND TOWN.
MUCH WONDERING.

Review: Ariel Levy. "Painted Whimsies." *The New York Times Book Review*, February 17, 2008.

Illustration: "Icons" by Herbert Muschamp. *The New York Times*, February 25–May 20.

SO LONG HERBERT.

Lectures at TED (Technology, Entertainment, Design) annual conference, March

Exhibition: *101 Dresses*, group show, Artspace, New Haven, Connecticut, May 9–June 23 (catalogue)

Illustration: "The Enthusiast: Kim Hastreiter's Downtown" by Dana Goodyear. *The New Yorker*, September 24.

Profile: Rachel Pulfer. "Drawing Power." *Azure*, October.

Exhibition: *The Principles of Uncertainty*, solo show, Julie Saul Gallery, New York, October 11–November 24

Exhibition: *Pricked: Extreme Embroidery*, group show, Museum of Arts and Design, New York, November 8, 2007–April 27, 2008 (catalogue)

Lectures at First Person Arts Festival, Philadelphia, November

Text and illustration: "Mind's Eye." *Aperture*, Winter.

Text and illustration: "Working It." *Time*, Winter.

Text and illustration: "The Splendid Garden(er)." *Culture + Travel*, Winter.

2008

Inducted into the Art Directors Club Hall of Fame, New York

WEARS JACK LENOR LARSEN
GAUZY WHITE SCARF.

Text and illustration: "Finding Lincoln," a forty-four-panel story based on the life of Abraham Lincoln, for the Rosenbach Museum and Library's web project "21st-Century Abe"

EATS LINCOLN APPLES.

Illustration: Page in the "Glass House" Moleskine® sketchbook (National Trust for Historic Preservation)

Exhibition: *Just Looking: The Art and Design of Maira Kalman with Dates*, Beijing Art Gallery, China (catalogue)

TRIP TO CHINA
GUMDROP MOUNTAINS.

Exhibition: *Lots of Things Like This*, group show curated by Dave Eggers, apexart, New York, April 2–May 10

Illustration: "Stem Sell: Alvar Aalto's Design Still Holds Water." *The New York Times Style Magazine*, May 4.

Text and illustration: "Mad about the Met." *Departures*, May/June.

POPPIES.
CHRIS NOEY
INGRES BLUE.

Text and illustration: "My Tel Aviv: A stroll through the City." *Tablet* (online magazine), September 5.

2009

Blog: "And the Pursuit of Happiness." *The New York Times* online (nytimes.com/opinion), January–December.

SISTER KIKA COMES UP WITH TITLE. AMERICAN JOURNEY.

Designs mural and reading room for library at Public School 47 in the Bronx, commissioned by the Library Initiative, a partnership between the Robin Hood Foundation and the New York City Board of Education

ALL the OBJECTS WERE in MY LIVING ROOM. FOR A YEAR.

Featured: *More Things Like This*. Edited by Dave Eggers, with an interview by Jesse Nathan. San Francisco: Chronicle Books.

Designs in-store art for MAC Cosmetics

EYELINER NAMED "MAIRA'S MOOD"

Interview with Linda Yablonsky for MAC Cosmetics' "Make-up Art Cosmetics Collection" press release

Performance: "Illustrated Music (Lincoln Center American Songbook)," selections from *The Elements of Style* and *The Principles of Uncertainty* set to music by Nico Muhly, The Allen Room, Jazz at Lincoln Center, February 18

Exhibition: *Maira Kalman: The Elements of Style*, solo show, Memorial Art Gallery, University of Rochester, New York, May 2–August 2

Exhibition: *Summer Pictures*, group show curated by Isaac Mizrahi, Julie Saul Gallery, New York, July 9–September 12

Profile: Holly Davis. "Guileless and Gutsy." *The Artist's Magazine*, October, cover.

Profile: Francine Prose. "The World According to Maira." *Aperture*, Winter.

2010

Exhibition: *Maira Kalman: Various Illuminations (of a Crazy World)*, Institute of Contemporary Art, University of Pennsylvania, Philadelphia, solo show, January 14–June 6, (catalogue)

INGRID SCHAFFNER CURATES. BACON LETTUCE TOMATO SANDWICHES. LADDERS and BUCKETS and LINENS and 100 DRAWINGS.

Book: *13 Words*. Text by Lemony Snicket. New York: Harper.

Book: *And the Pursuit of Happiness*. New York: Penguin Press.

Book: *In Love with A. Lincoln*. New York: Putnam.

ICA Staff

Shannon Bowser
Senior Preparator

Robert Chaney
Director of Curatorial Affairs

Eliza Coviello
Assistant to the Director

Lizzie Frasco
Spiegel Fellow

Lucy Gallun
Whitney Lauder Curatorial Fellow

Jamie Gorman
Development Associate

Claudia Gould
The Daniel W. Dietrich, II Director

William Hidalgo
Visitor Services/Education Assistant

Jill Katz
Director of Marketing and Communications

Kate Kraczon
Assistant Curator

Christianna Miller
Major Gifts Officer

Rachel Pastan
Staff Writer

Marilyn Pollick
Director of Development

Jenelle Porter
Curator

Nikyia Rogers
Business and Building Administrator

Ingrid Schaffner
Senior Curator

Interns
Grace Ambrose, Dong Chen, Patricia Cuevas-Gomez, Hannah Gilbert, Rachel W. Higgins, Kristen Kinstrey, Claudia Lauture, Evan Litvin, Ben Loughin, Sarah Margolis-Pineo, Linnea Rading, Rokssana Sukkur, Desiree Thompson, Angela Washko, and Francesca Zanghi

Board of Overseers

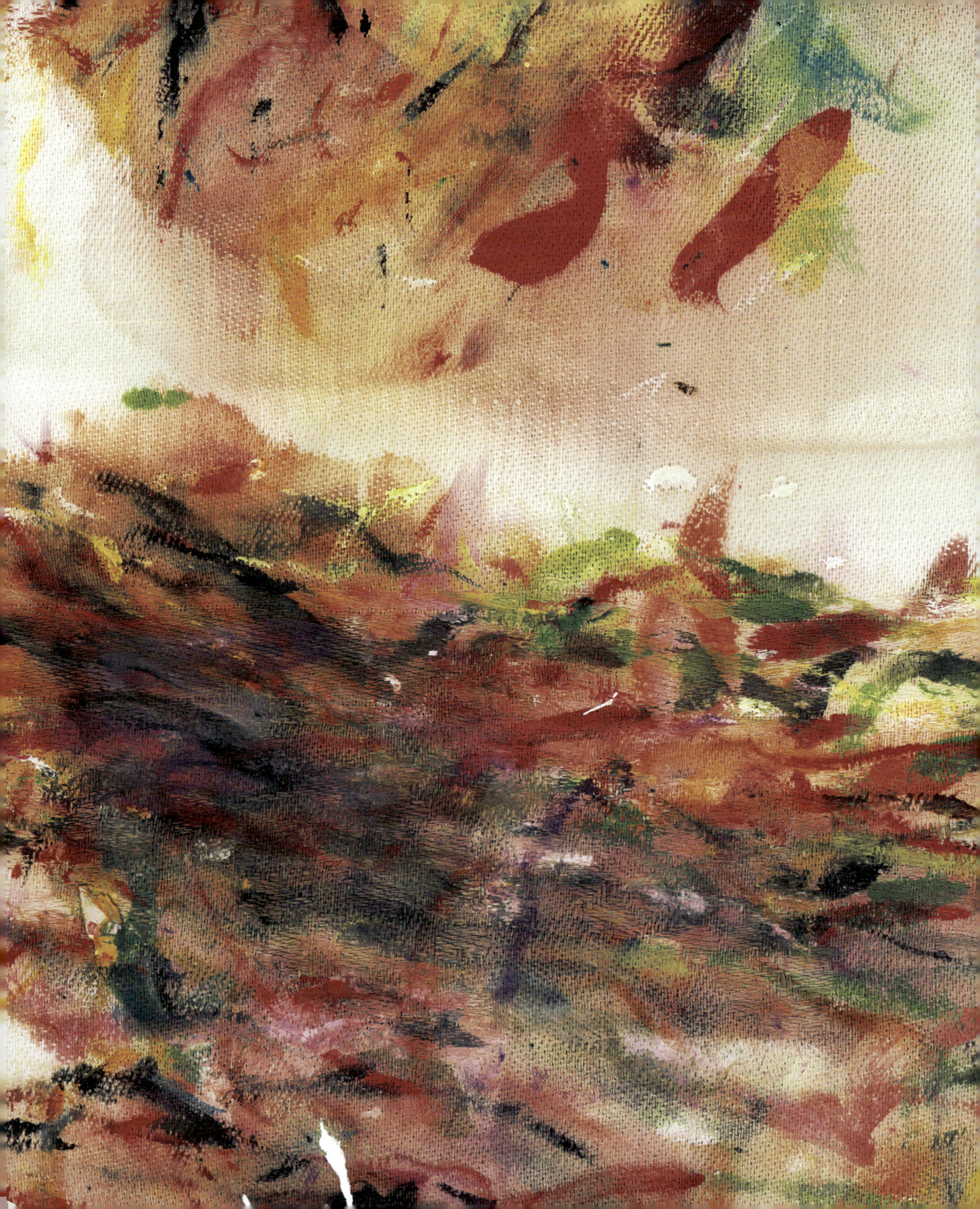